Advance praise for Angelo Pezzote and *STRAIGHT ACTING*

"There is no such thing as a 'real man,' only millions of men—straight and gay—trying to convince themselves and others that they have the right stuff. In *Straight Acting*, Angelo Pezzote peers behind the curtain to uncover the human costs of this relentless masculine performance. His immediate concern is gay men, but all men who seek love, intimacy, and most of all, self-respect, can benefit from the honesty and wisdom in these pages."

—Jackson Katz, creator of the award-winning educational film *Tough Guise: Violence, Media and the Crisis in Masculinity.*

STRAIGHT ACTING

GAY MEN, MASCULINITY AND FINDING TRUE LOVE

ANGELO PEZZOTE

KENSINGTON BOOKS
http://www.kensingtonbooks.com

The author's advice and opinions are not intended to substitute for professional consultations. Readers should consult with their physicians before embarking on any health, diet and/or exercise programs.

Names and personal information have been changed to protect the confidentiality of the individuals. The author has taken the information from actual letters and created composite profiles in order to illustrate his advice and opinions.

KENSINGTON BOOKS are published by

Kensington Publishing Corp.
850 Third Avenue
New York, NY 10022

Copyright © 2008 by Angelo Pezzote

All Kensington titles, imprints and distributed lines are available at special quantity discounts for bulk purchases for sales promotion, premiums, fund raising, educational or institutional use.

Special book excerpts or customized printings can also be created to fit specific needs. For details, write or phone the office of the Kensington Special Sales Manager: Kensington Publishing Corp., 850 Third Avenue, New York, NY 10022. Attn. Special Sales Department. Phone: 1-800-221-2647.

Kensington and the K logo Reg. U.S. Pat. & TM Off.

ISBN-13: 978-0-7582-1943-5
ISBN-10: 0-7582-1943-1

Designed by Leonard Telesca

First Kensington Trade Paperback Printing: March 2008
10 9 8 7 6 5 4 3 2 1

Printed in the United States of America

ACKNOWLEDGMENTS

I thank the following people, in alphabetical order, whose works have in part inspired this work: Dr. Alfred Adler, Dr. Sigmund Freud, Dr. Carl Jung, Jackson Katz and Jeremy Earp, Mike Lew, Dr. James O'Neil, Dr. Joseph Pleck, Dr. William Pollack and Dr. Ronald Levant, Dr. Terrence Real, Gabriel Rotello, MichelAngelo Signorile. Special thanks to inspirational teachers, mentors, colleagues, and friends, Dr. Michael Bernard Beckwith, Marie Keller, Dr. Leah Matson, and Dr. Arlen Ring. I've been influenced by their thoughts. This book in part contains some of their teachings, which I have adapted for gay men. Other acknowledgments are listed in the book where appropriate. A heartfelt thanks to all those who taught and believed in me: the formal teachers I've had in my life, clinical supervisors, colleagues, those who got Ask Angelo off the ground, my family, loved ones, and friends, and most of all, the people whom I've had the privilege to assist. I'm grateful to John Scognamiglio at Kensington Publishing for accepting my pitch, my editor, Justin Hocking, for acquiring my work and pushing me beyond where I thought I could go. He challenged me to chisel a statue (a book) out of a slab of marble (the words).

Contents

It takes a lot of courage to release the familiar and seemingly secure, to embrace the new. But there is no real security in what is no longer meaningful. There is more security in the adventurous and exciting, for in movement there is life, and in change there is power.

—Alan Cohen

1

The Inspiration

My "True Hollywood Story"

The journey home is never too long.
—A.R. Rahman and Don Black

Our journey begins in West Hollywood, California. Why there? West Hollywood is gay ground zero. The US Census last reported that California, followed by New York, has the highest proportion of same-sex couples in the states plus the District of Columbia. And West Hollywood upstaged San Francisco as the queen city, having the highest ratio of same-sex couples in the United States. A third of West Hollywood's residents are gay. There are over thirty gay bars in the city, which is just 1.9 square miles. It has one of the densest US populations, which can triple on weekends, and swell up to half a million for major events like Halloween Carnival and the Gay Pride Parade. The city is known as a front-runner in social justice legislation and as one of the gayest places in the country. In fact, it's Gay Mecca.

It was my life dream to move to West Hollywood (WeHo)—the shining city of Oz! It was going to be wonderful—a great, gay city! I had already traveled much of the globe, but I chose to live in West Hollywood. I was sure to make many gay friends and build a fulfilling life with my partner. Happiness awaited me.

After all, if I couldn't find it in West Hollywood as a gay man, then where on earth was left?

After ten years of California dreaming, I finally moved to the Emerald City from Boston, MA. After three and a half years together, my partner and love of my life unexpectedly told me he wasn't in love with me anymore. He walked out six months after arriving in West Hollywood and never looked back. He quickly joined the hot WeHo scene. When I bumped into him several months later, he was a stranger wearing another man's ring. I was heartbroken and felt hopeless. I was without a support system, and a severe depression arose in me. It hit me with the full force of a devastating blow. I would never hurt myself, but it was a time I could hardly bear. I wanted to die every minute of every day for many months. No one was truly there for me in the promised land. It was a dark, cold, and barren time.

I quickly realized I was not in Kansas anymore. I was tormented by the Wicked Witch of the West. She was disconnection, isolation, and loneliness. The three years I lived there were the most painfully lonely in my life. So many gay men, and yet I was so alone, treated with such indifference. Nicholas Snow, creator of *notesfromhollywood.com* and friend, put it best. He told me that American materialism, the Hollywood emphasis on appearances, and the fit body image of the gay male gym culture, all collide in West Hollywood with an intensity unlike anywhere else.

It seemed like most of the gay men there had a perfect Adonis appearance adorned with a perfect attitude. It was as if they were beautiful carvings of cold stone. Gorgeous, youthful, impeccably dressed, meticulously manicured, incredibly fit, and masculine to boot. They were calculatingly posed with an expressionless, emotionally unavailable stare that looked right past you as if you weren't there. They seemed to be sending out a strong contradictory message—I'm here and I'm fabulous, but don't you dare talk to me. I felt invisible. I may as well have been. It was nearly impossible to meet anybody. Unless alcohol or drugs were involved, the facades typically didn't come tumbling down on their own. It was an uninviting atmosphere, for the most part. While researching this subject, I interviewed many gay men with similar experiences. Interviewees named Johan and Doug shared their thoughts with me:

All kinds of people compliment me on my looks except other gay men. I feel a big difference when I'm surrounded by just gay men. They're all so stuck-up and stuck on themselves. Everyone's so guarded and it feels really unfriendly. I feel rejected by gay men rather than welcomed. I look around and feel worthless—like I'll never be good enough. I don't experience these feelings of insecurity in other places. I think I have good self-esteem, but I feel like I want to slit my wrists when I'm in a room full of gay guys. In fact, I'd prefer a Starbucks to a gay coffee shop, a gym to a gay gym, and a bar to a gay bar any day.

Doug shared:

I went on one of those big gay cruises thinking I was going to meet 2,000 great guys and I wanted to jump overboard after just a couple of days. It didn't feel welcoming at all.

Being lonely and being alone are not the same. Loneliness hurts, but being able to be comfortably alone with oneself is healthy. We create our own happiness from within. No one outside of us can truly make us happy, so it's important to learn to be alone. But I also know that it's a natural desire to share our lives with a partner and friends so we're not lonely. I'm not perfect, but with few notable exceptions, I could not meet friends, find dates, or hitch the future man of my dreams in West Hollywood. And I tried like hell.

I thank a power greater than myself for leading me to Dr. Michael Bernard Beckwith's Agape International Spiritual Center (*agape-*

live.com) in Culver City. I have been very inspired by Dr. Beckwith, both personally and professionally, adapting his teaching about love and authenticity for both my life and work with gay men. Agape was a magically supportive place. As a stranger walking in the door, I felt warm and welcomed by members. Everyone was like Glinda, the Good Witch of the North. It would be great if gay bars were embracing like that. We could straggle in, having been ravaged by the hostile antigay war outside, welcomed by our brothers.

Now, I'm sure West Hollywood can be a great place and that there are good people to be found there. But I was miserable in Gay Mecca. This deeply troubled me. I am a good person and a trained expert in building relationships. Yet I couldn't connect meaningfully with other gay souls in a preeminently gay city. Surely other gay men living there wanted deeper connection too. Something outside of me and them seemed to be getting in the way. I wondered what it was. I started to ponder this disconnect in our community. Didn't my experience in West Hollywood, the gayest of cities, reveal something about our sense of community as gay people in Anytown, USA?

I thought so. I started a gay, lesbian, bisexual, and transgender (GLBT) advice column, Ask Angelo, and Web site, *askangelo.com*, to address my concerns. Ask Angelo debuted at *westhollywood.com*, and soon after, I got invited for my first interview with *notesfrom hollywood.com*. Then Ask Angelo received its first online syndication at the *gaywired.com* network (now part of here! Interactive Media), and was printed in their international magazine *Gay Monkey* (now *here! magazine*). *Edgenewyork.com* network soon followed.

I began receiving letters from gay men everywhere. They also spoke of loneliness and feeling that there was something empty about gay culture. They too felt there seemed to be something missing in gay life. I listened to these men's voices. I'll be using Ask Angelo letters throughout the book to help bridge theory and real-life experience. The letters I use serve to represent the many I get just like them. I hear these same voices echoed again and again in my private psychotherapy practice, where I work almost exclusively with gay men, formerly in West Hollywood and now in Chelsea. The following letter is a composite.

I'm a good-looking normal guy, fairly new to the gay scene. From what I've been through so far, it seems to be mostly hooking up going on. I try, but I can't seem to find a healthy, lasting relationship. I think gay men don't want relationships because they are always looking for the next hot boy who comes along. Or they're such judgmental perfectionists that nobody's good enough for them. Or they are too full of themselves for anyone else. It's either about how much do you have, or what can you do for me, not to mention your youthful looks. I often feel down, empty, lonely, or angry. Sometimes to de-stress and escape I like to drink or get high. What floors me is that there have never been more ways to meet other gay men. The Internet, gay groups, sports leagues, political groups, personal ads, and the old ways such as the bars. But so much of our lives revolve around the bars/clubs/sex. Where does the relationship line start? I want to be first in line. Anybody talk? It seems like I hit the wrong mark a lot. They like me, but I don't like them. Or I like them but they don't like me. Or they just totally lie about themselves. I'm not 'discreet' about being out. Some of these 'straight-acting' guys won't meet you if you're too out. I thought it would be easy to find a gay relationship, but gay men treat each other like shit. I don't get it. Is it just me? I knew that being gay was going to be tough, but I didn't know I would be spending my life alone. I can't think of a time in my life when I have been more depressed. Gay life can be so lonely, and I'm doing everything I'm supposed to.

It saddens me how we treat each other in our community of gay men. It's like *Mean Girls*. A fair share of us seem to be flying high on BMW brooms much of the time, dressed in slimming black (Dolce & Gabbana) of course. It can be shocking, disappointing, and angering. But we can be empowered to change the situation if we understand what's going on.

When I felt most lonely, I needed someone caring to tell me I wasn't alone and that there was hope. So, I decided to share what I think is happening in our community by writing this book. Like the Scarecrow, the Tin Man, and the Lion, I realized that I already had inside what I had been seeking outside. I drew upon my education, training, and experience as a gay psychotherapist, pharmacist, and gay man. Like Dorothy, I left Kansas only to discover—there's no place like home. I went back east. My mission became to identify what's keeping gay men apart and to help them find one another's heartspace. As a community, we've focused a lot on the "gay" part of "gay man" but not enough on the "man" part. I hope this book changes that. Reliable statistics on gay men are still relatively scarce. The figures I provide are intended to show us the ballpark. This isn't meant to be a research or history book, or to represent every gay man's experience. It's just my take on things.

In my private practice for gay men, I observe that clients who suffer most have been, are, and fear being chastised by people for being gay. Much of our suffering comes from experiencing other people's negative reactions to us being gay, not from being gay by nature. I think almost all gay men experience social and psychological trauma because of prejudicial gay stigma, discrimination and oppression. We are significantly stressed and unfairly challenged by the toxic homophobic atmosphere of our heterosexist culture and negatively impacted by the dysfunctional responses of others.

For men both closeted and out, internalized homophobia levels have been found to be the largest impediment to mental health for gay men. The experience of societal stigma, discrimination and oppression makes gay men view their sexual identity in a negative way and produces shame. This results in low esteem, emotional distress, physical dis-ease and increased suicide risk. Further, coping responses like drugs, alcohol, unsafe sex, sex, porn, food, over-exercise, over-work, etc., mitigate the stress of living in a heterosexist culture, but are self-destructive. Compensations like overemphasizing masculine traits result in isolation, disconnection and loneliness. I work to free us all from horrible fear, humiliation and shame, toward recognizing the negative impact of homophobia on us and the importance of developing a positive sexual identity.

Having walked the walk, I help gay men thrive and sustain relationship in a sometimes insensitive world. I approach gayness as something that's positive, natural, and healthy. Thus, all of my work is in the context of being gay-affirmative. It's my goal to help change damaging experiences for gay men by: improving the poisonous homophobic atmosphere of our culture, alleviating symptoms or problems arising from these sensitive issues, fostering self-acceptance and self-love, affirming non-shameful authentic sexual identity, encouraging personal growth, and improving relationships.

Clients report that they are comfortable being themselves around me and that they find me easy to talk to. I deliver the rest of my message to you in this spirit.

You can search throughout the entire universe for someone more deserving of your love than you are, but that person will not be found. You deserve your love most.—Buddha

2

The Concern

I'm Fine. What's the Problem?

> *By seeking we may come upon the truth.*
> —Pierre Abelard

Maybe you just want more gay friends.

Maybe you're single, a great catch, and have tried everything you know to find true love—and still nothing's working. Perhaps you're fed up with "the scene" and wondering if there are still any good men out there. Maybe you worry you'll never find Mr. Right and you'll be alone—forever! Perhaps you're filled with envy every time you see a happy gay couple.

Maybe you're in a relationship and looking to feel closer to the man you're with. Perhaps you're tired of having the same argument. The passion in your relationship may feel like it's long gone. At times you may even wonder if you're with the right guy, but you don't want another failed relationship.

Maybe you can't quite put your finger on why it seems so hard to find a meaningful relationship that lasts with another man. You know you want deeper intimacy in your life. You're just not sure how to get it.

At times you may think things like: "Something's missing." "How do I make a gay relationship work?" "I'm tired of the bars, partying, and one-night stands." "Is it all about sex?" "I'm sick of all the attitude." "How do I meet more guys outside of the steam room?" "I'll always be single." "Why does it seem so impossible to meet a man for something more?" "No one wants me." "When do things get better?" "Something's just not right."

Don't spend another day racking your brain and beating yourself up. Want to know what's getting in the way of you and your man?

Meet Max. Max is a ruthless businessman. Like a hunter, he enjoys the "kill" of a deal. He was president of his fraternity and a star athlete. He is ruggedly handsome. The stubby shadow of his thick beard outlines his chiseled jaw. You can tell he is confident. Still youthful, he stands strong at 6'1", 210 pounds. He is muscular from pumping iron. He has large, rough hands. He sports a hard body complete with a six-pack of abs, a tatt, buzz cut, and cap. A rugby shirt covers his big, hairy chest. A pair of jeans hangs well on his solid lower body.

Max is tough. He keeps a serious face, a brooding scowl that can make him look mean and pissed off. He can be ready to fight at a moment's notice. He speaks few words. He remains stoic, careful not to reveal any weakness. He is an emotional mystery. He has a deep, commanding voice. He doesn't wear cologne. He moves in stiff and controlled strides. He needs no one.

Max is reliable. He provides for his wife, kids, as well as the family dog, in a decent neighborhood. He's a devoted husband, and while he and his dad are distant, he is a very loving father. On weekends he enjoys spending time with his family, attending a service at the community church, and fixing things around the house. He plays cards, drinks, and smokes cigars with the guys on Friday nights. They talk about the hot chicks they dream about screwing on the side. The guys like to yell out "faggots" if a preview for a *Will & Grace* rerun plays on TV during the boxing tournament.

Who is Max? Whether you're rich or poor, white or a man of color, to you Max represents an overriding all-American stereotype of a macho guy. He is "a man's man"—"all man"—a "real man." He represents a particular "model" of maleness—a myth propelled by the media; a composite image of certain masculine traits that represents an impossible standard of manhood. Picture the Hollywood characters portrayed by The Rock and Vin Diesel. Such "ideal" male images capture the stereotype of the "real man" in America.

Through powerful social forces, such "real man" images have come to define "all-American" maleness. Our culture shoves "his" traits in our faces countless times a day. He's presented to us in many different forms throughout our lives. The media bombards us with him. He's in print, music, TV, and the Internet. He's in art, the theater, cinema, cartoons, and video games. He's in our families, at work, and in our institutions. He tells us how to "be a man." He's everywhere, always—the yardstick for manhood we measure ourselves against.

When I ask gay men in my masculinity workshops for the qualities of this stereotype, here's the laundry list of masculine traits I typically get: *white, successful, good-looking, muscular, strong, big, tough, hard, dominant, powerful, virile, heterosexual, stud, partier, independent, a leader, decisive, logical, initiates, vocal, brave, protector, violent, aggressive, mean, angry, conquering, capable, active, athletic, competitive, unemotional, stoic, invulnerable, honorable, reliable, family oriented, believes in God*. While this list represents many traits of the "real man," it isn't absolute. There are many acceptable ways to be a man in the world. Each way represents a certain grouping, or constellation, of specific masculine traits. Different eras, cultures, and subcultures have varying constellations, or standards, for masculinity. For instance, today in America, many African-American and Latino men mimic a sort of hip-hop, urban street style that Richard Majors identified as a "cool pose." Yet, an overarching image of a stereotypical "real man" who is larger than life, like that portrayed by the legendary characters of James Dean, James Bond, Clint Eastwood, or Sylvester

Stallone has had extraordinary influence over American men, no matter what their race, ethnicity, economic status, or background.

However, the "real man" image is unachievable. You may have noticed that some of the "real man" traits in the list were exact opposites. No human man can be, or needs to be, all of those things. Since it's impossible to live up to all the attributes of the "real man," most of the men you're close to probably aren't like "him" behind closed doors. But make no mistake. Most men are heavily influenced by the "real man" image, try to measure up to it, and like to portray their version of its persona in public.

If you have any doubts about the profound influence of the "real man," watch and listen—the signs are all around you.

On the New York subway, it's a man's automated voice that delivers authoritative commands like, "Step away from the doors, please." A woman's voice provides helpful information: "This is an uptown C train." One day I was waiting with a friend in a long line for Broadway tickets. Suddenly, an unofficial-looking man across the street raised his hand and directed everyone to "move the line over here." In spite of the fact that he was wearing nothing that identified him as a ticket agent, about a quarter of the line obeyed the stranger without question and went to wait with him across the street. Turns out he didn't work for the ticket booth. He was just a joker. A significant number of people did what this person told them to do simply because he was a man. A woman would not have had the same influence so easily. I was flabbergasted that this could still happen in the middle of New York City in modern times.

TV is one of the biggest conveyors of information about maleness. In a span of just under three minutes, while surfing cable, I saw a father say to his son, "Face your fears like a man." An erection pill commercial told me to "imagine what it's like to be a real man in bed!" An officer told his squad, "I'll make men out of you." A commercial for a deodorant told me it was "tough enough for a man." A mother sent her son on his honeymoon. "Enjoy becoming a man, son," she said. One guy told another he was "wearing more cologne than any man should." A huge lite beer can fell from the sky into the middle of an outdoor men's party. It landed on the wimpy guy—crushing him. And a cartoon villain told a youth to take punishment "like a man."

I spoke with a young man who lost his father and newborn in the same year. I asked him how he was doing and if there was anything I could do for him. He said proudly, "No, I'm just trying to stay strong."

The influence of the "real man" is quite real, but one of "his" traits stands out from the others. The "real man" is unquestionably heterosexual. All heroes and mass media images of iconic men are heterosexual. It's no big surprise that all males are assumed to be heterosexual until proven otherwise. No parent hopes their son is gay. In these ways, we can see how homophobia—the fear, discrimination, and prejudice against gays—"colludes" with heterosexuality. Homophobia and heterosexuality are tied together. Many men "broadcast" homophobia so other people won't think they're gay. Most men don't want to be thought of as gay because they don't want to be seen as "feminine." A "feminine" man is seen as emotional and weak. So "endorsing" homophobia is tied to a man's desire to be seen as straight, masculine, strong, or manly, and not gay, "feminine," "weak," or "unmanly." In this way, homophobia works hand in hand with heterosexuality, and becomes another glaring trait of the ideal masculinity.

So the "real man" is homophobic, too. A straight guy can get away with being "soft" as long as he asserts his heterosexuality—his manhood. Today, he may be tough and sensitive, wear a pink shirt, spoof drag, or even befriend gays, but he still doesn't want to be perceived as being gay, "womanly," "weak," or "unmanly" himself. Tom Cruise, reportedly a "great respecter of gay rights," according to his lawyer, still filed charges and won millions in damages for defamation lawsuits against those alleging he was gay. Cruise's lawyer reportedly said Cruise was "tired of it and it hurts his children." Being gay is considered slanderous. Even mainstream gay publications arrive in our mailbox shrouded in opaque plastic wrapping, proclaiming inside, "Publication of the name or photograph of any individual or organization is not to be construed as any indication of the sexual orientation of such." After all, we wouldn't want to offend anyone.

So what's this all got to do with you? Many gay men seek to present a normative masculine image. A fair share of men in our community want to be perceived as "real men" who aren't "flamboyant." Many of us actually demand that our men don't look, behave, or sound "too gay." How's this for some ironic twists? Check out gay men's personal ads: "masculine for same," "straight acting, straight appearing only," "wanted: real man, muscular, who likes sports," "no fats, no fems." Some can be confusing, like "straight, total top looking for discreet man action." Others are downright contradictions like "straight gay porn" and "straight bottom." And what about this one—"straight men exploring their lust for other men." I don't know about you, but I'm a little confused. Doesn't "their lust for other men" make them gay—even if it's just a little?

More and more self-identified straight men have become part of the gay scene. There's a whole gay Web site called "normal gay" and many other sites exist with similar themes. Such "regular guys" may work as go-go boys, bartenders, or doormen. I recall going over to chat with a hot doorman of a well-known gay club. He said in a huff, "You know I'm 1000 percent straight, right?" Some male escorts say they're only "gay for pay." Many tell me it's simply because the money's better. I recall a recent conversation with a Latino I met in a popular gay establishment. When I got too casual, by calling him "girl," he responded in a threatening tone. "Don't call me 'girl.' I'm not one of your faggot friends."

It doesn't matter whether a guy's really straight or not. What matters is that a guy who acts straight, by having the masculinity of a straight man, a "real man," is highly valued. This is true whether he's straight, closeted, curious/exploring, out and proud, or someplace else.

Heterosexism, the bias that being straight is the "normal" sexual orientation, and homophobia are powerful overarching constructs that influence all men—straight and gay alike. But for gay men, heterosexist and homophobic norms are obstacles that are especially difficult to surmount. In the struggle to come out, we can experience two conflicting drives—the important need to belong, and the equally important need to be our true selves. We may get caught in the Catch-22 of conforming to belong, while being our authentic selves. We may be out, but we may also elect to conform, at times diminishing the signals that we're gay—to play it more mainstream and masculine. Coming out doesn't mark the end of the road. Coming out isn't an event that's over when we first out ourselves. It's a lifelong process. We're constantly deciphering how far to be out—when, where, and with whom. No matter how much work we've done to be out, the sly Gay Shame Monster can creep up on us at any time, and we may play it more straight to "pass" and blend. It's more comfortable. We're nearly guaranteed an easier time, especially around strangers and other men. Most gay men take it as a good thing, a compliment, if others can't tell they're gay. We don't always wear our rainbow colors.

Understandably so. American gays have grown up in a predominantly antigay culture. It still wasn't that long ago when homosexuality was illegal and classified as a mental disorder in this country. Even today, according to one Gallup News Service

Poll, fewer than half of Americans consider homosexuality to be a morally acceptable "alternative lifestyle."

While all people have lifelong challenges and are different in some unique and beautiful way, GLBT persons can face overwhelming hate, prejudice, and discrimination at almost every turn. Even though social acceptance is improving and the number of straight allies is growing, we can't get our love affirmed by federal marriage or enjoy the 1049 legal privileges marriage brings, like immigrating our partners, being taxed equally, visiting our partners in the hospital, and receiving our partner's inheritance. Meanwhile, dysfunctional marriages, infidelity scandals, divorce, broken families, and multiple marriages march on. Adoption can still be hard for gays because many don't trust "us" around children. At the same time, "their" children are abused or aborted every day. We can have trouble just being allowed to be near children— as teachers, day-care workers or summer camp counselors. Meanwhile, even though most sexual perpetrators are straight men, gay men who work with children are considered more suspect than straight men who do so. Gays are acceptable scapegoats in modernity, being battered openly as a matter of national discourse that includes hate speech, which, ironically, is sponsored by many lawmakers in the guise of love, family values, and religious morality. Our government uses religion as a weapon against us, and even proposed amending the US Constitution. We're not allowed to serve openly in the military with "Don't Ask, Don't Tell." Our love has to be kept silent, not to be asked about or openly expressed. Top soldiers in the US military have called us "immoral," while honorable GLBT soldiers serve, fight, and die for our country. Why is it that we can legally crush a gay soldier's spirit? Over 10,000 GLBT personnel have been discharged since 1994 because of antigay harassment, the majority in peacetime. Gayness is often associated with despised traits. Many of us are rejected by our beloved families, friends, co-workers, and religious communities. A study found that about 25 percent of gay youth are rejected outright by their own families. Unable to live at home, many wind up on the street. Nationally, 40 percent of homeless youth are gay. New York City alone has over 7,000 homeless gay youth. Many of us are denied housing, lose business, get fired from work, or just don't get promoted—for some "other" reason, of course. A Lambda Legal and Deloitte Financial Advisory Services survey found that 20 percent of GLBTs experienced barriers to being promoted and 40 percent reported job harassment. Many of us have been ridiculed, insulted, threatened, beaten—even murdered— in violent hate crimes. GLBTs constitute the victims of roughly 16 percent of all hate crimes that get reported. We may even do the job for ourselves. A Parents, Families and Friends of Lesbians and Gays (PFLAG) survey found that approximately one out of three sexual minorities has thought about or attempted suicide. While the situation is improving significantly, gays are probably the most besieged group in America, whom people can openly hate and discriminate against with little serious reprisal. No wonder we have problems.

In such an inhospitable climate, many gays themselves "ingest" that being gay is not a good thing. If I "feed" a plant poisoned water, it can't help but absorb some of the poison. We, too, take in toxic ideas about being gay from our polluted cultural environment. The way we see ourselves is in part a reflection of how we think others see us. Ultimately, as gay men growing up in a homophobic culture, we feel shame because we're not seen as "real men" and our self-esteem gets corroded. Sam stated:

I learned to see myself through the eyes of others like my parents. I felt they disapproved of me. I felt judged and I believed I disappointed them. I felt I was bad and wrong. I knew I wasn't considered "a man" and at times I felt like I wasn't even thought of as a person. I felt diminished. I was so ashamed. Growing up, I heard and read awful things that people were saying about gays. I thought they must be right because they were important people saying it. I grew up seeing terrible images of AIDS on TV and thought, "Is that my future?" I thought I deserved to get sick, die, and go straight to Hell. Death seemed like a better option than being gay, anyway. I thought if I didn't die, I'd surely be crucified.

Even if we're out, a part of us can secretly harbor the prevailing, negative social judgment of being gay and bear shame. Who can feel good about themselves when they're being oppressed every day in the news, at work, at church, and at home? How do we thrive in confidence and move toward same-sex relationship when we fear that the very society, institutions, communities, and loved ones that nurture us may exile us because of our true nature?

Sadly, a large number of us try to stamp out our "gayness" to appear more straight, masculine, or "normal" so we fit in. We downplay our "gayness" even after we admit it. There's a gay/straight blending that many of us do to be more accepted. Afraid to stick out too much, we try to blend like chameleons. At times we may offset, or balance, our "gayness" with masculinity. The use of such "normalizing," or "I'm gay, but I'm just like you" strategies, makes it hard to tell if we're really progressing socially and assimilating into mainstream culture, or if we're actually doing a type of social conforming, in which case we're moving backwards.

I have been perplexed by the recent plethora of articles in popular and gay literature saying in essence that "gay" is over because gays are so postmodernly homogenized into mainstream culture. The implicit attitude of these articles is that being gay is becoming so accepted and normalized, that there's no more need to use such arbitrary labels like "gay" and "straight." After all, we're all the same.

Articles like this have appeared in publications such as *Time*, *Newsweek*, and even our own the *Advocate*. They often point out that gay youth are coming out younger. Reportedly, more gay teens are having positive experiences with their peers. The journalists convey the idea that the bleakness of coming out that dominated the early years of men in my generation seems to be falling by the wayside. Today, there are many positive images of gay people in the media. The risk of coming out is run in a social atmosphere that is more uncertain than absolutely rejecting. Yes, they sometimes confess, there is still some hardship, antigay bigotry and antigay violence out there, but the cultural winds have shifted toward acceptance. In fact, they say, there are many gay youth who are rejecting the "gay" label today because they want to be seen as just normal. Such articles claim these younger gays are moving us forward to a postgay era.

I disagree. Yes, things have improved dramatically for us, but I think gay youth, like many other gay men, are still busy distancing themselves from the unmanly stigma of being perceived as stereotypically "gay," "flamboyant," or "effeminate" and it drives this feeling—I just want to be seen as normal, i.e., just like you, regular, masculine, not "too gay"—in which case we are really moving away from self-acceptance. While we all want respect and deserve to be treated just like any other person, I don't think the "gays acting normal" mentality is bringing us into equality as much as it's moving us back into an extension of the closet— the closet of masculinity.

"Normalizing" is a type of conforming to the prevailing social masculine ideology. We may twist ourselves into pretzels to fit in because we want to be treated like everyone else. So we might behave "less gay," and more masculine, like "regular," "normal," or "real men," because that's more "acceptable." This "gays acting normal" mentality fools us into thinking it's progressive and good because others can more easily relate to us. But by morphing our behavior into the shape of how others expect us to be, we're actually abandoning a part of ourselves in order to conform to other people's standards. It's "I'll be just like you want me to be so you'll love me" thinking.

Such an appeasement mode rings especially true for our community in an age of terrorism when people are stressed and fearing for their lives. In such worrisome times, the mainstream feels more punitive toward groups it deems as moral transgressors—like gays. Sexuality is shamed in general in this country, but homosexuality has been specifically targeted. Many gays understandably seek to normalize themselves by making their "gayness" appear less important than it actually is, or muting how much it's openly expressed in appearance, mannerisms, the way they talk, and so on. Many gay men are discreet and conform to the rules of masculinity as much as possible in self-defense because gays are often attacked.

Many gays struggle to fully embrace gayness. To make matters worse, gay culture doesn't seem to be fully embracing, either. Many gay teens and men report they find gay culture empty. They say they want more of a sense of community. They want to feel more like they fit in and belong. Some are being lured into the lion's den of ex-gay groups like Exodus International, Parents and Friends of ExGays and Gays (PFOX), and Love Won Out that promise to meet that need. Those groups are bent on making homos act like heteros with promises of salvation and a more fulfilling life. They're wolves in sheep's clothing that claim "reparative" or "conversion therapy"—the ultimate in conforming to the rules of masculinity—is the answer to feeling normal. They view being gay as a gender identification problem and prescribe nonsexual male bonding activities with heterosexual men, while repeating manly affirmations like "I'm masculine." Their popularity is resurging because (given gay stigma) gay men are shamed and often feel inferior as men.

Such "normalizing" trends miss the central issue—that the reason some gay persons seek to distance themselves from "gay" in the first place is because they're taught that "gayness" isn't something acceptable. While many gay people have worked hard to be out and proud, "gay" is also loaded with a collective and personal history of rejection, hurt, and pain for many of us. So we can love and hate the word. Labeling yourself "gay" means you run the risk of being "unacceptable" and not belonging. Belonging is an essential human need. It comes right after survival needs, like food and shelter, in American psychologist Abraham Maslow's well-known hierarchy of needs. Sure, we all want to belong. But wiping out the expression of one's "gayness" only deepens the shame that brought about the desire to get rid of it in the first place. Instead, our focus needs to be on embracing our "gayness" and fostering self-love. It's understandably difficult. What man would choose to be identified with something that's so stigmatized if he didn't have to?

People haven't stopped identifying as "gay" just because more gays are accepted and integrated into society. Quite the contrary. We are still fighting for equal rights. Not to mention, the words "fag," "faggot," and "gay," as well as phrases like "that's so gay," are commonly used today to refer to anything or anyone that's lame, stupid, freakish, inferior, or weak—unworthy of respect. They're derogatory words that demonstrate just how much gays are reviled in our culture. No wonder we want to normalize ourselves and aren't comfortable being associated with anything "too gay." Many gay people just don't want to complicate things by "putting it in their face." This would bring more burdens onto themselves than they already have with the "gay" label itself. "Gay is over," "I'm gay, but I'm just like you," and "repair being gay" are nice ideas. But I have a news flash. We're gay and that's a unique and beautiful thing to celebrate. "Gay" makes us quite unlike everyone else. If "gay" was over, if we were just the same as everyone else, or if gay wasn't considered a choice, then we wouldn't still be targets of blame. We wouldn't need to understate ourselves, obscure our "gayness," or "normalize" to feel more comfortable.

Shame is not intrinsic to being a gay person. It comes from a homophobic culture. People aren't bad, but a bad atmosphere can be "infective." Internalizing continuous antigay prejudice and discrimination can breed antigay sentiment in heterosexuals and a sense of inadequacy, shame, and a corroded self-esteem in gay people. In the face of gay liberation, the assaults of a conservative backlash have brought our "unacceptability," "inferiority," and consequently, our unconscious shame, to fuller consciousness. The more they see us, the more they judge us. It's unbearable. The shame and pain of social rejection makes some gay men unwilling to stick out too much by appearing less masculine. We can be careful not to "flaunt it." The need for such "discretion" can be carried into adulthood from childhood. Juan told me he learned young that he better "hide it":

> *One day I remember watching TV with my mother and a "gay" character came on. She said, "I'd rather have a dead son than a gay son."*

By "conforming," we're screaming out that we just want to be seen and treated as normal. We don't really wish to erase being gay—a core part of ourselves—our sexual identity. It's who we are. Gay persons, as well as mainstream American medical and mental health professionals, overwhelmingly say that being gay is not a choice. Scientific research is pointing toward confirming a biological cause. No one wants to "hide," convert," or "repair" the essence of who they are. In fact, that's damaging. What gay persons really want to change is all the hardship that comes with being gay. We want the pain that comes from the stigma to be taken away so we suffer less, living better lives.

In spite of all the obstacles, many of us triumph. We can be accepting of our sexuality and feel comfortable enough to pro- claim publicly, "I'm gay and not ashamed of it." But that may be just the tip of the iceberg. The struggles we've overcome to get there can leave emotional scars, or unconscious shame, that's invisible inside. That's like the bulk of the iceberg that remains hidden underneath the surface. Even if we're out, we may still feel somewhere deep inside, "I'm inferior, abnormal, sick, bad, and wrong for being gay." In short, we have to believe self-love in our hearts, not just our heads.

In a nutshell, many of us may "act" relatively more masculine because of hidden shame. "Straight acting" is a term I use to describe this phenomenon. Some closeted men, who may or may not yet be having sex with men, are literally acting straight. Other gay men are straight acting. They're out to varying degrees, but avoid the stigma of being "too flamboyant." The phrase "straight acting" customarily refers to gay men who don't exhibit stereo- typically gay, effeminate, or nonmasculine mannerisms, dress, or behavior, in order to be seen in a more positive light. I use the phrase "straight acting" broadly to refer to gay men, closeted or out, who portray their masculinity as if they were a "regular," "normal," or straight guy—a "real man" to whatever extent. A gay Broadway actor I treated captured the essence of straight acting with this comment about being out in his profession:

When you audition for a role, you have to be perceived as being straight. The casting director, director, and producer may be gay

*themselves, but they don't want an actor who's perceived as gay.
If you don't play it straight, you won't get many parts.*

Walter described straight acting like this:

*I was at my best friend's wedding. Everyone knows about me,
I'm out, but I was still playing it kinda straight. Like I remember thinking, "God, I really don't want to fag out on the dance
floor."*

A gay online profile put it more directly: *No fems. Looking for
normal.*

Lance Bass reportedly said to *People* magazine, "I want people to take that being gay is a norm. That the stereotypes are
out the window. I've met so many people like me that it's really
encouraged me. I call them the SAGs—the straight-acting gays.
We're just normal, typical guys. I love to watch football and drink
beer." I'm not criticizing Lance Bass. I respect him for being out.
This is just a perfect example of downplaying our gayness with
a straight-acting comment to be seen in a more flattering way.

The need to "be a man" seems to be of paramount importance and not only to gay men. Many straight men put out a
manly image too, a *"tough guise"*—a term devised by Jackson
Katz and Jeremy Earp. Katz and Earp identify the essence of
masculinity as performance. To perform is to carry out an action
in public. A large part of masculinity, then, is made up of how
men act in public. The "tough guise" is a tough-guy pose. It's
a social show men put on for others, namely other men and potential mates, to get respect and attract love.

There may be good intentions behind straight acting. Lance
Bass reportedly said he's proud to be gay and not ashamed. I

don't doubt it. But you can't say "I'm proud to be gay" and "I'm straight acting" in the same sentence. It's an oxymoron. Straight acting is engendered by gay shame. It means "I'm gay with a disclaimer." It's a gay decoy. Straight acting attempts to level the playing field. It helps us feel like we're still men, like we have more approval. Sure, we all want to defeat stereotypes, having a more trouble-free life. We want to be more accepted and to belong—to feel normal, have equality and a chance to be loved— just like anyone else. Things haven't customarily been that way.

Throughout history, to remain physically, mentally, emotionally, spiritually, and socially safe, gay men have grown accustomed to having to conceal their gayness from others to pass—to pretend. Based on our community's history, we can still harbor fear deep in our collective unconscious, which haunts us. A fear that we will be discovered and harassed if we're not low-key enough. Having our "cover" blown is still potentially dangerous in many ways. Thus, the primitive part of our brain in charge of keeping us safe may interpret being gay as a survival threat. Straight acting is a "gay instinct," an adaptive survival skill that's been imprinted in our individual unconscious minds over generations for protection. Consequently, many of us continue to raise our defense shields, cloaking our gayness with a pretense of straight-acting masculinity.

The straight-acting modus operandi is the subject of this book. Most of the straight "act" happens unconsciously. To the unconscious mind, our No. 1 goal is survival. In being straight acting, we are seeking to insure two important, fundamental elements in our survival—to stay safe physically from antigay violence and to belong psychologically. The straight-acting "tough guise" or "disguise" is gay men's camouflage. This online profile shows how we go underground: *Discreet. Masculine. That means I don't act fem, so neither should you.* This off-putting cover helps explain why many gay men are lonely. But we can undo the "act" to find true love by healing the inferiority, shame, and fear that underlie it with self-acceptance.

Self-love can be a lifelong challenge. The Cass Model (Vivian Cass, 1984), widely used for GLBT identity-formation and coming out, is based on an inner acceptance of a socially unacceptable difference. It shows how GLBT people decrease their gay shame and accept themselves more through a six-stage continuum model. The model places the burden of acceptance on the gay person rather than on society. It would be much simpler if others had to go through stages to accept us. We aren't the problem. But unfairly, we get stuck with a very big bill.

While people can vacillate among the six stages, they have to continue to fight gay shame throughout their lives in order to move forward in this model overall. Albeit to relatively lesser degrees, gay persons continue to conceal their gayness, or are straight acting, through at least Stage Four. Stage Five is a kind of middle ground where you're sort of straight acting. You're out, but not always, to anyone anywhere. Gays are not always out to everyone everywhere until Stage Six. But even amid the safety of metropolitan areas, there are many times more men who feel most comfortable in Stage Five or below, than there are in Stage Six (who are always visibly out, never straight acting) than there are below. So the straight-acting gay man is very real. He's the vast majority of gay men. Unfortunately, straight acting keeps gay men suffering, obstructed from gay relationship.

With awareness, we can better cope with, and change, the poisonous social attitudes that "gay" embodies, so we can accept our whole selves comfortably just as we are, and create more fulfilling relationships with full equality. To triumph over straight acting, gay persons need to hear gay activist Franklin Kameny's message—"gay is good"; and looking, behaving, or sounding gay is OK too.

There's nothing wrong with you. Just as you are, you are

every bit a man as a straight guy. Yes, heterosexism and homophobia can make it damn hard for many gay men, even if they're out, to let go of masculinity, openly express their full "gay" selves, and have satisfying gay relationships—if they buy into the "real man" ideology and think "gayness" is less masculine. But don't be pressured to adopt a straight-acting guise. Such blending, normalizing, or conformity is mistaken for gay acceptance, assimilation, and as necessary to further our "agenda," rather than being seen for what it is—shame and self-rejection.

You don't have to be effeminate if you're not. You just have to be yourself—a gay man without any facade.

3

The Culprit

Masculinity and Its Influence—The Birth of Straight Acting

> *"Man is the only creature that refuses to be what he is."*
>
> —Albert Camus

Masculinity is the villain behind straight acting. Exploring masculinity and its impact on gay men is the purpose of this chapter.

A hallmark trait of masculinity is being tough and emotionally strong. That quality lends itself to one of manhood's most honorable and heroic sides—the ability of a man to squash his feelings, thus sacrificing himself in order to benefit others or a great cause. This virtue is demonstrated in things like putting "women and children first," the heroism of 9/11, and devotion to work and family. But being less emotional is also a trait that has extremely negative consequences for men too. The "dark side" reveals itself in things like deadbeat dads, infidelity, divorce, destructive competition, crime, violence, war, and disease. This includes suffering from disconnectedness, separation, injury, illness, and death.

The story of masculinity mostly tells the dark side of the tale. Throughout history, great empires have been built upon the killing, conquest, rape, and pillage of others. This has been the rule more than the exception. Much of the blood has been spilled by rich white men in the name of ideology, especially religion. Male reign was often established using brute strength and power, even if it was to serve a queen. Women, children, and indigenous people were dominated and converted to the prevailing customs. Since men held all the power, that which was masculine held a high social currency. Significant social pressure to bow down to that which was masculine resulted in the subjected cultures. Social adherence to the ways in which men and woman were expected to behave, according to the dominant culture, developed. Today such conforming behavior is known as sex roles or gender roles. Gender roles are long-standing, deeply held, cultural beliefs that are like fixtures in many people's minds. Thanks to the American feminist movement, many expectations of traditional sex roles have given way to the times. But we continue to live in a male-dominated world. Our society still ranks men above women. People still expect men and women to behave in certain ways. The expectations that remain are old and powerful diehards.

Why do those that remain retain such power? Because they've taken root deep in our psyches. Sex roles were already in play well before the white man. In *Religion: What Is It?* author William Tremmel says that in primitive times, amid the uncontrollable, unknown, and often unpleasant forces of Mother Nature, our unsheltered ancestors needed security in a dangerous and terrifying tooth-and-claw world. He says that, without science, our ancestors used belief systems like superstition, magic, and religion in an attempt to manipulate unseen forces to gain a sense of control in their unpredictable environment. They needed something to ease their anxiety and bring them the comfort of security. They needed to make meaning from chaos.

According to the philosophers, one's life is ultimately built upon the place it gets its meaning from. This is an ideology, most often religion. From there we develop values. From values we derive goals. Goals direct behavior. And behavior is what makes up our lives. So people fiercely protect the ideology, or religion, from which they get their meaning, because their whole life has been built around it.

This is why people throughout history have automatically defaulted to religious bigotry as the basis for "the wrongness" of homosexuality. It's the reason homosexuality ultimately gets linked with being immoral. It's also the reason women suspected of being witches were slaughtered. People who cling to strict ideology, like religious dogma, are often fearful people who aren't strong independent thinkers. They believe that they will be rewarded by following a path of righteousness. They like the security that following the rules, conforming, and belonging bring. They erect strong inner scaffolding to ease the fear of what's unknown outside. Folks fear behavior that's foreign to theirs. Unconsciously, it threatens the foundation of their life, by challenging their core belief system—i.e., the religious ideology—upon which it's built.

A conservative conformist mentality may still run strong in the collective unconscious of a large group of Americans, since some of the first European colonists that settled America were Pilgrims. The Pilgrims were a group of English separatists called Puritans, who committed themselves to a life based on the Bible. They were persecuted in England for their relatively conservative religious beliefs and fled to establish religious freedom for themselves. However, they were rather intolerant of others who held different beliefs.

Many people, religious or not, find the security that conformity brings appealing, especially in an age of terrorism and uncertainty. To feel secure in a "dangerous" world, we cling to what we know, and demonize "the others" who contradict our ideology. After all, we're taught that the "fallen" descend into a place of darkness, flames, and eternal punishment. Conforming to the rules brings psychological security, comfort, and safety. A theme of the song "Stars" in the play *Les Miserables* is that we need sentinels to protect us, enforcing the rules. They can keep watch in the night so things remain predictable and fixed like the stars. This may help explain the popularity of some modern sentinels— the religious right and other conservative groups—against gays.

Think of gender roles and masculinity as a sort of routine mass conformity like something out of Pink Floyd's *The Wall*. Everyone follows the rules. The benefit is that it allows for order and routine, which reduce fear and anxiety. Such ritualized structure keeps people busy. It shields us from the petrifying silence. According to the existentialists, without such distraction, the uncomfortable age-old questions, "When will I die?" and "What is the meaning of life?" surface. Strict codes of behavior, like gender roles, provide a secure canvas, thrown against the backdrop of nothingness, upon which we paint our lives.

Social scripts also brought an advantage for our species. Traditional gender roles provided a structure, such as the division of labor, that was useful for extending survival. Babies were either molded into hunters and warriors or harvesters and fair maidens destined for motherhood. Over time, gender roles became automatic scripts that were played. Few brave souls bucked the system. For the most part, men did what men did, women did what they were told, and neither dared to cross the line. As it's commonly said, "it's just the way it is."

I ordered a chicken at the take-out counter in a restaurant on the corner of W. 23rd Street and Eighth Avenue. There's a whole separate section for dining in. But I spotted a row of empty bar-side tables near the take-out counter. I decided to sit and enjoy my chicken. There was nobody else sitting at these tables, it was self-serve, and no one was waiting for a table. Anyway, I was asked to leave because I had ordered a "take-out" chicken. Both the host and the manager demanded that I therefore "take it out." They couldn't give me any other reason as to why I couldn't sit at a vacant bar-side table and enjoy my chicken other than "those are the rules."

The rules of masculinity work the same way. They often don't make much sense, but everyone follows them and enforces them anyway. The rules of traditional masculinity in America represent a powerful social force that's hard to move against.

If you doubt the power one's sex holds in society, I ask you: What is the first question people ask when a new baby is born? That's right. They ask, "Is it a boy or a girl?" It all unfolds from there. People ask for the baby's sex because it's not always that easy to tell just by looking. Folks want to know how to act. Simple observation will show that they actually change their behavior according to the baby's sex. People talk differently to the newborn. They touch the baby differently. Individuals move differently around the baby. They expect different things from the baby. People respond to the infant differently. Folks describe the newborn differently. Individuals buy the newborn different toys. The baby is dressed as a boy or girl. Relatives and friends have different hopes and dreams for the infant. Many parents even opt to know the sex before birth. They prefer to prepare. They need to pick names, buy the right wallpaper, and get the appropriate toys. Knowing makes planning simpler, because it's all pink or blue from there. And try saying, "What a pretty little girl" when it's a boy. You will swiftly be corrected. So the words, "It's a boy," and all that entails, are as powerful today as they were to kings.

But what is maleness exactly? Maleness is not the same as masculinity. Maleness is our sex, our biology—the body we're born with. If you're born with a penis, you're male. Our masculinity, on the other hand, is not something we're born with. It's something we're taught to develop. It's a social invention. Masculinity is a socially constructed set of expectations based on one's being male. Masculinity is how males are socialized to express their maleness. It's our gender expression. The "real man" image of masculinity is a social "game" that children will learn to some degree based on what they see, how they are treated, and what they are taught. Since masculinity is learned, it can be unlearned.

In my training, a clinical mentor, friend, and colleague of mine, LA psychologist Dr. Arlen Ring (arlenring.com), helped me understand more about how masculinity works.

When I was a kid, we played this game called King of the Mountain. One boy would run to the top of a mound and proclaim himself king. The other boys would run up the sides and try to knock him off the top. Whoever toppled the king dethroned him and, in turn, became king. Masculinity is a social "game" that works in much the same way.

Men compete against each other for status—to be one-up. One's ranking as a man is achieved by scoring "points." Check out typical cocktail-party talk—men discuss work, titles, salary, houses, cars, pretty wives, children. They flex muscle, both intellectual and physical, show tattoos, discuss sports, sexual prowess, and so on.

Ironically, masculinity has much to do with men posing for other men's admiration. Perhaps it's because masculinity comes so close to being gay in this particular way that homophobia is so prevalent. There's a fine line between what's adoration of a man's masculinity, and what's gay, but it's clearly marked. Most men are quite mindful of the distinction. They know exactly where one ends and the other begins. The consequences of crossing that line can be fierce.

Ordinarily, the spirit of guys showing off for each other is good-natured. But underneath, there's a sense of battle readiness in case one needs to improve his rank. A friendly ribbing can turn into an offense to one's manhood and quickly turn violent. A man can be called upon to fight at any time. Men are vigilant. Their manhood is set on alert status. They are prepared, armed, and willing to defend their manhood at any moment. As the soldier, he has to be physically strong, emotionally tough, and endure pain. He will be punished for any "feminine" weakness. A man wants respect. He wants to prove he's tough, strong, and powerful in other men's eyes. He may be willing to stand there and protect his honor until his death.

Men keep close tabs on each other's masculinity, especially in all-male arenas where men are intimate, like on a sports team or in a fraternity. Here, men play together, shower, party, eat, sleep, and live in close quarters. In such circumstances, homophobia can be and oftentimes is severe. There's a pack mentality to masculinity where the men carefully police each other. Everyone is cautious, pitted male to male, jockeying for a status boost. One loses a lot of "points" for sissy stuff. Every man is circumspect. In a machismo world, there's no way out. It's kill or be killed. Each man is sure to convey some degree of homophobia, since his manhood is being monitored so closely, to maintain his status in the group. An experience with a teammate or brother can be quite different one-on-one.

The masculinity of the "real man" is a mask that boys, and later men, grow to wear to some extent. It's a man's facade, not his true nature. The true self hides behind the protective armor of masculinity forged by society. Behind the hard shield lies a man's true nature—a soft, gentle, sensitive, emotional, kind, loving human being.

In my interviews, I spoke with a lot of gay guys about the idea that masculinity is learned. Many strongly disagreed with the idea. The crux of their responses is:

Masculinity is an essence, not an attitude.
I'm just masculine. It's who I am. Gay or straight—it's my nature.

These notions aren't entirely true. If masculinity was yoked with one's identity, an essence, a man's nature, a part of his biology, then we would expect all men to be quite similar in their masculinity. We know from our experience that this is not the case. There are many different types of men. Some are quite masculine, some are quite feminine, and most are somewhere in between. This is partly due to genetics, but it's much more because there are many different standards of masculinity.

What it means to be a man in France is not the same as what it means to be a man in America. Even within America, being a man in Detroit is not the same as being a man in Beverly Hills. Heck, even in New York City, being a man in Harlem isn't the same as being a man on Wall Street. Standards of masculinity are heavily influenced by both the local and broader culture a man lives within, no matter what his genetics are. This results in many masculinities or ways of being a man all over the world. The same behavior can be acceptable in one place but seen as unacceptable or "feminine" in another. Plus the same male behavior can be viewed differently by historical time. What's seen as feminine today may have been seen as masculine in a different time.

In addition, both male and female animal behavior differs little outside of the process of reproduction. Any difference in animal behavior between males and females serves the purpose of rearing offspring. Human males and females, on the other hand, behave in many different ways that are totally unrelated to having children. This strongly suggests that behavioral differences in human males and females are social inventions that have little biological basis.

Moreover, contrary to stereotypes, human developmental research has shown that baby boys are more emotionally sensitive than girls. In Harvard experiments, boys have been shown to become, and remain, more emotionally upset than girls, when their mothers leave the room. Anecdotally, many moms say their baby boys are more sensitive than their baby girls.

Masculinity is, in fact, more a product of one's culture, than the "essence" of being male. American cultural forces, even with the best intentioned parents, strong-arm sensitivity out of boys over time. Our culture wants to make boys who are "nice and strong." And, like little toy soldiers, we act accordingly. Masculinity is a social script that we prefer to conform to. For if we don't conform, we may pay a heavy price.

A boy may not be born a real American man. But there's a lot of pressure put on him to become one. Certain behaviors are strongly rewarded and reinforced, based on our sex. It's about how we're supposed to act and what's permitted. While girls are given leeway to be boyish up to a point, it's much less permissible for boys to be like girls. While it's relatively more acceptable for a female to be more male, it's degrading for a male to be more female. Girls are given barrettes. Boys are not. Girls can cry. But "big boys don't cry." Girls can keep their hair short, wear jeans, and be tough. Boys, however, are strongly discouraged or flat-out prohibited from "girly" things like keeping their hair in pigtails, wearing dresses, and being too "soft." Boys may be forced to stop playing with dolls, using mommy's makeup or washing with pink soap that smells like roses. These aren't things that conform to the benchmark society has for males. Even lesbianism is relatively more tolerated in our culture than two men having sex, especially among straight men. Males learn—all too well—what's acceptable behavior and what's not. Maleness seems inseparable from being masculine. Anything feminine is highly discouraged for boys and men.

As we've discussed, we're simply told things like "that's just the way it is," "those are the rules." But I'd like to delve deeper into why. Why do we submit to the "authority" of gender roles so blindly?

Long before we are born, the stage has already been set and the scripts have been written for men and woman to play their parts. Our role is cast as man or woman. Throughout much of history, few have publicly resisted their lot. A well-known rebel is the infamous Joan of Arc. But she was burned at the stake for not playing by the rules. A few cultures have celebrated a third gender, a mix of male and female. Such two-spirited individuals were revered in those cultures. They were given high-ranking positions as liaisons between their people and the gods. Today, at the Los Angeles Gender Center (LAGC) (lagendercenter.com), founded by clinical mentor, friend, and colleague Marie Keller— one of the few places like it in the world—gender isn't so black-and-white either. As a former core staff member, I began the New York Gender Center as part of my private practice in the city I most think of as home. However, I continue to model the LAGC's philosophy.

Its philosophy is that we all deserve our place in society as we actually are, not as puppets controlled by the strings of a narrow ideology to be this kind of man or that kind of woman. We must acknowledge the wide spectrum of possible life paths by respecting and supporting the integrity and uniqueness of each individual.

While it's easier to categorize people, we have to appreciate that we're much more complex beings. When people refer to a "real man" in the everyday sense, they actually lump four things— biological sex (male or female reproductive organs), gender identity (an inner sense of being a man or woman), gender expression (the way gender is expressed as masculine or feminine) and sexual orientation (straight or gay)—together. But each of those is actually a distinct phenomenon. We can't simply clump them all together. We need to tease them out and appreciate their subtleties.

To help us understand this better, below is the "Sex and Gender Diagram" developed by colleague Janis Walworth of the Center for Gender Sanity (gendersanity.com).

BIOLOGICAL SEX

male_____intersex_____female

GENDER IDENTITY

man_____two-spirited_____woman

GENDER EXPRESSION

masculine_____androgynous_____feminine

SEXUAL ORIENTATION

attracted to women_____bisexual/asexual_____attracted to men

From this diagram we begin to see that all of these lines are separate. Let's have a good time with this.

Imagine you went to sleep one night (as usual) a man. The next morning, you awake safe and healthy. Nothing about your mind has changed—just your body. You look down and see large breasts and a vagina. You have soft, smooth skin and most of your body hair is gone. You have wide hips and delicate, round curves. I bet you're saying something close to, "Oh, my gosh!" Somehow your body has changed to the opposite sex. You now find yourself a man trapped in a woman's body. How would you feel when everyone uses feminine pronouns to refer to you? What would it be like to be expected to dress and behave as the opposite sex 24/7? Would you still want to dress like a man? Would you still be attracted to men? If so, would you be straight now or still gay? How comfortable would you be having sex with men with a woman's body? Who could understand your predicament? I bet before long you'd be running down the streets screaming, "but I'm a man inside, I'm really a man!" The pearl in this experiential exercise is seeing that sex, gender identity, gender expression, and sexual orientation are separate.

Now let's plot some points on the Sex and Gender Diagram together. Yes, go get your pencil. This will be fun! A "normal" male is born with a penis (biological sex, plot point left), identifies as a man (gender identity, plot point left), appears masculine (gender expression, plot point left), and is attracted to women (heterosexual orientation, plot point left). All points align left. A "normal" female is born with a vagina (biological sex, plot point right), identifies as a woman (gender identity, plot point right), appears feminine (gender expression, plot point right), and is attracted to men (heterosexual orientation, plot point right). All points align right. Let's do a couple more. A transman is born female (biological sex, plot point right), identifies as a man (gender identity, plot point left), may present himself as masculine (gender expression, plot point left), and may be attracted to women (heterosexual orientation based on gender identity, plot point left). All points don't align left for this man. A transwoman is born male (biological sex, plot point left), identifies as a woman (gender identity, plot point right), may present herself as masculine (gender expression, plot point left), and may be attracted to women (gay sexual orientation based on gender identity, plot point left). All points don't align right for this woman. And they don't need to.

There are countless deviations from these four configurations. People can fall in any position on these lines. A position can also change for people over time. Moreover, no line depends on another. Each line is independent. This makes for endless variation in the human population.

Homosexuality is just one more natural variation. Being gay is not a preference or biological mishap. Like left-handedness or eye color, it is just another genetic expression of human life. It just so happens that the gay man is "out of alignment" with the expected heterosexual orientation and may be "out of alignment" with the expected masculine gender expression usually associated with males. He is born male (biological sex, plot point left), identifies as a man (gender identity, plot point left), may appear in the range of masculine to feminine (gender expression, plot point anywhere), and is attracted to men not women (gay sexual orientation, plot point right). Depending upon how he expresses his masculinity, he aligns somewhere between three points left and one point right to two points left and two points right. So he doesn't "match" most men. So what? How come diversity isn't more celebrated?

Because the rule is that if you're born with a penis (male) you're supposed to be a man who is masculine and straight. Except, maleness isn't inseparably linked to being a man, masculine or straight. But that's what people expect.

What gets into people? It's seen as something "unnatural" if a man is "feminine," i.e., "gay." The simulated gay sex acts abusively perpetrated by US soldiers at the Abu Ghraib prison, were reported as "horrific crimes of nature." Why were the "simulated gay acts" referred to as "horrific crimes of nature" and not the abusive actions of the inhumane soldiers who perpetrated them? Homosexuality is called an "abomination"! What is so horrible about it? Why is a man who breaks with traditional gender roles so upsetting to people?

Remember from earlier, that the unknown is profoundly unsettling for many. An unfamiliar world—a queer world—frightens them deeply. It threatens everything familiar that brings them a sense of comfort, safety, and security. In the musical *Les Miserables*, prisoner Valjean shows mercy by sparing the life of Javert, the policeman who's hunted him for years. Valjean's kind act shatters Javert's unyielding principles of justice, which are the foundation of his life. He believes that those who have fallen from grace, like Valjean, must pay the price, not be spared by personal redemption. Without a sense of meaning and purpose, Javert's world of order and light no longer makes sense. He no longer feels safe enough to live in such an unfamiliar, unpredictable, and terrifying world. He jumps to his death. We also see this same fear in those against gay marriage. They argue that the whole fabric of society will be destroyed by gays getting married. They claim, "it will bring the end of the world." The power of masculinity lies in fear instead of love. Fear of breaking the rules. It dares you to go against what's customary and do something else.

Great, but right about now you may be asking, "What does all this have to do with why I'm alone on Saturday nights?" Well, a lot of gay guys themselves fear the fallout from being less masculine. Since gay men aren't considered "real men," many think they have to "prove" their manhood by accenting their masculinity. This straight-acting front makes it hard for gay men to find true love. Anthony, an Ask Angelo subscriber, describes the scene at his gym, which illustrates how masculinity can keep you alone on Saturday nights anywhere. He wrote:

I can't stand the gay gym. It's such a scene. It's just like a bar. You may as well hang disco balls from the rafters. Everyone's there to be seen with their straightest attire, short hairdos, facial hair and tatts. Everyone looks like they just came out of a college frat house, sporting event, or military zone. Most are just showing off. They walk around as if they were banging their chests like King Kong. What's funny is that I'm intimidated by the really huge guys. But if they open their mouth and a purse flies out, I feel better. But most guys make sure to use a deep voice. The sad part is that there are so many gorgeous guys and hardly anyone talks. Everyone is too busy posing, looking mean, working out, listening to their iPod, or guzzling their water. Most guys look in the mirror at themselves, at the floor, or stare into space between sets. So it's hard to even catch someone's eye. Then there are games. "I don't see you." "I don't hear you." And my personal favorite, "I don't want to know you." It makes no sense. Everyone's so concerned about acting cool and tough on the floor. Then you'll see all of them later in the steam room silently "connecting" in the vapors where they're invisible. I know that being masculine is attractive, but how's anybody supposed to meet with all this bullshit going on? Maybe everyone looks so pissed off because they're lonely.

Acting more masculine comes from a desire to protect ourselves. While it doesn't matter where you fall on the lines of the Sex and Gender Diagram, there's a lot of fuss about those who deviate from the "norm." The public has a strong punitive response to it. People commit murder over it and parents disown their children because of it. They fear crossing the lines of a traditional belief—men should act like men.

If you think this isn't real anymore, consider that three-year-old Ronnie Paris was beaten to death relatively recently by his twenty-one-year-old father in Tampa, Florida. In a story about it, "A father's homophobia turned deadly" in the *Miami Herald* by Leonard Pitts Jr., the father was said to be terrified his son could grow up to be gay. So, to avoid this, he beat him to toughen him up and make a man out of him. Now his son's a dead boy who won't be a man at all. The grandfather (father of the killer) reportedly said, "I raised my son in the right way. We played football, went fishing, went to wrestling matches, boxing, all that." Apparently, Pitts wrote, he thinks he's blameless because he raised his son like a man. Quite the contrary. A toddler is dead because his son beat him to make him a man like himself. Now he has no son. What happened to talking to our sons while we're playing games? Teaching them? Hugging them? Pitts wonders.

Also consider that Kevin Aviance, a prominent drag queen singer in the New York gay scene, was attacked during Gay Pride month in 2006. *HX* magazine reported the attackers threw garbage cans and trash at him before dragging him to the curb, and kicking him at least fifteen times in the face. *HX* reported that he suffered a broken jaw, a fractured knee, and neck injuries. According to *HX*, Aviance's publicist reportedly said, "They all kept saying he was not 'diesel.' We think that it means 'masculine'—and they were basically saying Kevin's not masculine, that he's not strong." There are hundreds of other victims we never get to hear about. Sadly, several gay men told me they thought Kevin's beating was just a publicity stunt like the rappers do. I think this is a form of denial that runs strong in our community. It's just too painful and scary to see the level of hate out there.

In the mid-nineties, Gabriel Rotello wrote an article titled "Transgendered Like Me" in the *Advocate*. He focused on the bottom line. Gay men are discriminated against for transgressing masculinity, their expected masculine gender role, not for who they sleep with. He was a bit ahead of the crowd, but he couldn't have been more on target. Gay men are hated for crossing male gender lines by loving men. The social "rule" is that women, not men, love men. This goes against the grain of long-standing, deeply held, cultural beliefs about how men should behave. If you act masculine, but secretly sleep with men, you won't be suspected of being out of the accepted male role. Therefore, you won't be ridiculed. We're straight acting in fear of what might happen if we travel too far outside the territory of the "real man".

There's tremendous social pressure to toe the line. Other than in sports, universal tragedy, or in the company of a female confidante, men are usually putting up a tough-guy front to dodge the humiliating and potentially dangerous ridicule that comes from stepping outside the box. Men can be shamed, shunned, and punished for being outside. We may be laughed at, taunted, picked last for the team, cast out from our families and communities, fired from work, harassed, beat up, maimed, or killed. The danger comes mostly from other men.

"Take your places" as they say. Masculinity is ultimately about preserving a prejudicial system of control that subjugates women for male dominion. Men in general, but more specifically rich white men, have historically used their power to dominate others (patriarchy). Sexism is at the core of masculinity and homophobia—a preference for maleness and the devaluation of that which is deemed "feminine."

Emotion is probably considered the most "feminine" trait. Customarily, emotion is relegated strictly to the realm of the feminine. The rules of masculinity say men can't be "too emotional." Sports is one area where men are allowed to display emotion. This may be one reason the sports arena is so popular with guys. The sports channel is literally that—sports are a channel for emotion. Sports is one of the only venues where men can express their feelings openly, including physical and emotional affection for one another. No one's manhood is questioned against the "all-man" backdrop of sports—even if they're walking with a limp wrist, patting asses, crying, or jumping into another player's arms after scoring. Masculinity is a given on the playing field.

Truth is, men are emotional, just like women. A human being gets trapped behind everyman's false front of masculinity. The incongruity between the personal needs of the self and the public demands of masculinity causes a discrepancy between a man's inside and outside. A man's vulnerability is strongly discouraged from being shown in public. This creates an internal struggle. The conflict is great because the risks are high. If a guy shows emotion inappropriately, he will be called "gay," feminized, branded as weak, and humiliated. *The Wizard Of Oz* presented a public image that was very different from the reality of the man behind the curtain. Most men are trained to present a false public self—a "tough guise" that's superimposed on a real private self.

Do gay men know this experience? You bet. We're all raised as men. In 1997's *Life Outside*, author Michelangelo Signorile identified a "cult of masculinity" in gay culture. This refers to a group of gay men who project a hypermasculine image, which in turn has a disproportionately large impact on all gay men. Thanks to his groundbreaking work, we have a solid sociological account of hypermasculine behavior among gay men through the mid to late 1990s.

The "cult of masculinity" has grown to be more intense than ever for many gay men over the last ten years. It's getting worse. What's been fueling the increase over the last decade?

Hypermasculine behavior is on the rise in our community as we're gaining more visibility. As we're getting closer to equality, the backlash has gotten more severe. Like in the beginning of any new relationship, when we're feeling more emotionally exposed, our insecurities can come to the forefront. We may try to cover them up by acting as "sane" or "normal" as possible. As our community is building a new relationship with the mainstream, our insecurities come up. Since gay men are considered emasculated, our biggest insecurity is our manliness.

Take a look at the images in any gay rag and you'll notice an emphasis on two extremes of manhood—the stereotypically feminine gay man (the drag queen) and hypermasculine man (a thug, military dude, rugby player, etc.). Sometimes the two polar images are even placed side by side. We seem to balance flamboyant images with images of pumped-up studs. It's as if gay men have something to prove about their masculinity. It's like the straight actor playing the gay role, always pointing out his heterosexuality— just in reverse.

If we're closeted, we may think our reputation will be wiped away once we come out. If we're out, we may want to clean the "stain" on our manhood. In either case, we desire to recoup the respect that can get ripped out from under us when we identify as gay, salvage our esteem, and be treated like any other man. We have faith that being masculine will save the day, avoid humiliation, fix our shame—rescue us. By being hypermasculine, we're honoring our manhood, doing everything we can to normalize ourselves, dodging all the garbage that can come with being a more "flashy gay." Hypermasculinity is an overcompensation for eroded male self-esteem from not being thought of as "all man." Hypermasculinity is straight acting.

Those of us who pay homage to the icons of masculinity may be overly judgmental of peers who don't. Ironically, we're more judgmental of men who don't conform, expressing themselves "more gayly." Clients frequently report that an all-gay crowd can be less friendly and nurturing than a regular crowd, if you stand out too much. When I gave transgender talks in LA, we were treated worst at the LA Gay & Lesbian Center. Such harsh judgment creates a divisive masculine hierarchy within our own community. It's interesting how messed up that is—gays denouncing others for being who they are, especially if they're "too gay."

How can this be? Since all of us are actually "queens" relative to straight men, many of us can feel damaged as men. We seek to regain our lost male status in our own beaten-down peer group. We may do everything we can to rank "all man" in our gay world. We end up ranking ourselves in the exact same way the dominant culture ranks us: As straight men are more valued than gay men, masculine gays are more valued than "effeminate" gays. Society hurts us with masculinity. Then we use masculinity to hurt each other. It's monkey see, monkey do. The oppressed has become the oppressor.

Dreading to stay outside of the box of masculinity, we try to conform as best we can to stay on top. Gay men can be fiercely competitive with one another. We can actually overdo masculinity by emphasizing it too much. When we hypermasculinize, we become gay men in male drag, playing dress-up in the closet of masculinity.

Unless you're a drag queen, there's extraordinary pressure in our community to be less "nelly" and more masculine, like a "regular" guy. Gay men can feel pressured to measure up even more than straight men. Gay men can continuously feel the need to prove their manhood. Here are some quotes from gay men in my Straight Acting workshops who were asked about their experiences of the pressure to measure up as "real" men:

Jim: *I feel like I'm a peacock that always has to show his feathers.*

Steve: *We're not even thought of as men. We're faggots. So why bother?*

John: *I got beat up in school. Always picked last in gym class. Body building helps me to feel more masculine.*

Peter: *You can get anyone to love you if you have drugs, a hard body, and a big dick.*

Angel: *I've always felt like a misfit. I was their sissy. I never really fit in or fought back.*

Drew: *I like to get high and dance all night. I feel on top of the world.*

Tom: *Money makes it better. I'm short and small, but I can shop and buy big toys.*

Robert: *I stay closeted at work or I'll lose everything. I even wear a wedding ring.*

Jake: *It's too hard to fit the mold. A few pills and it's all better.*

Don: *Gay men are so competitive. But I'm the best, so put those nails away, girls!*

Ned: *It's all about the gym, clubs, partying, and one-night stands.*

Bill: *I'm not your typical gay man. I just focus on my straight friends.*

Luke: *I just stay busy, so I don't get depressed. My family still doesn't know I'm gay.*

Ted: *When I was young I was different. No one played with me. But now I'm popular for my A&F looks.*

Craig: *I wonder if this is why we're all so damn insecure.*

Eric shared his story through Ask Angelo about fitting in:

I was teased on the school playground and in the lunchroom for not fitting in. I was a small kind of meek kid. I wasn't like one of the guys. So after I came out, I really got into always working out. I became strong and developed a great body. Then I delved into the whole gay scene that eventually led to drugs. I never looked better in my life. But at the same time, I never felt worse. I was a shell of a man. I felt so hollow. Everything was to fit in. Sure, I had a lot of sex, but it was all empty. There were rigid rules to follow about looking and acting a certain way—masculine. It was like being in a military camp or prison. I never really felt I had true friends there. Eventually I tested positive. Then when the party drugs stopped and my body changed with age and by HIV medication, I found myself alone again, on the outs. It's like I was chewed up and spit out by some heartless machine.

Many gay men think of masculinity as all-or-nothing. It's black-and-white, this or that. It's clear that the more masculine you are, the more value you have. You're masculine or inferior, a drag queen or a homo-thug, a "Mary" or a jock. A line is drawn in the sand between the straight-acting men and the "flamboyant" ones. Some gay men don't want to come across as, be around, or date men who are less masculine. They dread being outside the box. This exclusivity can shut others out, amplifying feelings of inferiority. "Peter Pansy," wrote to me to say that it seems as though he doesn't meet men because he's not straight acting:

> Dear Angelo,
> Why are gay men afraid of "feminine guys" like me? Did I miss something? I can't meet anyone.
> Signed, Peter Pansy

Straight acting is about being "all man" in order to mend a broken manhood. But "the femininity" that some guys dislike in others is actually something they were taught to dislike in themselves. Looking outside of themselves to the "real man" to feel worthy, straight-acting men may strive to embody "his" image as best they can. In time, they can lose touch with their authentic selves by overidentifying with the false self, i.e., the masculine self they use to "pass." In this way, gay men can split apart from themselves and each other.

Masculinity excludes other men—it's about being one-up, the alpha male, or top dog. It's about being tough and emotionally unavailable. The sad thing is that we're straight acting to win more love, but it leaves us feeling more incomplete and further alienated instead. Toughness, macho rules, and "attitude" only serve to block us from ourselves and others from our hearts.

What drives the manly divide? Homophobia, antifemininity, and trauma take center stage. They're the steam engine behind the train wreck of gay relationships.

4

The Roots of Straight Acting

At the Core—How Antifemininity, Homophobia, and Trauma Drive Straight Acting

> *"Do not wait for the last judgment. It takes place every day."*
>
> —Albert Camus

Antifemininity

The seeds of homophobia are planted deep in men's minds. In this chapter, we will discuss how they take root. It's important to understand what homophobia is ultimately about, because gay men have grown up with, and continue to exist in, a culture of homophobia, and straight acting is one coping mechanism that gets in the way of our relationships.

Homophobia boils down to the fear men have of being feminized. Being feminine for most men is considered a fatal weakness. It's a direct threat to manhood. Since being gay is equated with being feminine, being considered gay is a direct threat to manhood as well. Homophobia is really a form of a fear-of-the-feminine. Its "job" is to keep men adhering to the strict codes of masculine behavior. Brett, a gay athlete, told me: *Masculinity conquers. Femininity is to be conquered.*

Men's fear of the feminine is strong and pervasive. Shakespeare beautifully captures the awesome power this fear has over men with this male banter in *Two Gentlemen of Verona:*

Act 2, Scene 1. A heartbroken Valentine is feeling quite depressed. His servant Speed tries to snap him out of it by giving him a "be a man" speech. Speed tells Valentine he's being pathetic and not acting like a man worthy of respect. He uses the threat of being womanlike to shame and inspire his master back to his sense of male pride and dignity:

> *Marry, by these special marks: first, you have learned, like Sir Proteus, to wreathe your arms, like a malecontent; to relish a love-song, like a robin-redbreast; to walk alone, like one that had the pestilence; to sigh, like a school-boy that had lost his A B C; to weep, like a young wench that had buried her grandam; to fast, like one that takes diet; to watch like one that fears robbing; to speak puling, like a beggar at Hallowmas. You were wont, when you laughed, to crow like a cock; when you walked, to walk like one of the lions; when you fasted, it was presently after dinner; when you looked sadly, it was for want of money; and now you are metamorphosed with a mistress, that, when I look on you, I can hardly think you my master.*

We can see how "masculinity" uses the power of the feminine to insure that males aren't feminine, performing like tough, strong men. The phrase "Be a man!" means "toughen it up," especially emotionally. Recall that the male socialization process teaches men to be emotionally stoic. After all, emotions are for the "weaker" sex—women. Emotions go along with being soft and feminine. "Real men" don't show emotional weakness. Men are trained to disconnect from their feelings and separate from others. Not being emotional goes along with being hard and manly.

Emotional or not, if a man behaves in any feminine way, it's taken as evidence that he's unmanly or "gay." This is true whether he's had sex with a man or not. Femininity and gayness are erroneously equated. Feminine men are seen as gay. Gay men are seen as feminine. Gender (femininity) and sexuality (homosexuality) get mistakenly fused.

It's practically a contradiction to say "effeminate straight guy" or "manly gay guy." Many people erroneously think that being feminine equals being gay—period. How did being feminine get equated with being gay? The misconception that feminine equals gay may come from the incorrect belief that since some gay men dress and express themselves like women, then all gay men must do so. People may also mistakenly think we want to be women because we love men. The preeminent psychologist and psychiatrist, Dr. Sigmund Freud himself, espoused the notion that homosexuality was an "inversion" of gender roles. Even today, ex-gay movements use a similar argument, purporting gay men just need masculinity training.

The history of the word "faggot" may also help shed some light on the link between feminine and gay. The word *fagot*, or *faggot*, was first used to mean a bundle of sticks that one carried on his back. Such sticks were used for fires. Contrary to popular tale, there is no evidence to suggest that gay men themselves were used as the kindle wood for public burnings. Later, the word was used as a derogatory term for an overbearingly emotional woman. Next the term was used as slang for someone who whined like a woman, such as an effeminate man. Since gay men are considered effeminate men, the word "faggot" has become the derogatory antigay slur we know it as today.

Whatever its origins, not being feminine or "gay" is a culturally permissible, underlying way of male thinking that has produced stifling conformity to masculinity standards. The "gay" label has the ultimate power to emasculate.

Often when *Eminem* and other rappers use "fag," it's aim is to make a statement about gender—"you're not a man." It's meant to cut a man down. The word humiliates him, stripping him of his manliness.

"Fag" status taints manhood for most. It "feminizes," "softens," and "weakens" a man. It's not flattering to most straight men to be called "gay." In fact, it can be quite offensive. Perhaps unable to separate their masculinity from their identity, straight men can feel it's an attack on who they are. Being called "gay" can be dishonoring and shameful, and can bring one of the worst forms of social humiliation on a man and his family. It's the lowest of the low. A "fag" loses respect in the male community. For some men, this "downgrade" is unbearable. Most men go to great lengths to avoid this—even to their deaths. Many would rather "die with honor" than be seen as "weak" and stripped of their male identity.

The mere thought of being feminized is enough to stop most men in their tracks. The threat of masculine failure, being seen as a "weak" man, results in a massive loss of reputation and humiliation and shame. Being unfeminine is masculinity's insurance, guaranteeing that men will conform to its standards.

Why do men tremble in fear of the feminine? Perhaps because they think femininity can annihilate them. After all, it made them.

In the book *A New Psychology of Men*, Dr. William Pollack and Dr. Ronald Levant examine masculinity. One intriguing theory about men's fear of the feminine goes something like this. Since women have the capability to give birth to men, men despise women because they ultimately have that power over them. Thus, they dominate women to protect themselves, keeping control, always fearing an insurgence.

Another theory is that men fear the feminine because it annihilates their identity. Manhood itself can be defined as not being feminine. Since industrial change has created more absent fathers, there are few if any male role models for sons to identify with. The lack of a personal male role model in the nest is a traumatic breach in the early development of men. Mothers are relatively more present, but boys can't identify with their moms. Everyone discourages it—even mothers. So the very foundation of manhood may be built upon not being like a woman. This Ask Angelo letter reveals that no boy is comfortably raised to be "a mama's boy":

Dear Angelo,
I think my son's gay. He spends a lot of time imitating me. Did I do something? How can I fix it before it's too late?
Signed, Soccer Mom

Gay men know that they don't want to change their gender. They ultimately want to reaffirm their whole selves by expressing their masculine and feminine parts. But the general public doesn't understand that difference. It's confusing for many people. So it's just easier for everyone to bunch feminine and gay together.

As we've touched upon, many people in the general public think gay men forfeit their manhood by choosing to be like women, stepping down from the masculine platform. They think we emasculate ourselves by gender trading, that we take the easy way out. They may think we deserve what we get. In being straight acting, gay men are shouting back, "Yah, I'm gay, but I'm still a man." While gay men may call each other "girl," they can still be quite sensitive about being feminized by others. No matter how effeminate a gay man looks or behaves, he still has the ego of a man. Two workout buddies wearing one-piece lavender leotards at the gym may be silently competing with each other to see who can lift more weight and who has the biggest bulges. Mark told me:

I sleep with a lot of drag queens. You'd be surprised. They all flip me over. They want to be the top.

Some gay men can get quite defensive if you say they embrace femininity because they're already stereotyped as not being "real" men. George said:

> *I'm a regular guy, and I like a man who's a man, not a woman.*

No one likes to be outside the box of masculinity.

In my masculinity workshops, I ask gay men to list words that describe men who are outside the box. Here's the laundry list of the ones they come up with most frequently: *fag, gay, homo, fruit, sissy, wimp, pussy, wuss, weak, passive, emotional, sensitive, sweet, feeling, effeminate, flamboyant, twinkle toes, lispy, swishy, pumpkin, artsy, gentle, soft, mama's boy, pansy, a Nancy, long-haired, pretty boy,* and Schwarzenegger's *"girly man."* A major theme is having feminine characteristics or being womanlike. The guys have a much easier time pinpointing what a man isn't than what a man actually is. "Being a man" is definitely being unfeminine. Zack told me:

> *Being a male nurse and being gay, I already have two strikes against me as soon as I walk into the room. I have to work twice as hard to get the respect of the doctors and patients.*

It can seem like we have no choice but to be masculine. We've discussed in chapter 3 how masculinity demands conformity to its rules. Men who openly deviate from its rules are reviled. As Rotello wrote a decade ago, hatred will come at us for transgressing our expected gender role—not for whom we sleep with. Prejudice and discrimination can take their toll. Troy, a subscriber to Ask Angelo, wrote in and described the cost:

Dear Angelo,
I hate being gay. I hate the prejudiced world we live in.
Depression and suicidal thoughts are increasingly common.
What can I do?
Signed, Hopeless

It's antifemininity that drives homophobia. And homophobia is hurtful and harmful.

You may want to pause for a moment to reflect on these questions. Did you feel inside or outside the box growing up? How was your masculinity invalidated by others? Today, do you invalidate your own masculinity in any way? Do you notice any links between how you were invalidated then and how you invalidate yourself today? How does this impact your relationships?

Homophobia (Outside and Inside)

Many men carry deep emotional scars from the psychological violence that's been inflicted on them for being "effeminate" or affirming a gay identity. Once out, we can be reduced to someone else's homophobic picture of what gay is. Others project their gay stereotypes onto us. For instance, many straight people tend to stereotype being homosexual as just being about sex. When some straights see us with a companion, they picture us in bed. I don't know about you, but when I see a heterosexual couple, I don't usually imagine them in bed. But gay coupling is often reduced by many nongay people to a sexual thing rather than a loving bond. To them, a gay relationship holds less value than a heterosexual relationship because it's just about sex. The stereotype is we're sex fiends. Our relationships are thought to be "inferior" to straight ones. This demotion leaves us quite vulnerable to people who don't support gays. A minority of Americans overall, just 39 percent, according to one Gallup News Service Poll,

support legalizing our love relationships. We're more straight acting because we want to be treated as whole persons, not devalued. Hateful bigotry against gays continues and it has the potential
to grow into something more insidious. When we're downgraded
to a "fag" or "gay," we're objectified, depersonalized, and dehumanized. We stop being part of the human race. It becomes
"them" against "us." We're "the other." Not only does being
demeaned damage our esteem, but it can also lead to physical
violence. This demotion is the basis of all human atrocities rang-
ing from hate crimes to massacres.

The derogatory homophobic slur "fag" is routinely used today
to mean any "freak," "loser," or "low-life." Gay men are psychologically abused by such toxic "faggot" messages every day.
A school study determined that being called "gay" was the most
psychologically disturbing thing for students, especially boys. If
you want to know what group is reviled as the lowest group in
a culture, look to its insulting language and its degrading jokes.
The "innocent" gay joke reflects our inferior status in our culture. This seemingly "harmless" homophobia found in everyday
conversation hurts gays.

While there is decreasing tolerance of it, verbal gay bashing
is still socially permissable in our culture compared with abuse
of other minority groups. Antigay ridicule happens with such fre-
quency that it is frightening. A government survey on lesbian,
gay, bisexual, and transgender (LGBT) youth issues found that
nine out of ten gay youths reported hearing homophobic re-
marks in their school, and over eight out of ten reported being
verbally harassed. Two out of three LGBT youths reported experiencing some form of physical harassment or violence in their
school. Many reported experiencing it daily. Males who exhibited
nongender-conforming behavior were harassed more. Massachu-
setts surveys found that gay, lesbian, and bisexual youth were between two and four times as likely to report being threatened or

injured with a weapon on school property than heterosexual youth. GLB youth were also found to be over four times as likely to report missing school because of fear about their safety. A California survey of sexual minority youth found that nearly seven out of ten didn't feel safe in their school because of their sexuality. It has also been shown that often school faculty doesn't intervene, and may even contribute significantly to the prejudice.

Even beyond the school yard, name calling and hate speech are typically unrestrained as if it were all right to insult gays. It goes in tandem with an implicit attitude like "doesn't everybody hate these people?" Credible people can still openly attack gays— compared with other minority groups—with little serious consequence.

As of the printing of this book, we still weren't allowed to March in the St. Patrick's Day parade in the old Irish enclaves of New York City and Boston. We still couldn't donate our blood, even if we were tested and shown to be disease-free. Are we sub human?

As we know, the threat of physical violence doesn't end after high school. Manny told me a story:

While I was out on a smoking break with the guys, one of them jokingly asked me, "Would you rather screw a dog or another guy?" It was sort of menacing. I was stunned that it was better for me to compromise and say I would fuck an animal than another dude. So that's what I said. I was too scared to tell the truth.

A wide-ranging workplace fairness survey, conducted by Lambda Legal and Deloitte Financial Advisory Services LLP, announced that, of those GLBTs responding to a survey, almost 40 percent said they experienced harassment or discrimination in the workplace. No federal law (Employment Non-Discrimination

Act) has been able to pass Congress since 1974, leaving us un-protected at work.

Since 1981, the Federal Bureau of Investigation (FBI) estimates that one out of every six hate crimes targets GLBT Americans. This only represents reported crimes. GLBT hate crimes go drastically underreported.

In the HBO hit drama *The Sopranos*, Vito, a high-ranking member of the mob family, was brutally beaten and killed after it was discovered that he was gay. This was done to protect the honor of the mafia. Vito was worth more to the family dead than alive, even though he brought in the most money. It would be dishonoring to the family if they knowingly spared the life of a "fag." Others would think the mafia wasn't masculine. Vito was murdered to save face. While this is a dramatization, it reflects the modern antigay attitudes of some people. Such attitudes are highlighted by a survey of adolescents that found that nearly nine out of ten considered gay sex "disgusting," and nearly six out of ten reported they wouldn't be friends with a gay person. In other studies, nearly half of all high school students admitted being prejudiced against gay people.

In many countries, homosexuality is still a crime punishable by prison, torture, and death. For instance, the government of Iran routinely tortures and murders gay men. Gay Iranian youth are sometimes even sentenced to death by hanging. We do nothing about these sanctioned gay murders as we fight wars, even next door in Iraq, in the name of human rights. Gay men all over the world receive a powerful message that's loud and clear— "We're unimportant. Being gay is considered so low that we're disposable human beings. You can still be stoned and killed." Gay activist and ACT UP founder Larry Kramer has asked rhetorically, "Who cares if a faggot dies?"

If you live in a major metropolitan area, you may not ever worry about leaving your house and being harassed, assaulted, or hung out back for being gay. You may not even think that most of the things I've talked about directly affect you. But that doesn't mean they don't. It's like being unaware of a massive computer program that's running in the background, slowing your computer down. Consider the possibility that all the anti-gay hostility and violence out there still gets stored in your memory, impacting you and your relationships.

It seeps in. Some men may be very aware it's all there and feel unsafe to come out. So they act straight and remain in the closet. Others may be so overwhelmed by the bombardment that they block it all out and grow comfortably numb. Still others may have overcome the trials and tribulations to be out and proud. They may not want to go back in time to the painful past. But the reality—that we're targets of blame simply because of who we are—doesn't just go away. It gets recorded deep inside of our hearts and impacts our ability to love ourselves and each other. As a result of homophobia, many closeted, curious, and questioning men can be frightened about merely having gay thoughts. They're confused, concerned about their masculine identity and scared of what having gay thoughts means for them. They write in asking me questions like this:

Dear Angelo,
Is it wrong to be gay?
Signed, Questioning Metrosexual

Movies like *Brokeback Mountain,* based on E. Annie Proulx's story, help change people's minds. By contrasting American culture's most celebrated man's man—the Marlboro man—with a gay love story, *Brokeback Mountain* makes us question the very foundation of our concept of manhood. That's what makes it uncomfortable for many. It dares us to deny the men their love, their manliness, or their humanity. What keeps the gay lovers apart is the fear of what other men will do to them if they find out.

In the part when Jack Twist asks Ennis Del Mar to live with him, the terror of homophobia comes to life. Ennis says "no." He's terrified. He says he can't because he doesn't want to end up dead. He tells Jack about two old guys he remembers who ranched together. When he was nine years old, his dad made sure he took him to see one of them dead in a ditch. His body was mangled, having been beaten and dragged by a horse from his penis until it pulled off. This is what "real" men can do to queers. Ennis says he wouldn't have put it past his dad to kill the rancher, and he wouldn't put it past him (his dad) to kill him now if he found out.

It isn't wrong to be gay. What's wrong is the social stigma gay men face. The powerful movie *Brokeback Mountain* brings the consequences of homophobia into broad daylight.

Brokeback Mountain also portrays that being gay is about love, not sex. It's a love story between two men. Their gayness is portrayed as a natural expression of who they are, rather than a lustful perversion. Ennis and Jack respectably try to squelch their "compulsion," attempting to live the "right lifestyle," and do "the right thing." They act straight and stay closeted. But being gay is part of their essential nature, so they suffer. Unfortunately, innocent women get hurt too, and children.

We have to challenge homophobia every day by being the gay men we are so this doesn't happen anymore. Otherwise, fear can manifest itself as confusion that may cloud our entire lives. Take this letter for instance, and my reply:

Dear Angelo,
How does one really know they're gay?
Signed, The Quest

Dear Quest,

While it is true that gay men are attracted to and have sex with other men, this is not sufficient to define being gay.

Being gay is not just about sex. For example, a gay person can be celibate for life and still be gay. A gay youth can know he is gay years before his first sexual experience. Alternatively, a man can have man-to-man sex in prison for life but not be gay.

Being gay is not just about attraction, either. There are many men who are attracted to other men, but they never act on it. They identify as straight. Having same-sex fantasies doesn't mean you're gay. Fantasy is normal, especially while masturbating. Dr. Alfred Kinsey published *Sexual Behavior in the Human Male* in 1948. Even in those conservative times, Dr. Kinsey found that a large percentage of men he surveyed acknowledged having a same-sex experience. Almost half said they experimented with another male at least once in their lifetime, and over a third said they had reached orgasm with another guy by age forty-five. Dr. Kinsey believed that male sexuality is fluid. Freud himself thought everyone was bisexual. Most men aren't simply gay or straight. Same-sex behavior is common. It's having an openly gay identity that's so taboo.

So what makes you gay? The essence of being gay is about feelings. The key is more how you feel, not so much what you do or whom you do it with.

A gay identity is forged when you are predominately attracted to the same sex AND when you feel that you want to romantically love and share your life with a member of the same sex. When you desire to truly love another man. When you dream of waking up next to a man and creating the moments of your life with a man. When you wish to create a union and perhaps a family with another man. These feelings are at the core of being gay.

It's also political. Being gay is a mind, body, spiritual, and political orientation, not just a sexual one.

You may have trouble identifying you're gay because the powerful stigma around it can make you "confused" about your feelings. To get more clarity, give yourself permission to explore what you already know about yourself. Following what you know will lead you to what you don't know. Gay-affirmative counseling and coming out peer groups like PFLAG can also provide very helpful support.

All the Best, Angelo.

Antifemininity, Homophobia, and Straight Acting

Straight acting is a coping mechanism for our public emasculation by antifemininity and homophobia.

Many of us covet masculinity, accessorizing with the latest masculine "couture." If you're "womanly," "queeny," or "nelly," then you run the risk of rejection by your own kind. Victor, an Ask Angelo subscriber, wrote:

> *I'm not attracted to flamers. In fact, I can't stand them. They give us a bad name—not acting like men. I'm gay, but I'm not a faggot.*

It makes sense that many gay men like Victor prefer masculine men because they are attracted to men. But this preference is tagged with the stigma against feminine men. It's not the preference for the masculine that's wrong. It's the discrimination against our "effeminate" brothers that's wrong. Many men tell me they can't help it—they're just more attracted to masculine men. I help them tease out—how much of it's based on a healthy, harmless preference—like choosing chocolate over vanilla ice cream—and how much is prejudice from toxic internalized homophobia? How much of it's simply a sexual turn-on and how much comes from shame and fear—of sticking out and being guilty by association? How much is discriminatory, to distance ourselves from "those" "Mary's"—protecting our already fragile self-concept from being like those "other" "faggots"? Are we not being separatists, adding to the hurt, shame, and isolation we may have inside from being outcasts ourselves? Are you really nondiscriminating if your friends are all like you?

It seems ironic that gay men use the same masculine standards they were excluded by to exclude each other. It doesn't seem logical that gay men can reject other gay men who are "too gay." But that's exactly what a fair share of us do.

Many of us try to behave the way men are supposed to behave—adopting the "tough guise"—so we're not stigmatized as "flamers" or "sissies." We're responding to what we've been taught about how men are supposed to behave. We reject our more "feminine" brothers to set ourselves apart from them so we're relatively more accepted—"I'm gay, but I'm masculine." Yet with straight acting, we're actually rejecting the "feminine" part of our own nature, the "gayness" inside, the "nelly" part of ourselves, that we may have learned to dislike. But in the end, it's we who suffer most. We may end up lonely, shutting each other out for falling short. How can two "masculine only" guys like Heath Ledger's character, Ennis, in *Brokeback Mountain,* connect heart to heart and soul to soul to really find love?

Gabriel Rotello wrote an article called "The Enemy Within" for the *Advocate*. It features the results of a study conducted by the University of Georgia's Dr. Henry Adams, showing that male students who tested homophobic got 60-80 percent of full erections within four minutes while watching gay porn. In contrast, students who tested nonhomophobic were left limp by the same videos. Rotello said this implies that homophobia is a "maladjustment to something deep inside yourself." He continued, "The men who hate us the most are us. And that seems terribly sad."

Gay shame is so powerful that it can turn you against yourself and others like you. As we've discussed, most men distance themselves from anything feminine, especially about themselves, to preserve their masculine identity; and gay men's dislike of the feminine can be much greater, since they're told they're not "real men." This may cause a reaction formation. This is when a person seeks to cover up something "unacceptable" by adopting the opposite stance. Many gay men conceal their "femininity" by being masculine or straight acting. We protect our Achilles' heel with a display of manhood. If we don't, we risk verbal or physical harassment from others, mostly other men, for colluding with the enemy—femininity.

All of us are impacted by homophobia and the threat thereof, mentally, emotionally, physically, spiritually, and socially. Homophobia lurks in the shadows of our minds and hearts. It's no wonder many of us try to some degree to be more straight acting. Who can blame us? We're put through a lot. Miguel put it this way: *I wasn't born a bitch, I became one.* Miguel captures, in a nutshell, how much hardship gay men endure to survive.

I know the magnitude of all this can be a downer. But it's also quite important. We're talking about something—homophobia—that is so powerful that it can drive strangers to physically harm us and loved ones to reject us. Such personal rejection by those we love most can leave us relationally impaired as adults. Homophobic ideology makes tragic things like this possible. But we can overcome our trials and tribulations to triumph over social abuse. If we better understand homophobia, we can free ourselves from the heavy, thick, and cold chains of masculinity to find freedom, happiness, and true love. So let's press on just a bit more.

If homophobia doesn't literally kill a queer, it certainly kills his sense of manhood and of belonging to the male community. As a result, he has a massive amount of inferiority, shame, and fear. This makes him feel bad inside about who he is and drives straight-acting behavior.

Dr. Michael Kimmel's research on masculinity and the school shooters of Columbine High School may help us better understand how strongly homophobia affects men. His research reveals how the forces of masculinity and homophobia are strong enough to pressure young men into school shootings. If the forces are strong enough to do that, we can understand how easy it is for them to keep gay men on a straight-acting path.

The male shooters were ridiculed and rejected socially for being unmanly. As a result, they felt inferior as men. They pathologically turned to violence to verify their manhood, since violence is a culturally permitted, even encouragable and excusable male outlet. Their horrible crime actually stemmed from a deep need for acceptance as men. They were desperate to avenge their masculinity.

Gay men face similar social pressure because they're ridiculed and rejected socially for being unmanly. This causes a painful internal conflict. The conflict is that maleness and heterosexuality are not aligned for gay men like they are for straight men. The gay man knows that he wants to be seen as male, but he also knows that being gay is viewed as "feminine." He may fear that if he admits to the world he's gay, it won't treat him like a man. But he doesn't want to be stuck suffering in the closet, either. So he's left with this conflict between his gayness and his maleness that seems impossible to bridge.

The need to be a man and the need to be honest are in direct conflict. How can he, as a gay man, be true to himself by loving men, and still be a "real man"? The public's definition of what makes a man a man is narrow and rigid, leaving him feeling like he's inferior and that he doesn't belong. Perceiving a clash between his maleness and his gayness, he can become fearful, anxious, confused, and isolated. He may think it's either-or. He must either sacrifice himself by abandoning his gayness and keeping his manhood, or sacrifice his manhood by revealing that he's gay and being true to himself. He may also fear sacrificing others by losing their love when he comes out. It can be difficult to climb out of the disparity between being the man that others expect him to be, and being the man he is. He may struggle to define himself one way with these people here, and another way with those people there. It's a very confusing and stressful situation, but he may try to straddle both worlds for as long as he can.

Except he discovers that when he attempts to meet the straight male standards of the dominant culture, he frustrates gay male standards. And when he attempts to meet the gay male standards of his culture, he frustrates straight male standards. Which set of standards is to be his reference group? Where does he fit? What kind of man is he? He may stay in this type of purgatory, not meeting either set of standards. For if he comes out, he will be treated as different, be discriminated against, and risk antigay violence by the straight male community. But if he acts too straight, he will be closeted, negated by the gay community, and sell himself out. Until he's fully out, the gay man suffers greatly from such gender strain or conflict when he wears two faces.

In a deep desire to end the painful conflict (driven by social stigma), many gay men, like the school shooters, try to vindicate their masculinity. They want to take action to set the record straight. But, fortunately, they go about validating their manhood in a very different way. Unlike the school shooters, gay men don't decide to avenge their manhood through pathological violence. Instead, some peacefully conclude that others are right about them. They are unmanly. They take action to reclaim their manhood simply by portraying a more "acceptable" straight-acting persona to fit in. Being straight acting is the tool they fight with. It's their "gun." They arm themselves with straight-acting masculinity and go on a proving spree, saying, "I'm a real man." Pathologically self-hating gay men may actually use that "gun" to hurt others with hypocrisy, betrayal, or crime. But most of us mean no harm. We do our best. We want to maintain our masculine identity. We want equality and to be treated with respect. We want more love. We think it's more attractive to be straight acting. This desire comes from the desire to heal the wounds of homophobia.

Now that we've discussed how masculinity's homophobic fear of the feminine affects men, making gay men straight acting, we need to better understand how profoundly gay men can be affected by it all. Many gay men may in fact be suffering with a chronic form of stress from the effects of trauma. Trauma is what causes us to be straight acting, hampering our relationships most. Until we recognize, name, understand, feel, and release this injury, we can remain frozen, numb, alone, and hurt.

Trauma

When we think of "trauma," we think of accidents, war, natural disasters, and other major events. According to the *Diagnostic and Statistical Manual of Mental Disorders IV* (*DSM IV*), Post Traumatic Stress Disorder (PTSD) is in part diagnosed when a person experiences or witnesses an event that involves "actual or threatened death or serious injury." The person's response to the event must involve "intense fear, helplessness, or horror." The *DSM IV* also states that "Individuals with Post Traumatic Stress Disorder may describe painful guilt feelings about surviving when others did not survive or about the things they had to do to survive." The National Center for PTSD states that "PTSD is complicated by the fact that it frequently occurs in conjunction with related disorders such as depression, substance abuse, and other problems of physical and mental health. Sufferers may feel detached or estranged from others."

In *Alternatives* magazine journalist Daniel Hill published an article titled "Bug Chasers." In it, he says that many gay men may have a form of PTSD from experiencing, witnessing, and surviving the "event" of the AIDS crisis. Despite miracle medications and the notion that HIV infection is "just" a chronic manageable disease, HIV/AIDS still has the potential to cause "actual or threatened serious injury or death" for us all. AIDS certainly involves "intense fear, helplessness, or horror." Mental health professionals find that many men who survived the AIDS crisis have "survivor's guilt." These men face a tremendous number of challenges including loss, grief, anguish, despair, shame, rage, health, work, money, making new friends and lovers, and more. They can experience feelings of alienation and depression, and have other problems like substance abuse. AIDS may have traumatized an entire generation of gay men—but it's impacted all of us. All gay men have "collateral damage."

In spite of this, we don't see classic PTSD symptoms in most gay men. It's not that AIDS isn't potentially traumatic; it's that the experience of trauma and its symptoms don't always fit the criteria for PTSD. We may still experience trauma, but differently than PTSD describes. The scope of classic PTSD is incomplete.

Leading trauma experts like Dr. Bessel A. van der Kolk concur that any negative life event—not just big events like AIDS—can be traumatic if we aren't in control during the situation. In fact, the trauma doesn't even need to be something that happens. It can be just an idea. It doesn't even have to be an accurate or probable idea. Just the perception matters. Whether or not something is a trauma is about how we perceive our ability to survive it and stay safe. Can we effectively fight, escape, or find a solution? It's not the life-threatening nature of the event, but rather the degree of helplessness we have during the event that matters. Trauma goes into the brain the same way, whether it's big and obvious or relatively "small" and "subtle." A 9/11 can register the same trauma to the brain as severe rejection by significant people.

Not belonging can be a traumatic experience. John Bowlby, English psychiatrist and father of attachment theory, established that it's a human instinct to want love. It's built into our physiology. We need lovingly accepting relationships to remain healthy. Rock bottom, we all want someone we can count on when the chips are down. Isn't this what we all ultimately ask for in the powerful bonds we shape with others—will you be there for me? If a gay child feels different, a gay youth feels significantly rejected by his family, or a gay adult faces job discrimination, the answer is no. His survival brain reduces it to an unconscious thought sequence as described by Scott Peck and Pia Mellody. To paraphrase the sequence: "I'm unlovable, I'll be abandoned, my survival needs like food, shelter, and safety won't be met, and then I'll die." Gay men can experience trauma in this way by rejection, disconnection, isolation, and loneliness, at the hands of those closest to them and our culture at large. A study showed that 50 percent of gay and lesbian youth are met with parental disapproval or rejection when their sexual orientation is first disclosed. These feelings are unbearable and have negative consequences.

Admittedly or not, gays live with "intense fear, helplessness, or horror" in a society that can be hostile and violent toward them. I often hear, "I don't tell them I'm gay because my sex life is no one's business." That's ridiculous. Sexuality encompasses a whole lot more than a sexual act. Heterosexuals talk about their straight "sex lives" all the time at work—what they did over the weekend with their families, stories about their children, special occasions, what they're going to do on their date next weekend; they place pictures of their loved ones nearby. No one would ever think to say, those things are no one else's business. When you implement a "Don't Ask, Don't Tell" policy in your life, you limit a huge part of yourself and your life. This increases a sense of shame and affects how well people can get to know you, inhibiting your relationships. We mute ourselves because our lower brain, the primitive part that operates outside our intellect, senses potential danger and thinks our very lives may be threatened by being gay. It knows we don't hold the power. It recognizes that we aren't in control, that we're relatively helpless at the mercy of social opinion. Living like this qualifies as a kind of stress disorder in my opinion.

Despite intellect, on an unconscious level, our brain fears for the very safety of our lives. Survival mode takes over and our basic brain puts us on automatic pilot (straight acting), reacting as if we were in danger—no matter how illogical it seems to our situation now. The part of our brain that takes over to protect us operates on feelings and sensory data, not logic.

Just because this happens under the radar, doesn't mean it has no impact. You can put a dog down in the basement, lock the door, blast the stereo, and forget about it. The dog will bark, howl, whimper, scratch, urinate, defecate, and more. It'll tear your basement apart. You don't see, hear, smell, or feel any of it. You don't even think about it as you tune out upstairs. But the dog is still "silently" causing a lot of havoc down below. Out of sight isn't always out of mind.

Many of us can exhibit symptoms characteristic of people who have survived trauma. Based on lectures by trauma expert Dr. Shelley Uram, such nonclassic PTSD traumatic stress response symptoms can include blocking intimacy, coming close to others but then running away, fearing rejection and abandonment, thinking something's so wrong with you that no one will love you, feeling alien, getting in your own way, being on guard, worrying that something bad is always about to happen, thinking there's no end in sight, tuning out, losing focus, not seeing the big picture, not listening to body signals, illness, and much more. This is in addition to fear, anxiety, irritability, rage, sadness, depression, and so on. Studies show that a significant number of gay men report such nonclassic PTSD traumatic stress response symptoms. Research has also shown that one in three people who experience trauma turn to cigarette smoking, alcohol and drug abuse, sexual compulsivity, and other self-destructive coping strategies for relief. Since studies show specifically that one in three gay men report turning to cigarette smoking, alcohol and drug abuse, sexual compulsivity, and so on, for relief, it supports the idea that gay men as a group experience trauma.

I'm not claiming that being gay is a mental disorder or that all gay men have a mental disorder. What I am saying is that many of us can experience mental, emotional, physical, spiritual, and social trauma from gay stigma and may turn to self-destructive coping strategies for relief. Growing up feeling socially rejected can be severely traumatizing. We can develop a deep wound in the core of our being from not being loved for who we are. In addition, we disproportionately experience personal life traumas like childhood abuses or other victimizations, losses, or life setbacks that can exacerbate and deepen our well of shame, creating a chain of pain and suffering.

For instance, meet Tim, a small boy who likes to play with dolls. It makes Tim so happy to dress his dolls. He wants to take them everywhere. But people tell him how bad it is to play with dolls. He may be hated for it. Sure enough, he's teased, bullied, and laughed at in school. He sees people talking about his kind on TV. They say he should be reading the Bible instead. His parents, schoolmates, teachers—even his priest—are ashamed of him. They constantly scold, "boys don't play with dolls." His mom pulls him aside one day and says, "I'd rather have no son than a son who plays with dolls." He doesn't understand. "Why don't you love me, Mommy? Why can't I play with dolls?" he asks, tearfully. He's firmly told, "Wipe your tears; boys don't cry."

No one holds him. No one tells him it's going to be OK. All of his dolls are taken away. But luckily Tim hid a few away. His dad knocks him around to toughen him up. He is so ashamed to have a son who plays with dolls. What will the neighbors think? He signs him up for Little League hockey to make a man out of him. Tim feels ashamed too. He thinks he's a failure as a son. Maybe playing hockey is for the better. He wishes his dad was proud of him and would brag "that's my boy." Tim often wonders, "What does he want from me?" "Who should I try to be?"

Tim's heard about other grown-up boys who don't stop playing with dolls. Almost everyone's against them—even presidents, popes, and other leaders. Few want to legally recognize their relationships with other boys who play with dolls. They're not accepted. They don't fit in. They don't belong. They're not listened to. He's even heard about some being murdered. A terrible disease has killed many of them. The worry of getting it, or having it, can make life even harder for them. No one's doing as much as they should to help save them. He knows some of the grown boys slowly destroy themselves with drugs, unsafe sex, and other things because it gets so bad at times. You'd think most of the boys who play with dolls would get together. But many don't. To stay safe, they act like they don't play with dolls. They avoid each other like people avoid them. Many of these boys are very sad and lonely.

Yes, Tim better learn to play hockey instead. But he knows inside he can't run away from what he is—a boy who plays with dolls.

How crushing and agonizing do you think this situation is

for the boy? What other conclusion can he come to except the thought sequence as described by Scott Peck and Pia Mellody: "I'm unlovable, I'll be abandoned, my survival needs like food, shelter, and safety won't be met, and then I'll die." His very self isn't accepted. How devastatingly painful is it when you can't be yourself? Tim's mind, heart, and soul are scarred forever by the values of masculinity. Maybe yours are too.

Larry shared a story with me about his childhood:

People seemed to know I was gay before I did. I was teased, called "fag," threatened for no reason, slammed into lockers. Later, I had to move away from my family. They said I was making my father sick with cancer. I think maybe he wouldn't have died if I were different—tough, not effeminate. It didn't make me hate them. It makes me hate myself.

If it weren't potentially dangerous and traumatic to be gay, fear of coming out or being "too gay," and straight acting, wouldn't exist. We wouldn't "hide"—but we do.

Trauma and Straight Acting

Metaphorically speaking, we're careful not to overexpose ourselves, not to be seen naked on the streets in broad daylight. Many gay bars used to be hidden in filthy parts of town. Ousted by society, gay men were forced to sneak out late under the protective cover of darkness to meet. We went to disgusting damp cellars, piers, truck stops, rest rooms, and other secret, seedy places that were well hidden. The outer pierced the inner and we internalized being "disgusting." We worried about having our lives ruined by police raids until we fought back at Stonewall, a bar in New York that was the birthplace of the gay civil rights movement, in 1969. Yet sodomy laws remained on the books

until 2003 in thirteen states—that's 25 percent of all states—
until the Supreme Court struck them down.

Even literally, we can still keep ourselves out of sight. Gay
nude beaches are usually in the most secluded of places. Even
traditional gay beaches are well delineated. There are clearly
marked-off areas where we can be "free." I recall a family that
strayed too far on Miami Beach and entered "the gay section."
The mom beckoned her children, "C'mon, hurry up!" as if there
were sharks in the water.

We're in a cultural war and homosexuality is at the center of
it. Being "obvious" or fully out is potentially harmful. Whether
we're gay or sleep with men as only part of our overall sexual
orientation (being more straight than gay, bisexual, or being more
gay than straight)—we seek to conceal the part of the truth that
says we sleep with men. This is an effort to dodge the gay stigma
that sticks to us even if we admit to sleeping with a dude just
once. Our lower brain hasn't "forgotten" the dangers. It's possible that we could lose everything—our family, friends, church,
membership to the "All Men's Club," job, love, health, and life.
Such banishment can result in unbearable inadequacy, shame,
self-dislike, and the fear that propels straight-acting behavior.

The Center for Disease Control (CDC) found that nearly a
quarter of African-American HIV-positive men who have sex with
men don't consider themselves to be gay. But it's not just African-
American or HIV-positive men who "duck." There are a significant number of all types of men who keep the fact that they
have sex with men secret or on the "down low."

I read Keith Boykin's *Beyond the Down Low: Sex, Lies, and
Denial in Black America* to see what he thought about this. I
found that he concurs. The "down low" is not just an African-
American thing. There are many men of all races, ethnicities, and
HIV-statuses who secretly sleep with men and still portray them-
selves as straight.

Having said that, arguably, the need to be straight acting may impact racial and ethnic minorities harder. Not all gay men of color have the same experience. We can't draw simple conclusions about all minorities. Yet in order to honor some gay men of color's experience, it can be useful to make some broad observations. This is not to stereotype, but rather to give us a way to talk about minority issues.

Gay men of color may accent their manhood or compensate more since they have extra hardships to overcome: relatively strong subcultures of machismo and homophobia, family and religious values, sexual values, economic challenges, and racism. Such factors may make the "gay" label even harder to accept for men of color. So they may feel the need to be even more straight acting. Recall the hip-hop, urban street "cool pose."

Brent told me about his understanding of how being gay is seen as an attack on masculinity for guys in his community:

The "down low" (DL) is a term that originally described black bruthas that messed around together but kept what they were doing very quiet, low-profile, and secret between themselves. You have to keep in mind that it's extrahard to be black and gay. It's like two slams against you. You don't want to be disrespected as a man and to bring shame on your family. The culture is very macho or masculine. They don't want to be rejected. It's worse if you were raised Baptist too, 'cause you're going to burn in Hell forever if you're gay. The Bible says it isn't right. These guys keep the image of being masculine but they sleep with men. They're not of the gay community. They don't associate with it, they don't act gay, and they don't go to gay bars. These men are not even gay in their minds. They don't use the word. There's too much stigma. Call a down low brutha gay and your ass will be beat down. The only thing they think they have in common with gays is that they sleep with men. They have girl-

*friends or are married and many have kids. I remember get-
ting it on in a peep booth with a brutha who had the channel
set to lesbian porn.*

As Brent's explanation of the "down low" illustrates, gay men
of color can push back even harder against the effeminate gay
stereotype, being more straight acting.

There are some reasons for this. While both gay men of color
and white gay men can be rejected by American mainstream culture, gay men of color may be further alienated within their own
race or ethnic group for being gay. Some are rejected by their
families and churches, which may still have traditional ties to their
roots. As gay men of color grow up and adopt values of the
American culture, they give up aspects of their traditional culture. If their family moves at a slower place in this process than
they do, the gay son is put under tremendous strain. He is caught
between the old and the new, between bondage and freedom.
Often strict religious values are involved. Being gay can be much
more difficult under these circumstances. There is a pressure to
not bring shame on the family and to carry on the family name.
Additionally, gay men of color can be rejected by the mainstream
for being nonwhite. Still, within the gay community, they may
be discriminated against, too. Consider that a white gay man can
actually go "invisible," being straight acting, passing when he
needs to, to escape discrimination. He can still access most white
male privilege. Gay men of color don't have this advantage.

Derrick told me:

*I suffer from racism in America at large. Then when I came
out, I suffered from the homophobia of my family and ethnic
community. When I started going out to meet gay friends, I
suffered again from racism in the gay community. I get it from
all sides. It gets pretty lonely.*

Some African-American men tell me how extrachallenging they find it out there.Take these two letters:

Dear Angelo,
I'm a black man down south and finding a black man who's not on the DL to have a relationship with is like winning the lottery. Any suggestions?
Signed, Southern Belle

Dear Angelo,
Hey Angelo. I'm a black gay man. I don't understand how a gay person can be racist.
Signed, White Boys Only

We must celebrate difference, turning toward each other with acceptance, compassion, and love. Prejudice of any kind is wrong. Challenge racism and discrimination whenever you run into it.

As men of all kinds, we may have been pressured by masculinity to squash our emotions and shove our "gay tendencies" down. We're taught they're "feminine" and "weak." This oppression and rejection of the self can be traumatic. In being straight acting, we may think we'll be safer and belong better if we come across as more acceptably male, escaping discrimination.

The straight-acting coping mechanism goes all the way back to childhood. We hear from a young age that gayness is unmanly. We know that sissies lose all respect. Even though we may not have known we were gay yet, we know we felt different when growing up, not like the other rough-and-tumble boys. Maybe we didn't want to play sports, army, or roughhouse. Perhaps we'd rather play with the girls. Maybe we just didn't fit the man code. Perhaps we felt inadequate compared to the other boys, ashamed. We naturally wanted to fit in and be like everyone else. We didn't want to be targeted, called a "sissy," and treated like a misfit.

We learned to be more masculine to escape dangerous threats, cruel ridicule, and discrimination. Being hardwired to keep safe from harm, we began to distance ourselves from getting too close to obviously effeminate boys to "cover." We may have even joined in to tease them to score "man points" and save face for ourselves. Maybe you didn't escape anything. Maybe you were the one who was alienated, horribly teased, or attacked because you were effeminate. In either case, we grew up to believe that we were inferior and unacceptable as we were. We came to feel shame, humiliation, and inferiority. There may have been no one we could turn to with our secret. We may have retreated into disconnection, moving more into ourselves, maybe tuning out altogether, escaping into fantasy. We came to feel a sense of separation from both the "unacceptable" parts of ourselves, other people, and the world. We began to "duck" parts of ourselves. We began to "duck" each other. Such an isolation or distancing pattern like straight acting can last into adulthood and interfere with gay relationship-building. We can end up shell-shocked—paralyzed like deer in headlights—from being continuously assaulted by the heavy artillery of a culture that shoots antigay propaganda, which rains down on gay men.

We might believe a straight-acting path is the road that will restore our stripped manhood and sense of belonging. After all, it's socially encouraged. We can get relatively more social approval and less flack if we're undetectable. Perhaps knowing no better way, we may abandon our true self to be more straight acting. But the straight "act" only eats away at our self-esteem more. The gay man gets hit by a double whammy. Being both detested by some people and partly self-reviling, the gay man is in crisis. And straight acting is our main coping mechanism to fix it all.

Moving from Trauma to Healing

It might be hard to get in touch with the magnitude of the things we've discussed, now that you're grown up. You may think it was so long ago, that it doesn't matter anymore. If you had the misfortune of experiencing alienation, mistreatment, or abuse growing up, it makes sense that you would want to distance yourself from a painful childhood, never looking back. Perhaps you don't want to go back because you've worked too hard to be strong and move on. But even though you've moved on in your life, carrying a distressed past can get heavy. You may think that you can go it alone, believing it is unmanly to share your feelings and weaknesses in exchange for unknown benefits. You might think that you should have been tougher and protected yourself. You may fear that one small crack will break the dam, and the flood of emotion will never stop. You may worry about falling apart and not being able to put yourself back together again. You may wonder what people would say. Or you might never worry about being harassed, attacked, or killed. But you know how sometimes you feel afraid, nervous, confused, sad, or broken? How you may sometimes feel like you're different than other people, or like you just don't fit into the world, and you can't put your finger on why?

What I know is that there can be long-term effects from childhood wounds like trauma. Even though things happened long ago, they can still be affecting your life today. But I also know that it is possible for you to take your power back now. To feel good again. To break through shame and self-blame. To safely rediscover and befriend the you that was not touched by the suffering. To have a fulfilling life with healthy relationships and a great sexuality. You can harness the strength you used to survive to move forward and get to the other side.

It's unresolved hurt and shame that unconsciously drive our desire to act more masculine so that we can restore our dignity once again, being strong and tough, and fighting back. We want to scream, "I have value." "I want respect and esteem." This is understandable. But like straight men who aren't allowed to be truly intimate with other men, a gay straight-acting mentality inhibits a gay man's close relationships with other gay men. This makes us more lonely.

The struggle to reconcile our maleness and gayness hinders our ability to openly love other men. How the gay man deals with this struggle will determine how far he is able to step outside the traditional masculine role, to be able to find emotional closeness with other gay men. The more a guy stays inside the box of masculinity, doing "damage control," the more disconnected he will be from other gay men. The more of a "real man" he has to act like, the more lonely he may feel. Since many of us, closeted or out, try to stay in the box of masculinity to some degree to avoid being relatively more stigmatized, many of us may find ourselves perpetually single—seemingly unable to bond lovingly with other men. We may long for close relationships. We may find ourselves lonely in the area of gay romance and maybe even gay friends. So we have to ax the "real man" to find the right man.

Right about now you may be feeling like there are way too many obstacles to find happiness, let alone true love. But I know it's absolutely possible to thrive as a gay man and have a successful relationship. You may have doubts. But I know it's 100 percent possible to find true love. Colleague Kathryn Alice, author of *Love Will Find You*, teaches in *Releasing a Person* and *Manifesting LOVE* (kathrynalice.com):

> *If I were a fortune-teller and predicted your future correctly in the past, and I told you that your true love is coming, but you*

just didn't know his name yet, it would be easy for you to believe it. Well, believe it. Put out a soul call to "the one." Imagine him standing in front of you. Imagine looking into his eyes. Invite him to come into your heart. See the two of you surrounded by a deep beautiful shade of red, the color of love.

Look forward, not back, to all the new people and fresh opportunities ahead, waiting to bring you what you want. You'll fare much better thinking positively, rather than believing you'll never find love.

Support is already out there for us. Several states and foreign countries have legalized gay marriage or recognize it. Many more places have civil unions, domestic partnerships or something similar. I've treated gay couples that have been together for as long as fourteen, thirty-one, forty-seven, and sixty years without any ceremony. Carlos and Fernando are two male flamingos at the Wildfowl & Wetlands Trust in Slimbridge, England. They have been happily together for over six years and have raised many adopted chicks over several seasons. If states, countries, humans, and animals can do it, you can too. It's not hopeless. Successful gay relationships are certainly possible—yes, even for you. I have no doubt.

Meanwhile, many gay men are self-sabotaging and self-destructing from stress, shame and loneliness. They attempt to relax, distract, escape, and soothe the pain with risk-taking behaviors. They hope to obliterate the challenging feelings relating to the "unacceptable" part of them they've learned to feel bad about. This is why it's so important to examine the many facets of homophobia, seeing it on the pages of this chapter. Not to reinforce us as victims, but to validate our experience as gay men in the world. Homophobia makes life as a gay man hard. In fact, it complicates life for all of us. Don't think you're alone or that it's only you. Knowing it's not you, that it is difficult, can empower you to turn it around.

5

How Masculinity Increases Gay Men's Health Risks, Stress, and Self-Destructiveness

"It is not easy to find happiness in ourselves, and it is not possible to find it elsewhere."

—Agnes Repplier

I often use the following analogy in my work when guys tell me they don't want to take a closer look inside.

Imagine a closet door. Behind the door there's a huge pile of stuff you've been collecting for years. You know that if you open the door everything is going to fall out. So you normally keep it shut. But you've really been wanting to clean that closet out for a long time. In order to have the clean closet you want, you might decide to deal with the mess that opening the door makes at first. Once the mess falls out all over the place, you can sort through everything, keeping some items and tossing others. It might be a big challenge, some things may even hit you on the head. But in the end, you can put back what you want and organize your closet just the way you like it. It will be a much better situation afterwards.

Reorganizing your "closet" is the purpose of the next two chapters. Before we can move on to the solutions and advice in chapters 7 and 8, which are roughly the whole last half of the book, we have to open this closet door. We'll look at the connections between masculinity, stress, men's health, gay men's health, self-destructiveness, and loneliness. We'll see how the potentially traumatic pressure to measure up to masculinity standards leads to a variety of self-destructive coping strategies that hinder our relationships in many ways, which is at the core of why it can be so difficult to meet a man.

Masculinity, Stress, and Men's Health

The "real man" causes real problems. In order to evaluate how seriously male gender-role socialization impacts our lives, we'll first take a look at the health of the average man, and then we'll examine the health of gay men.

The stress of being a man kills.

Men die roughly five years younger than women in America. The death rate for American men is significantly higher than for women through age 74. Between the ages of 15 and 24, a time when masculinity is highly influential for young men, the number of male deaths is nearly triple that of female deaths, and between ages 25 and 34 it more than doubles. It remains elevated by at least 150 percent through age 64.

Nearly four males commit suicide for every female who does. There is not a single age group in which the numbers of boys or men committing suicide doesn't significantly surpass the numbers of girls or women. Each day, sixty-eight males die by suicide. Male suicide rates have risen dramatically over the last half century, along with changing gender roles.

There's a connection. Amidst a changing world, the pressure of knowing when it's expected to maintain the "real man" image (most notably being emotionally strong), and when it's OK not to, causes significant stress in men. The intensity of male gender-role stress, strain, or conflict can actually be measured by psychological tests. The pressure to not fall short of male gender role expectations affects our mental and physical health, producing significant stress.

There's a clear link between stress and health. According to ETR Associates, 80 percent of all doctor visits are related to stress. Behavioral (mind-body) medicine has found that chronic stress negatively affects health and well-being. Stress has been shown to impact many men's health problems: frequent illness from a weakened immune system, high blood pressure, coronary artery disease, heart attacks, migraines, irritable bowl syndrome, duodenal ulcers, diabetes, poor eyesight, arthritis, back, neck, and shoulder pain, bronchial asthma, eczema, psoriasis, low libido, erection problems and more. Stress has been linked to several leading causes of death for American men—heart disease, cancer, accidents, stroke, lung disease, diabetes, and suicide. To make matters worse, men in general avoid the doctor. It may be "a man thing." According to Web MD, men in general seek a doctor 20 percent less often than women. Thus, negative consequences on our minds and bodies are some of the *Hazards of Being Male*, a classic book on masculinity of the same title by Dr. Herb Goldberg.

The ways in which men vent their stress have devastating consequences as well. According to information compiled from *Tough Guise*, the CDC, and the FBI: fatal accidents from risk-taking behavior are a leading cause of death for men. Since men act out or express their feelings through action, rather than talk them out, many fatal accidents may in fact be passive forms of suicide, like speeding down an icy road while drunk or drowning while swimming drunk. Many fatal accidents involve substance use. Eighty-six percent of all drunk-driving fatalities are male. More than 75 percent of young adult men binge drink. Men are at higher risk of dying from cancer, heart disease, and other illnesses related to smoking, drugs, alcohol abuse, and other poor health habits they use to relieve stress. Twice as many men use drugs as women.

Men are eight times more likely than women to commit a violent crime. The vast majority of offenders are under the influence of alcohol or drugs. Ninety percent of all violent acts are committed by men. Ninety percent of murders are committed by men. Ninety-five percent of road rage cases are committed by men. Men often unload on those that are less strong—like the dog, children, women, the elderly, the disabled, etc. More than one hundred women are killed every week and ninety of them are murdered by men. Of convicted rapists in prison, 99.8 percent are men. Around 90 percent of all child physical and sexual abuse is perpetuated by men.

We even assault our own. Most victims and perpetrators of homicides are male. And given that males are responsible for 95 percent of all domestic violence, the incidence of intimate partner violence is estimated to be significantly higher among male-male couples than male-female couples.

Something more than an aggressive temperament driven by testosterone is going on in the lives of men. The pressure of the tough guise takes its toll.

Masculinity, Stress, and Gay Men's Health

Often, the amount of stress a person has is relative to where they stand in the public eye. Since gay men are considered by many to be the "lowest of the low," growing up gay in a very homophobic culture can be quite stressful. Studies have shown that growing up under stress can have a powerfully negative impact on one's health many years later. Research shows that stress from an adverse experience in childhood is highly related to traumatic stress response symptoms like cigarette smoking, alcohol and drug abuse, loneliness, anxiety, depression, suicide, sexual compulsivity, unsafe sex, STDs, obsessive body image, and intimate partner violence. Gay men report traumatic stress response symptoms at higher rates than their heterosexual peers in adolescence and adulthood.

Reliable statistics specifically about gay men's health are lacking because we are excluded as a category in national health surveys taken by the CDC or National Institutes for Health. But here are some truly disturbing statistics I was able to find on gay men's health that reflect the experience of people who have undergone trauma.

University studies show that nearly twice as many gay men (one out of two) than straight men (one out of four) smoke cigarettes, alcoholism is estimated to affect one out of three gay men, and approximately one out of three gay men is addicted to drugs. Drugs as a category includes prescription medications, steroids, poppers, marijuana, ecstasy, special K, mushrooms, and acid. It's not just the "hard stuff" like GHB, cocaine, crack, heroine, and crystal meth. University estimates regarding the prevalence of alcohol and drug addiction among gay men are exactly in sync with separate studies showing that one out of three severely stressed people eventually turns to alcohol or drugs for comfort. Additional studies reveal that the prevalence of drug addiction and alcoholism among gay men is at least double, and may range up to six times higher, according to some studies, than among the straight population. Gay men do a lot of self-medicating and partying to unwind from the stress of being thought of as gay and not "all man."

But something else is lurking beneath the partying. A Boston study reported that nearly half of gay youth reported depression within the two years preceding the study. Other research found the overall depression rate for gay men was 17 percent—twice the rate of the general population. Depression itself has been linked to risk-taking behaviors like cigarette smoking, alcohol and drug abuse, compulsive sex, unsafe sex, obsessive body image, and violence—which are already in play as a result of the "gay" stress that helps fuel the depression in the first place. The issues are all connected and compound themselves.

Depression can lead to suicidal ideation and behavior. Research studies have shown increased suicidal ideation and behavior among sexual minority youth. Multiple surveys have shown that gay youth were over four times more likely—and up to six times more likely, in some studies—to attempt suicide during adolescence than their straight male counterparts; and four times as likely for the attempt to be serious enough to require medical attention. Suicide is the leading cause of death among gay teens. Gay youth may account for one out of every three youth suicides in the nation. A survey by PFLAG found that one in three sexual minorities—no matter what their age—has considered or attempted suicide at some point in their lives.

While sobering enough, this isn't the end of the road. Gay men, like straight women, can suffer from body-image issues, since both groups are trying to attract the eyes of male suitors. Not measuring up can be depressing and stressful, especially with age. As one of my clients put it, "If you don't look fabulous, you may as well be dead." Gay men can fall prey to things like obsessive exercising, eating disorders, "diet" pills, "vitamin" and "supplement" abuse, steroid use, distorted body image, unnecessary cosmetic surgery, expensive clothes, high-end products for grooming, and professional services to improve appearance. This can be costly in many ways.

Since gay men may overemphasize sex appeal, rather than emotional intimacy, sex is often the grand prize. It's often accompanied by alcohol and drugs to relax, lowering inhibitions. And clouded minds decrease safe-sex practices.

HIV infection continues to ravage the gay male community disproportionately, in the face of AIDS education. Men who have sex with men (MSM) accounted for approximately 70 out of 100 estimated HIV infections among all American male teens and adults in 2004. But only around 6 out of 100 men in the United States identify themselves as MSM. These figures show the MSM community has been disproportionately impacted by HIV. The numbers also imply far more MSMs than men who acknowlege it openly. Gay stigma, fear, shame, and male pride may help explain the low numbers. But even those who identify as MSM may be afflicted by depression from these same issues, because they are acting out by not practicing safe sex. A New York City survey reported that just 55 percent of MSMs reported using condoms in their last sexual encounter. While most MSMs report having far more sexual partners than straight men, only 35 percent reported having an HIV test over the last year.

HIV infection and AIDS have hit nonwhite MSMs especially hard. Even though only about 30 percent of MSMs are non-white, MSMs of color made up nearly 60 percent of all MSMs living with HIV/AIDS in 2004. The African-American community has been impacted most. The CDC estimates that almost half of African-American gay and bisexual men are HIV-positive. As Tyrone told me, "a mainstream cough turns into pneumonia in my [the black] community."

Not having access to health care compromises gay men's health further. The ratio of uninsured GLBT individuals is about twice that of straight people, according to an article in the *Advocate* by Jeremy Quittner called "Insurance Insecurity." He wrote that in spite of the rise in domestic partner benefits, many employers still don't offer them. He points out that even if couples can get the benefit, some may not want it because of extra costs involved that married folks aren't subjected to. He also says that some may not want to be out at work because they fear being gossiped about or fired. Quittner points out that gay doctors are quick to say that lack of insurance will force people to delay getting treatment, which in turn leads to more medical problems and higher death rates among GLBT persons.

We may not go to a doctor, even if we have insurance. Gay men may be reluctant to deal with a doctor, dentist, or other health-care professional, since their sexuality may come up and the specialist might be homophobic.

Seem overwhelming? It is. But things are definitely improving all the time. The "real man" image is being challenged by brave, iconoclastic men such as soccer star David Beckham, who embrace a more fashionable and often effeminate "metrosexual" aesthetic. Men in stereotypically macho male professions, like the heroic rescue workers of 9/11 and Hollywood's leading men, can be sensitive and are even shown shedding a tear nowadays on screen. We hear about "man dates" and "man crushes" in the mainstream media. Our health is getting better because men are living better and longer. Being gay is getting easier with lots of favorable gay images now flooding the media in shows such as *Ellen*. This is wonderful and long overdue. We can finally see ourselves more accurately reflected as part of the world. This is so healing for us. Encouraging change is happening continuously all around us. But we still have work to do before we kick up our heels and celebrate. While most of us aren't self-destructive and have developed strong coping skills, many of us are behaving in ways that negatively impact our health and well-being.

Self-Destructiveness

Significant health risks still exist for us as a group because a fair share of us are still coping with the stress of not being considered "real" men in self-destructive ways.

Internalizing the gay stigma affects our minds, bodies, and spirits. When an oppressed group believes the negative prejudices the dominant culture harbors about them, then self-hatred, low self-esteem, numbness, anxiety, depression, rage, and self-destruction emerge among them. Experiencing significant social adversity also creates the desire to eliminate what is "unacceptable." The oppressed group "stamps out" what makes them different to be more "normal," like the oppressor. In being straight acting, we muffle the so-called "feminine" part of ourselves. But by limiting the expression of our whole selves, we stifle our lives and acquiesce to the negative evaluations the general public has of gay men. This "ducking" is stressful and painful. Our need to neutralize the stress of being gay combines with the desire to mitigate the pain of silent shame and low self-esteem, and we self-destruct from coping strategies like cigarette smoking, alcohol and drug abuse, anxiety, depression, suicide, sexual compulsivity, unsafe sex, having to have the perfect appearance, gay partner abuse, and so on.

Perhaps not liking what is inside, we may self-soothe by turning to things outside of ourselves to make us happy. We may resort to artificial means to de-stress, avoid, distract, escape, or dampen our painful feelings. We seek, at least for a while, to remove all the shame and self-loathing that inhibits us from embracing all of who we are. The ways we choose to cope with the high stress levels and self-dislike often restore an inner sense of power, confidence, joy, and peace.

Nothing exists in a silo. The straight-acting routine that we already have in play biases us toward selecting coping techniques that channel our pain in ways that project an image of invulnerability and demonstrate our manhood—we usually don't just sit down, share, and cry. So we may turn toward self-destructive, male risk-taking behavior, and turn away from our feelings, especially if they're unpleasant. In this way, we can lose touch with who we are, and how we truly feel, developing a lost self. Getting split, gay men can feel incomplete and emotionally numb. Such inner deadening only drives us to engage in more self-destructive, male risk-taking behavior, to stimulate us back to life, leading us into a vicious downward spiral.

Self-destructive coping strategies contribute to the broader problems we see in the gay community today like overemphasizing sex, body image issues, eating disorders, ageism, dissatisfying relationships, emptiness, loneliness, anxiety, depression, self-sabotage, addiction, STDs including HIV, poorer health, suicides, and other premature deaths.

We are trying to cope with our shame. In the book *I Don't Want To Talk About It*, author Dr. Terrence Real explains that men who are hurting may use self-destructive behavior to shift a constant, underlying sense of shame in order to make themselves feel better. No one wants to feel bad all the time. Dr. Real describes two roads that men can take to shift their esteem called "merger and elation." Both merger and elation are stand-ins for the core issue, hidden shame, creating a mirage of good self-esteem.

To paraphrase Dr. Real, merger is when we seek to become one with a force that's larger than life. When we are one with "the force" we feel good. When we are high on alcohol or drugs, in a "cult" on the dance floor, or submissive at the hands of a hot sexual partner, we feel the ecstasy in uniting with something more powerful than ourselves. We are connected to something greater. It makes us feel worthy to be connected to something so fantastic. We feel that we are magnificent too. Elation is when we act like we *are* the powerful force—a power that's larger than life. When we are that force we feel terrific. Acting like God, possessing a perfect body, living the high life, having an important title, dominating a sexual partner bareback, and being on the hunt for sexual conquests are examples of elation.

These grandiose strategies may sound like fun—but they don't work. In fact, we usually we end up feeling worse afterwards. We can't catapult over our shame and land in self-confidence. The fix doesn't last. When the effect of our high is gone, we fall back down into shame. Since being gay isn't going away, and shame is an intolerable emotional state to stay in, we have to keep repeating the behavior. This is what turns a coping technique into an addiction.

People can be addicted to anything. Not only obvious things like alcohol and drugs, but things we don't normally think of as addictions, like food, sex, exercise, work, shopping, etc. I think it's an addiction if it repeatedly acts as an escape to make us feel better, causes problems in our lives, and is beyond our control.

Life can be hard and scary. We want to feel OK. As I've touched upon, we're not trying to hurt ourselves with self-destructive behavior. We're trying to take care of ourselves. I learned that from a graduate professor of mine, Jared Kass, at Lesley University in Cambridge, MA. Drugs like marijuana can calm our rage or depression. Crystal, cocaine, or other stimulants bring us back to life and end the numbness. Alcohol warms us and reduces our bitterness and emptiness. Unsafe sex makes us feel closer to someone. Perhaps knowing no better way, we self-soothe our pain with pleasure. We comfort ourselves to restore an inner sense of balance, harmony, and wholeness. Everyone wants to feel an inner sense of love, happiness, and tranquility. We do this "bad" stuff to stay out of the woods where it's dark and scary, transporting ourselves to an island of fun and pleasure in an ocean of stress and pain.

Except, self-destructive coping strategies are often harmful to our mental and physical health. They get us in the end. Plus, they will never take away the underlying pain that drives them. They're only temporary escapes.

Moving from Self-Destructiveness to Self-Care

Dr. Terrence Real explains that the experience of childhood or adolescent trauma is often responsible for a man's hidden pain.

The experience of trauma causes boys or young men to think something like, "If only I were more of a man (stronger, tougher, faster, smarter, or whatever) this wouldn't have happened to me." This produces a sense of inferiority, shame, and low self-esteem, to which, as we've discussed, men often react in self-destructive ways to feel better.

As you know from chapter 4, gay men can experience a social trauma (not being considered "real" men), causing them to feel insecure about their masculinity. This can lead to the aforementioned pattern of inferiority, shame, low self-esteem, and self-destructive behavior.

Thus, traumatic stress, subsequent self-dislike, and coping strategies contribute to a wide range of gay men's suffering.

When we're consistently overwhelmed by the symptoms of trauma, self-destructive coping strategies, and other personal problems, it's harder to develop good relationships. Our connection to each other is filtered through our issues. There's simply too much that gets in the way of making a healthy relationship. This can lead to the pain of mistreatment, disconnection, isolation, loneliness, and emotional unfulfillment, which only compounds the issues, leading us to tune out even more with self-destructive behavior. We may get trapped in a vicious cycle of self-destruction and loneliness. Unfortunately, while you're escaping yourself, you can't really be fully present, emotionally available, and committed to another man for a relationship, until you stop the cycle.

Just because you're out of the closet doesn't mean you've dealt with your "real man" issues, packed your bags, and left the closet of masculinity behind for good. Out or not in the traditional sense, you may still be using harmful coping strategies to deal with any unresolved masculine shame about being a man who loves men. If your mind's elsewhere, you don't have to think about it or feel it—you tune out. Being in fantasy land helps us escape masculinity and remove the man mask. We can ditch the gay stigma and fully embrace all of who we are and who we are with. We can tear down the facade, being comfortable enough to express our whole selves. We can finally find solace in another man's arms without any shame—at least for a while.

If you don't avoid, distract, or escape, you have to stay in reality and face yourself. Some men tell me that porn, smoking marijuana, drinking, or getting high on crystal meth just serves to make sex better. I say they make sex possible—to accept the "forbidden love" they need that's still so taboo in their hearts.

The relationships we do have can be based more on sex and fantasy than emotional intimacy. It's not because gay men aren't capable of intimacy or because they don't want intimacy. Quite the contrary. It's just easier. While we're doing the best we can, we're dodging the real thing because gay intimacy is hard. To avoid addressing internalized homophobia, many gay men focus on sex and not on love. Sex can be a vehicle that readily fills our voids with the illusion of intimacy. Sex isn't bad. But sex becomes a problem when we prefer to tune out and escape into a world of make-believe, rather than facing reality. Going on the Internet, in particular, can be like taking a trip to *Fantasy Island*. The hard part is staying present with a real person for a shared experience and dealing with all the issues that that entails.

You have to drop the "real man" to get the right man, facing yourself. The straight-acting routine we perform in our dog and pony show of masculinity may get applause from the crowds, bringing a temporary reprieve from stress, but it feeds into a major problem—finding true love. Since straight acting is so widespread, loneliness is too. We've discussed how self-destruction leads to more loneliness, but in the cycle of self-destruction and loneliness, loneliness begets self-destruction as well.

To illustrate how profound the problem of loneliness is in our community, leading to self-destruction, I want to discuss an extreme case of self-destructive behavior in a very, very small group of gay men, known as bug chasers. Bug chasers seek to become infected with HIV. Daniel Hill, the author of the article "Bug Chasers," which I mentioned in the last chapter, credits Michael Scarce (who wrote a separate article for *POZ* magazine) with saying that "the sharing of semen" for these men reflects a real desire for intimacy. Scarce goes on, "charged loads . . . offer a kind of permanent partnership, a connection outside of time." Scarce also quotes an HIV-positive man as saying, "It turns me on knowing how much he wants my cum and how much he's willing to deal with to get it."

These men bug chase to bond. Being Poz affords a gay man a lot of community support, relatively much more than an HIV-negative man receives. In that support, he can finally feel a part of something—joined with a tribe of men known as the gay community. Hill writes that some bug chasers even go so far as to choose a "gift-giver" (the HIV-positive person) in a sort of ceremonial rite of passage into the gay community.

Without getting into a debate about Scarce's point, I would note that it's so sad that bug chasers feel that they have to compromise their health and become infected with HIV to experience the deepest level of intimacy with another man. Is it not possible to share a high level of intimacy with a gay man without having to become infected with HIV? A healthy relationship between a Poz guy and a Neg guy can exist without the Neg partner becoming infected. How far do some gay men have to go in our community to feel loved? Hill wonders some of the same.

The reasons for bug-chasing behavior are complex. Some claim it ends their anxiety about becoming infected. If they contract HIV, it's over and done with. I think bug chasers have something to teach us all about our gay "family" if we pay close attention.

We're all familiar with the "problem child" in a family. The interesting thing is that the family wrongly blames the child. This allows the family to overlook the issues in the family that are actually causing the child to "misbehave." If they look more closely, they'll see that the child's behavior is really telling them something very important about what's wrong with the family. In our "family," the reckless behavior of this very, very small group of bug chasers ("problem child") reflects the excruciating pain of deep emptiness in our larger familial community. In being straight acting, we've emotionally abandoned one another. Bug chasing is a self-destructive behavior that underscores the lack of available intimacy in the gay men's community. You don't go to Holland to buy tulips if they're down at the corner store.

Bug chasing is a desperate call to be rescued from the pain of loneliness. Bug chasers are seeking to fill their hearts with "infected" intimacy. They feel it's the best they can hope for. These men are walking in a wasteland looking for love. They're dazed by despair, crying out for love in a barren land.

Our alienation is intensified because, as we've seen, it's not only hard to feel safe and comfortable enough in our society to love each other openly, but it's also hard for gay men to feel enough love within our homophobic society to love themselves. Hence, many of us find ourselves feeling all alone with a constant craving for intimacy. We have a burning desire for love in a community that seems to have lack and limitation around it. Being alone, or single, only reinforces an underlying sense of inferiority—that there's something wrong with us.

Becoming infected may make it easier for bug chasers to act out, finally nurturing and healing such inner emotional pain. Hill implies that it may be easier for bug chasers to manifest a physical disease because they can tend to that better than an evasive, invisible internal wound of profound emptiness and loneliness. Many gay men say learning they were Poz turned their life around.

They say it was a wake-up call and a blessing. They finally had a reason to take care of themselves.

Bug chasing isn't a large-scale behavior. But more prevalent self-destructive behaviors like partying and unsafe sex abound in our community for the same reason—a deficit of affirming love from society, loved ones, the self, and each other.

The larger-scale practices of partying and unsafe sex can be a misguided attempt at intimacy. Some men who "party and play," or PnP, for short, are seeking emotional closeness. The raw sex and "high" help them feel connected to someone. Many of us can understand the desire to experience deep intimacy with another man. It can be easy to turn to unsafe sex for fulfillment, mixed with alcohol and drugs to cope. But substance use alters our judgment. We can't really connect with another person through the fog of a clouded mind. Similarly, I tell my clients that raw sex is only an illusion of intimacy, unless you're in a trusting monogamous relationship. I say, "If he cared about you, he'd use a condom." If he doesn't insist on using a condom, he may not be that concerned with your well-being. You don't know what someone else is thinking.

> Dear Angelo,
> I am twenty-one and newly POZ. There is something I wanna ask you. If I am with someone and they don't put on a condom, I slap some spit on my dick and slide it right in. I seem to lose control. I assume they know the risks?
> Signed, Bareback

This behavior is wrong. If someone fails to protect himself, it absolutely does not mean that he is assuming the risk, asking for it, or that he doesn't care. Perhaps he doesn't know how to talk about safe sex. He may be starving for love so bad that he fills up his emptiness with sex, doing anything to end the awful pain of loneliness—even if it's unprotected. Maybe raw pleasure counteracts his unhappiness, depression, and inner pain. Perhaps he wants to feel powerful, like a "real man," or experience freedom by letting go. In any event, there's a lot of good information out there today about safe-sex practices. All gay men, Poz or Neg, have the responsibility to talk about HIV-status with each other before having sex. We must all take the responsibility to protect ourselves and our partners. Caring and love are actions, not just feelings. We care about another person when we weigh their needs on the same importance level as ours and carry out the responsible action. A safe time to talk about ditching the condoms is when you're in a long-term, trusting, monogamous relationship where both partners have tested negative. Otherwise, we're acting out or representing an emotion by irresponsible action.

We continue to fight against a resurgence of unsafe sex and substance use in our community. The safer sex and antidrug messages of gay organizations over the last twenty-five years or so, have not quite hit the mark. The focus seems to be more on risk reduction, rather than eliminating the behavior. We've seen confusing messages like—"If you're gonna do _____, here's how to do it safely." The logic is that we have to trust in and respect people's decisions. That can be read by someone who's lost and confused as—doesn't anyone care enough about me to tell me to stop doing drugs, having unsafe sex, and messing up my life?

De-stressing, low sense of self-worth, and desperation for love are behind our self-sabotaging, self-destructive behavior and loneliness. Clear direct messages are needed to assist men in making healthy choices. Our community campaigns have missed the bull's-eye, which is increasing gay men's sense of self-worth and esteem in our community.

The crystal epidemic has brought more self-affirming messages by advocating self-love and abstinence from the drug. It's vital to continue to increase the collective esteem of our community. We need a burst of gay pride 24/7, not just once a year. Messages that target rising self-esteem need to be coupled with information about how to resolve shame and find available intimacy in the gay community, safely and soberly.

Meanwhile, it's vital that we use tools to beat stress, live healthier, and get more out of life. So I have Five Quick and Simple Tools to Beat Stress for you.

First, realize that stress is your friend. Stress is your friend because it's trying to warn you that something is wrong. It's alerting you that it perceives a threat or danger out there. Anxiety works like this. I tell my anxious clients to imagine living in a small room their whole life, having to avoid one small forbidden area smack in the middle of the room. They'd be nervous all the time, worrying about not bumping into the taboo zone. Similarly, anxiety comes from avoiding some important area that's threatening in some way. It's a warning signal saying, "you need to pay attention to me over here." Carl Jung said, "What you resist persists." In other words, we get more of what we're not dealing with. When we dodge feeling bad stuff, we feel more bad stuff. So face anxiety head on. If you're not sure what "it" is, insight therapy is a good place to start.

Often we interpret our stress symptoms in catastrophic terms instead—"Oh my gosh, something feels terribly wrong, I'm going to die." This thinking only makes us more anxious. Recognize that anxiety is an uncomfortable feeling that peaks and then dips. It's like a roller-coaster ride. It has an ebb and flow to it. If you know it will run its course and be over with, you can avoid escalating it. Stress isn't bad, but it's bad for us when our stress level is always elevated. So it's wise to know how to shut the stress response off and return to square one—the relaxation response. The following strategies tell you how to do just that.

The second strategy is to move. Stress is mental and physical, so exercising your body goes a long way. You can walk, run, work out with weights, stretch, do yoga, aerobics, or dance—whatever you like. The point is to just get physical and get your body moving. Also be sure to avoid excessive caffeine, which can be found in coffee, soda, and energy drinks. Caffeine makes anxiety worse. Eat well and get enough rest overnight.

The third strategy is to breathe. You have to do it every day anyway, so you may as well make it fun. Try breathing from your belly. Deep breathing counteracts stress by turning on your relaxation response. How do you do it? When you breathe in, imagine expanding a balloon in your belly, or place a hand over your belly button and feel it rising. When you breathe out, flatten your tummy. Imagine the balloon flattening, or feel your hand sinking. Focus on minimizing the movement in your chest until you get the hang of it. Animals and babies naturally breathe from the belly because it's calming and refreshing. Another technique you can try is to take deep breaths, exhaling twice as long as you inhale.

The fourth strategy is to visualize. Find a soothing space to imagine something pleasant in your mind's eye. What image brings you joy and peace—a waterfall, a rose, a newborn? Focusing on pleasing images helps change your brain waves to alpha levels, which brings about a sense of calm. Aromatherapy can also be effective to combine with visualization. Just picture what you're smelling.

The fifth strategy is to cultivate a meditation practice. Studies have shown that happiness, loving kindness, and tranquility don't just happen to us. They're states of mind that can be cultivated by meditation. A meditation can be anything as long as you're practicing mindfulness. Mindfulness is being fully in the moment with whatever you're doing—focusing your attention on the rhythm of the rise and fall of your breath, brushing your teeth, taking out the trash. To experience mindfulness, try eating a piece of chocolate or fruit. Now try absorbing yourself in eating another piece. Really look at it this time, smell it, feel it in your hand, your mouth, taste it, savor it slowly. What do you notice? Meditation is about mindfully anchoring your attention in the here and now moment. When you do that, your mind automatically clears itself. Meditation isn't about trying not to think. It's normal to have a constant stream of thoughts. Just watch your thoughts stream by like the symbols on a stock ticker, but don't keep your "eye" on any of them. Let them whizz by. If you drift away in a thought, gently acknowledge it and bring your attention back to your anchor each time. Don't judge yourself, just observe. It's common in the beginning to get swept away in thought like a boat in a storm that's not tied down. Just return to your anchor. Meditation takes patience and practice. Exercising the mind is like exercising a muscle, playing an instrument or cooking. You get better results with consistent effort over time.

I hope you use these tools to better manage your mind. You'll fare better when you're not overwhelmed. A terrific book on living mindfully to beat stress is *Full Catastrophe Living* by Jon Kabat-Zinn. Remember to take care of yourself.

6

How Masculinity Affects Gay Male Relationships, Including Isolation

> *In true love the smallest distance is too great, and the greatest distance can be bridged.*
>
> —Hans Nouwens

Loneliness and masculinity aren't separate, they're inextricably linked. Many gay men are lonely. Something is hampering us from forming the romantic relationships we say we really want. This is the shame-based straight-acting phenomenon. It masquerades itself in the gay men's community as "normalizing," leveling the playing field, but it creates distance between us and contributes to our lonesomeness instead. Ironically, many gay men have more of an issue with masculinity, and feel its divisive consequences more acutely, than many straight men. Loneliness and our culture's warped perceptions of masculinity are the two greatest problems facing the gay community.

A substantial chunk of advertising in the GLBT market is geared toward helping men meet men because there's a significant need for it. The No. 1 thing men confide in me about is not sexlessness. It's loneliness. Gay men tell me that what they really want to find is a relationship with another man that is deep and lasting. Hooking up for just sex is an activity that comes easily for many men. The gay sex business is booming. Pornography, peep booths, sex clubs, bathhouses, phone lines, escorts, body workers, chat rooms, the Internet—gay men buy sex in abundance, but they are in search of something else.

According to Michelangelo Signorile in *Life Outside*, a sex survey in the *Advocate* reported that 71 percent of gay men surveyed said that they preferred "long-term monogamous relationships to other arrangements." Despite myth, gay men indicate they don't want to spend their lives cross-pollinating all the pretty pistils in the flower bed. A recent *Advocate* sex poll still found that 69 percent of gay men polled chose the statement "sex is best when building intimacy with a single partner." However, the poll also reported that just 46 percent said they were actually in a committed relationship. Another poll, where 75 percent of respondents were male, reported a similar number of men in a committed relationship—44 percent. This leaves more than half of gay men single. Most of us claim we want a committed relationship, but at the same time, most of us don't have one. Many gay polls, besides the *Advocate's*, also report that the majority of gay men are single. In order to compare the number of gay male partnerships in a meaningful way, it's helpful to know that just an estimated 27 percent of straights may be single—only about half the number of gay singles!

Most gay men are concentrated in the big cities. So you'd expect that it would be easy for us to meet and have relationships, but it's not. Unable to fully let our hair down, it's no coincidence that the majority of us aren't in a committed relationship.

Today's gay man lives in paradoxical times. We have never been more at liberty to live openly satisfying gay lives. We're moving into the suburbs and leaving the safety of the gay ghettos behind. We're having families, getting married, and mixing into mainstream culture. Never before have there been more ways to meet other gay men. Yet, whether I am based in West Holly-wood or Chelsea, loneliness is the No. 1 reason men write to me or come to see me in my private psychotherapy practice. "Is being gay lonely?" is a hot topic.

In spite of an unprecedented number of ways to meet, it seems that we have never been more disconnected from each other. How can both of these things be true at the same time? While we have never been more visible, why is a sizable and influen-tial segment of gay culture beset with troubling problems: self-absorbed, displaying mean-spirited, cliquish high-school "attitude," alcohol and drug abuse, unsafe sex in the face of AIDS educa-tion, isolation? You may think you're lonely because something's wrong with you. But you're not the problem. "Masculinity" rears its ugly head again.

With the help of biological attraction, most gay men are able to escape the role of the "real man" enough to have sex with men. But they protect their masculinity to some degree. Being gay places a man outside the box of acceptable male behavior. This invites social ridicule, violence, and other repercussions that are often sanctioned by our culture. Sex can be kept private, se-cret, discreet, and it's short-term. Showing physical intimacy in public, being emotionally close, and forming long-term intimate relationships with other men are much harder things for many guys to do because they can't keep those things hidden. Obvi-ous togetherness, public displays of affection, and cohabitation make it easier for people to know two men are gay. Having a quality same-sex relationship means coming out more visibly to ourselves and others.

So sex isn't so much the problem for men who have sex with men. Many men have sex with men and don't think of them-selves as gay. Engaging in same-sex behavior isn't the same as identifying as gay. Consider this letter:

Dear Angelo,
It started out as an innocent professional massage session
(he stated he was straight). He claimed that he has never
been with a man and couldn't explain why he had lost himself
with me.We continue to have sex (for free). We have
overnight "sessions." He makes me breakfast in the morning.
We do things together such as jogging, going to the beach,
gym, lunch, etc. But now and then, he says "Remember now,
I'm straight. It's just that you're so masculine!" He makes it a
point to flirt with women as we pass them by, or at straight
clubs. I am so confused. He's a sweet guy, but apparently he
has issues which I certainly don't quite know how to handle.
Do you?
Signed, My Muddled Massage Man

In certain circles it's only the passive, submissive, or receptive partner, referred to as the "bottom," who's seen as gay. For them, bottoming is "womanly" or unmanly. The men who are the "tops," the active, dominant, or insertive partner, identify themselves as relatively straight. Like President Clinton in regard to the Monica Lewinsky scandal—these men like to clarify who's having sex with whom. The issue isn't about the actual position as much as it's about internalized homophobia and who has the power and control.

It's more than the physical act of two men having sex together that really matters. It's more the fear of being perceived as gay, and revealing a stigmatic gay identity, that is the problem for many men who like men. In the eyes of many, "gay" is shameful. As discussed in chapter 4, our culture incorrectly equates gayness with femininity and weakness, which are traits that are disgraceful in men. Manhood is about strength. We have a tough culture of violence, crime, and fear. Billions of dollars are spent on macho "machines": guns, war, oil, rockets, skyscrapers, football, and *The Apprentice*. They flex our brain and brawn. The vast heartland of America, albeit a Christian and conservative nation, isn't to be mistaken as feminine, emotional, and weak. The stigma of losing face, especially with the male community, is the primary reason that the "man" in many men inhibits "womanlike" physical intimacy and emotional closeness with other men.

"Normal" American men don't exhibit "feminine" behavior and leave their arms around each other's waists, dance together, gaze into each other's eyes, hold hands, kiss, or often say "I love you." Men may do all of these things abroad. No one makes much of it. Not so for guys in the good old U.S.A. Some American guys still leave a seat between them at the theater, avoid prolonged eye gazing, and don't touch tenderly in the sports locker room. George Lenker of the *Republican* newspaper in Springfield, MA (my hometown), wrote in "Loosen Up!" that two macho guys may eat nachos side by side at a bar, but probably wouldn't dine face-to-face by candlelight in a romantic restaurant, "even if they both liked the food there." With regard to what physical contact is perceived as acceptable, he wrote, "the dividing line is sometimes a matter of inches." A man might walk a short distance with his hand on his buddy's upper back, but not on the small of his back. Presidents have walked before the world hand-in-hand in friendship with Saudi Arabian crown princes for diplomatic meetings. But in our own country, two men would never attempt this far from the zip codes of places like Chelsea, Provincetown, Boystown, or West Hollywood—if at all. Football players routinely touch each other's butts on the sports field in front of millions on national TV. But two gay men could be beaten to death for doing the same thing in the wrong place at the wrong time.

It's risky to break the rules of the "man code" in public—namely by being physically and emotionally intimate with other men.

There can be dire consequences. We discussed in chapters 2 and 4, how the "survival instinct" is a reason why many men who have sex with men are straight acting, having trouble moving their same-sex relationships beyond the testosterone-driven sexual aspect.

In further support of this idea, it's worth noting that the great psychologist and psychiatrist Dr. Carl Jung believed that the conscious history of a shared culture is "spontaneously" transmitted into the unconscious mind of individuals in that community generation by generation. He called this the "collective unconscious." The gay stigma may remain embedded in our collective unconsciousness as gay people. Gay men may be "programmed" not to be "too obvious," shunning others like us and steering clear of them to avoid trouble. Unlike sex, we can't easily hide our appearance, mannerisms, and voice if we allow ourselves to express ourselves naturally as men who are gay. So, to avoid potentially serious consequences, many of us try not to look "too gay," behave "too gay," or sound "too gay," in public. To some extent, many of us inhibit the natural expression of who we are, to fit in more and be more accepted. We withhold a part of ourselves according to inhibiting social rules.

Yes, gay men do live in paradoxical times. We are entirely free to be gay up to a point—as long as we remain "respectful" of the man code. There are potential consequences if we stray too far away from what's considered "acceptable" masculine behavior. We're free to be gay, but we still have to be careful not to go too far and express or "act on" our sexuality in the same way that straights do. Not only are we denied federal marriage equality, but it's frowned upon just to be "too flamboyant," "flaunt it," or "put it in their face." Our displays of affection for each other are often stifled in public. A fair share of gay men say they "cover" or hide their "forbidden love" in public. If they're not low-key, they risk trouble: a look, a snicker, a remark, ridicule, a reprimand, a threat, an assault. As reported by the *Advocate*, a gay couple was told to stop cuddling, since it was upsetting other passengers on a flight from Paris to New York. This would never happen to a straight couple. In spite of the fact that American Airlines is the unofficial "gay airline," an American Airlines captain reportedly told the gay couple that the plane would be turned around if they didn't stop arguing with the staff about the incident. In this way, we're still not free. We still shoulder "a love that dare not speak its name."

Unfortunately, gay men are caught in the net of a straight world. We feel the pressure of the man code in spite of our same-sex attraction. Even though we are gay, we are still men, socialized by the same masculinity standards as straight men. We share the same manly taboos. We dread the same negative consequences if we break the rules of the man code. We're taught to act masculine and it's hard to unlearn.

It's sad that men cannot openly express too much affection for one another without a level of fear and shame. I left my apartment one morning to go to the post office on West Eighteenth Street in Chelsea. I walked by a construction site. I stopped in my tracks. I could not believe my eyes. There were a bunch of hot hunks right before me. I was so taken by this fine grouping of male specimens that I stopped for a while to watch them work in the pit. It was great eye candy and made for some good daydreaming. Once a beautiful woman walked by, I was slapped back into reality when they all began to holler, hoot, and whistle at her. "How's your day going, baby?" they asked. She didn't appreciate it. I understand that this behavior is degrading to women, reducing them to a piece of flesh. But I thought to myself, she's lucky in the sense that the guys openly let her know that they think she's hot, and that they try to talk to her. If even just one of those men catcalled me from the tar pits—well, it might feel good to experience that kind of thing at least once. It can be self-affirming. Maybe gay men might have an easier time finding romance if men were allowed to just yell out that they liked each other all over the city and ask each other, "How's your day going, baby?" Can you imagine how much easier it would make it for gay men to meet if it were permissible for a guy to flirt and hit on another guy anywhere in public? If we could kiss, hold hands, and dance with other men in the streets without fear and shame? Of course those things hardly ever happen so indiscriminately, even in the gay ghettos. But wouldn't that feel "umm so good," if it did happen, to have our very selves affirmed? Straight people get this luxury and it may be taken for granted.

The saddest part of the gay stigma is that it taints something beautiful and magical like the healthy expression of our full selves and our love for one another. It stifles who we are. Outside of a gay neighborhood, when two gay men walk into a restaurant to eat together, like anyone else, they are immediately conscious of what makes them different from everyone else. Two out of three gay men polled in the *Advocate* said they "covered" or felt that they had to restrain their same-sex affections in public. What an awful feeling. That something so wonderful as our love has to be "hidden" because it may be looked upon as something that's shameful, ill, wrong, dirty, and bad. It can be unsafe to show our love, since that's unjustly seen as "flaunting" it. Yet, straight couples do it all the time because it's natural. Add people's fear and the stigma of AIDS to the mix, and you have a recipe for a group of gay men who may understandably have trouble showing love openly toward one another, especially in public. Everybody should have the right to love. It's just love. But many gay men live in fear of reprisal for loving other men. A large segment of our community alters our behavior by conforming to the rules of masculinity to fit in and feel safe. So we're not rejected for our "preference." It's no wonder we're more straight acting. There's a big benefit. You suffer far less grief!

The rub with straight acting is that in order to appease everyone else, we have to act more masculine and less "gay" to "pass," which causes us to be more inconspicuous. Since many of us prefer to turn our "gayness" down as low as possible and slip by incognito, it's hard to definitively recognize, acknowledge, and move closer to one another—to fulfill our natural need to connect meaningfully in lasting relationships with other gay men. Even among openly gay men, the straight-acting wall doesn't necessarily come down. We may leave it up because we think it's more appealing and attractive. We feel more adequate. So a cool, emotional distance between us predominates. After all, it's manly.

We've discussed how a "tough guise" disconnects men. Macho fronts and "attitude" only serve to keep other men from entering our hearts. Holding on to those aspects of traditional masculinity impedes gay men from building emotional intimacy with one another. We can't reach each other across such thick, cold walls. Straight acting leads to the pain of loneliness for many men in the gay community.

For instance, I found myself in a trendy Chelsea Starbucks location one summer evening. I sat sipping an iced, half-caff, grande, sugar-free-vanilla, skim latte. Suddenly, a strikingly handsome young man walked in. He was muscular, had a crew cut and wore a baseball cap, sweat pants, and a Greek fraternity-lettered tank. He seemed to like sports. After grabbing his order, he walked over to another guy who had been sitting along the window enjoying his beverage. This guy had a goatee and shaved head. He was also muscular and sported well-placed tattoos of skulls and thorns. He wore army pants, dog tags, and a plain white T-shirt. They both looked quite masculine.

I thought for a second there was going to be a terrible rumble between the preppy jock and the soldier. Perhaps, I mused, I should take cover? Instead, upon seeing each other, the two gracefully jumped into the air and screamed in high-pitched tones that only bats could detect. They danced on their toes like ballerinas and then proceeded to shower each other with hugs and kisses on each cheek.

Then something shifted. They seemed to "catch" themselves. They each stepped back. Settling back into more controlled movement, they sat down beside one another at the window. They looked out the window instead of facing each other. Their demeanor suddenly became very butch and less emotional. They sank into trite conversation while gazing at the endless parade of men passing by. It's like they displayed their excitement briefly, and quickly reverted to their "roles." It struck me how dramatic yet ordinary this scene was. It's a reflection of the everyday life of many gay men in America.

We're straight acting to save face. Many of us are "gay" here and behave more masculine there. It feels safer. While it may be more comfortable, this "no fems" attitude separates us from "the gay" or "feminine" part of ourselves and puts a wall between us and other gay men, becoming an obstacle to finding true love. By "hiding" parts of ourselves in "disguise," we make it hard to acknowledge one another openly in public, and we become more disconnected as a group. In concealing our essential nature and needs as gay men, we remain emotionally divorced from one another. Distance grows between us.

How does this happen? Since we are shamed for our same-sex feelings growing up, a same-sex attraction, experience, or relationship will stimulate, or trigger, those old feelings of shame, no matter how inappropriate that may be to our present situation. Recall how the primitive part of the brain that protects us doesn't think logically. It just perceives familiarity via the senses, that this seems, or feels, similar to what hurt us before. So when one gay man encounters another, old shame inevitably surfaces inside of him. This shame need not be in his mind (intellectual). It's the shame in his heart (emotional) that matters. I have to feel, not just think, I'm lovable for who I am or the shame doesn't get fully released. If I'm out and proud, but haven't processed the deep belief that I'm no good because someone important to me thinks so, or because of things I see, hear and experience every day, then the shame lingers. If this is happening for each guy in the scenario, the shame gets multiplied by two. This puts a big pile of shame between gay men, which makes it quite hard for us to form deep, lasting intimacy together. The shame is too big and too intense to bear for too long. So guys have trouble sticking together. This is how shame gets in the way of gay men connecting emotionally. Until they each work through their shame, quick, meaningless hookups and fly-by-night relationships may abound with substance use, while deep, long-lasting, sober relationships are in short supply.

Since our inner sissy gets triggered daily by homophobia, we can be straight acting much of the time to cover for the "gay," "effeminate," "weak," or "unmanly" part of us that we've learned to be ashamed of. Even though some gay men prefer to date effeminate men in order to feel more manly, many more don't like to date effeminate men in order to feel more manly. In either case, straight acting's about "correcting for" the "girly part" of ourselves to feel more masculine and not so inferior. More "man" equals less shame. If a man "cracks," or opens up emotionally to another man, he runs the risk of being seen as unmasculine. So finding a man to "crack" for a relationship can seem hopeless, since no one's willing to be less masculine. We often settle for a "wham bam thank you" instead.

Even when two men do connect for a relationship, it's not uncommon for gay couples to hit a wall after a while. Some couples get emotionally close, but only up to a point. Then there seems to be a stalemate.

I think this emotional threshold is where one's childhood wounds and life story, or personal experience with emotional intimacy, combine with internalized homophobia (gay shame) and masculinity pressures (the "real man" image). The couple seemingly hits a wall at this collision point that can stand indefinitely without proper intervention. Rather than cross the line in the sand and move toward each other emotionally (which is the solution), the men may do the opposite and strongly assert, i.e. proving, their masculinity instead to compensate. This counterbalances their intimacy fears and unconscious shame about being "unmanly," "inadequate," "gay," "feminine," or "weak" for being with another man. As part of the "man thing," the two men can battle for power and struggle for control. Competition, criticism, arguing, contempt, divisiveness, and emotional distance can emerge in a couple. This may lead to gay dead bed (when the couple stops having sex), cheating, an open relationship for the wrong reasons, or an end to the relationship.

Gay and blended families can have special challenges. Except for a heroine, Rosie, we have virtually no family role models. It's important for the health and well-being of your family to have gay-affirmative support.

Coupled or single, closeted or out, the problem of gay loneliness persists until we're ready to redefine manhood, stop playing the gay shame game, deal with our issues, love ourselves and our brothers just as we are, realize that loving men doesn't mean we're "feminine" or weak, and live our lives on our own terms.

Meanwhile, our inability to meaningfully connect with each other can leave us feeling alienated, separate, and lonely. Too often we choose friendship or sex with one another because it's easy and avoid long-term romantic relationships because it's hard. Tribal parties, substance abuse, sex, and other comfort behaviors act like medication, bringing down our guard for a while so we can come together to get the love we need. They're our substitutes for love. Unfortunately, these "intoxicants" create further emotional distance between us in the end. As discussed in chapter 5, the pain of loneliness is murdering us in the form of substance abuse, barebacking, suicide, and other self-destructive behaviors. We self-destruct, trying to soothe the pain from a lack of real emotional intimacy in our community with other gay men. It is essential that we, as men who are gay, start doing what we need to do to find one another's heart space. Meanwhile, we're killing ourselves by running and putting on a butch show. This can no longer be.

Now before you think of swan diving off a balcony wearing your very best white Armani, I absolutely know that you can turn this around. But you're right; when you really think about this stuff, it's unpleasant and very scary. It doesn't leave you feeling very good about yourself or optimistic about finding true love. But the sense of inferiority and shame you may carry belongs to society. However, blame isn't the same as responsibility. You aren't a victim. You can take responsibility to free yourself from social expectations of manhood. You can unleash yourself from the shackles of masculinity to lead a more happy, fulfilling life. It's undoubtedly possible to find gay love. There are lots of good men out there to find, but we have to open up our hearts to each other.

We can focus on making connections for friendship and love, not just sex. The gay community needs more helpful role models than porn stars, exotic dancers, bartenders, DJs, and celebrities. While there are many notable exceptions, I find it sad that some "gay icons" become so only for their looks, entertainment, or escapist value, not necessarily for what they've done to advance our community. We have to start looking on the inside of ourselves and each other for merit.

It can be challenging to move beyond the superficial. Having been rejected and hurt early on in our closest relationships, we can shut out love as adults to protect ourselves. An already fragile self-esteem may become overprotective. Getting close is risky. Many gay men fear that if they care, they might be rejected again. So they don't take the risk. Letting someone in may not feel safe. Allowing ourselves to be vulnerable can feel like suicide. But we want relationships with others. We need love. Otherwise we're left in a cell—alone surrounded by our walls. What are we to do? This can be a tough corner to find yourself in.

I wrote this poem as a teen in the mid '80s. I secretly loved my best male friend:

The mystical power you have attained,
Keeps me intrigued
Not to mention sustained,
That power.
It seems to originate in your eyes,
Holding me still
Quite paralyzed.
Next it radiates from your face,
Pegging my body right in its place.
Then it comes from beneath your clothes
From all of you,
Head to toe.
It lures me
It grabs me
It reels me in
What is this power?
And is it a sin?
Like a web it engulfs me
But not in despair,
The place in your heart—
Take me there.
Keeping control
I go with the motion
Now I'm lost—
No, suspended

In you,
An ocean.
The feeling I get is something quite strange,
Something I like
Not a thing I'd change.
Real love?
A dream?
Crazy?
Just Passion?
Do you feel it too?
Or will your power be my assassin?

As my adolescent poem illustrated, the fear of intimacy can keep us alone. When we're afraid to let other men in emotionally because we don't want to be hurt again, familiar and protective patterns of isolation from childhood can carry on. And on top of that, as men, we're socialized to be separate from others. Thus, we can remain isolated until the pain of our loneliness outweighs the risk of being hurt again. Meanwhile, it may seem like we're waiting at an empty station for a love train that doesn't come.

But the straight-acting express train keeps stopping by. We've become so conditioned not to let our "gayness" show too much, that we may not even realize we're doing it. We don't know how to shut it off. We're on automatic pilot, reacting instead of responding. Even when we're in each other's company, at gay places, with our straight allies, a lot of us continue to be concerned with making sure we come across as masculine.

That psychological split—the straight acting compensation—manifests itself into "games" we play with each other. We can't have relationships with each other when we're defensively flipping the gay light switch on and off, being "all man." As long as we compensate as straight acting, we abandon ourselves and each other.

Psychologist and psychiatrist Dr. Alfred Adler, an early ally and later rival of Freud, would propose that we compensate in one of three ways. First, we may believe we're less than everyone else and develop an inferiority complex, or low sense of self-worth. Second, we may overcompensate, or make up for what others believe we lack, to prove them wrong. Third, we may develop a superiority complex, or artificially high self-worth, to mask our low sense of self-worth. All three stem from a core sense of inadequacy. Everyone does all three of these things to some degree. They may overlap, but one pattern can predominate over the others. We will discuss how a core sense of inadequacy from the wound of not being considered a "real man" carries itself out in straight-acting men, contributing to gay men's loneliness.

Inferiority Complox

Some gay men are straight acting to compensate for an inferiority complex.

Knowing we are different from an early age, gay men arc constantly reminded that it's a straight world out there. We get the message countless times a day that's it's not OK to be gay—that it's not OK to be who we are. Being a minority of any kind doesn't feel good. It's easy to understand how under thc circumstances some of us can become overwhelmed by feelings of inferiority.

Some of us can feel devalued, as though we are worth less than "normal" guys. Being overwhelmed by the gay stigma, some guys may simply acquiesce to the prevailing masculine norms. They might feel defeated in life and may not even bother to change things. After all, they may think, "What's the point? Things will never change." And certainly if they feel inferior, they fcel power-

less to make a difference themselves. They may settle for an un-
fulfilled life. Perhaps thinking they have no special talent, and
are "unacceptably" gay, they may not like themselves very much.
They may beat themselves up with self-destructive behaviors like
addictions, unsafe sex, or abusive relationships. Self-destructive
behavior allows them to validate their sense of low self-worth,
punish themselves because they think they deserve it, vent stress,
and escape everything. A part of them self-sabotages their lives
like a gremlin, causing havoc. I received this letter from a gay man:

Dear Angelo,
I continued on a destructive path until I ruined my fourteen-
year relationship. I truly feel he is better off without me. There
were times I didn't care, and there were times that I just hated
the world. No matter where I went, I felt the same. I wanted
some sense of escape. I acted out a lot of my frustrations and
feelings of self-deprecation. I was depressed, suicidal, para-
noid, hypervigilant, defensive, scared, insecure, you name it.
More importantly, I believed in my core being that I was
worthless. Worse, I feared that everyone else would find out I
was worthless. I had some idea of what I was doing all along.
I felt compelled to ruin everything before anyone could ruin it
for me. I did whatever I could to make my life worse. Knowing
and looking at me, you probably wouldn't ever have suspect-
ed this. I'm just like a regular guy.
Signed, Beautiful Disaster

I also received this letter from a man who likes to be mis-
treated:

Dear Angelo,
I have a passion for being spanked. Sex without it is like a
Margarita without salt—why bother? Also, I can never like the

"nice guy." I always fall in love with mean guys—the straight
type. Please explain this. I toss a lot of good catches, but
they're just too soft.
Signed, Redbuns

In some gay dungeon XXX videos, degradation and humiliation are eroticized. "Oh yeah, treat me like shit, Daddy, I deserve it." Men dominating and demeaning each other becomes a turn-on. Other men can be reduced to sex objects, or even further, to sex organs, with the close-ups. Caring emotions and relationship are nowhere to be seen in this genre. After all, what's the point, since we may think, "I'm so undeserving of relationship anyway." We feel totally inferior since we don't believe we're "all man." We can be drawn to such machismo because we feel we lack masculinity. The gay porn industry capitalizes on this inner lack of masculinity by marketing horse-hung masculine men having sex—mechanics, boxers, thugs in jail, marines, straight guys, cops, jocks, bikers in leather—the list goes on.

Guys with low self-esteem may like A-List type guys who tend to be emotionally unavailable and show no interest in them. Rejection reinforces their negative self-perception that they really don't deserve someone that good to love them for the low-life they think they are. They can also feel like they're "in love," but his unavailability allows them to stay in the safe zone of fantasy. There's no risk. Being fully present with another gay man might bring up too many difficult feelings to manage. Maybe he couldn't handle them "like a man." That would only worsen his self-esteem and he already feels inferior enough.

Some guys may be so buried in low self-esteem that they can't even imagine the opposite—that they're hot and some people might check them out. Some gay guys can't even make eye contact with other gay men. It's too shameful. Alan told me in an interview:

*There are times when I smile at another gay guy and he reacts
defensively—like I think something's wrong with him or I'm
making fun of him. Doesn't he know I like him?*

Recall our discussion about bug chasing. It's the epitome of
self-destructive behavior—a passive suicide attempt that may be
conscious or unconscious. It comes from feeling inferior. It's an
unconscious way of making one's outer life circumstances proof
of negative inner beliefs—"I'm unlovable. No one would want
me. I deserve to suffer and complicate my life. Besides, gay love
is scarce. I have to settle for what I can get." Perhaps a "messy"
relationship is easier to manage emotionally than a successful one.

You don't have to be a bug chaser to self-sabotage. Alcohol
abuse, drug use, and unsafe sex are only some of many other
examples. For more about inferiority complex, you may want to
refer to the section on self-destruction in chapter 5, which ties
in here. You may also want to reflect on the ways you self-sabotage.
How can you choose to take better care of yourself?

I know that it is fully possible to turn an inferiority complex
around. Love does not equal suffering. It is not hopeless out
there. You can have the fulfilling life and relationships you really
want. I witness the men I assist embrace themselves, stepping more
into self-esteem and love every day. If they can do it, so can you.
You're not an exception. I tell you exactly how to go about this
soon in the last half of the book, but let's just discuss a couple
more complexes first.

Overcompensation

This pattern of overcompensation ties in most with being straight
acting, and thus has the longest discussion of the three compensations.

Many gay men cope with feeling less than real men by compensating for their gayness by being straight acting. A prime example of an overcompensation in popular culture is the Short Man's Complex—the 5'5" badass. This is a short guy who acts big to make up for feeling small. Picture Danny DeVito's character in the sitcom *Taxi*.

Along the same lines, some gay men act more masculine, at least in public, to make up for the gay stereotype of femininity and weakness. Some of these men compensate by working out and developing awesome, strong bodies to make up for being seen as feminine and weak. Many of them were ruthlessly teased as kids for being effeminate.

Many gay men prefer to display things like buzz cuts, facial hair, muscles, tattoos, and big chains. They may look like jocks, GIs or leather daddies. They may be seduced by steroids and military workout regimens, and suffer from eating disorders and distorted body images. The gay media also pushes masculine images of physical perfection on gay men. We may think if we're rough, tough, and look masculine, then no one will think of us as sissies or hurt us anymore.

In a sort of coalescence, men who subscribe to the straight-acting image form an influential gay subculture, Signorile's "cult of masculinity," which disproportionately influences what the image of physical perfection is for many gay men.

A physical strategy works nicely for men since men respond well to things they can see, measure, and keep track of. They're skilled at reading visual-spatial cues by nature. This strength likely evolved from our primitive past because it was quite useful for hunting prey, protecting, and fighting—a survival skill.

Men may also be hardwired to look for physical signs that signify virility in a mate to produce the fittest offspring. Physical signals of health and beauty are recognized and understood instinctively by sight. We prefer to see attractive attributes. Straight men seek partners who are young, pretty, and well-proportioned.

Men who are gay do the same. Even though we can't reproduce with one another, we're still programmed to screen for youth, attractiveness, and fitness.

Things that demonstrate our manhood like a buzz cut, facial hair, muscular body, tattoo, well-endowed penis, notches in the bedpost, having resources, and so on—are meant to send a strong attractive message. They display that we're "all man." They're social signs of manhood that other people can see, measure, and keep track of. A man can better acquire high-ranking social status, power, and mates, if he has "all man" signs. It isn't much different than male robins flashing their bright red breasts to lure females. Being "the big boss" means getting the best. If a competitor wants to move up the ladder, he has to challenge the leader's position. It's like deer having antler fights. Such male competition is common social behavior in many animals. Males openly show signs of their maleness to ward off competitors. Such acts of male bravado in the animal kingdom, which we're a part of, involve visible signs of maleness like spots, horns, antennae, size, a fancy car, house, designer clothes, being straight acting—you're getting the gist.

No matter what our species, when we do the macho thing, we're simply trying to be one of the guys. To be man enough and fit in. To be a top dog and get a mate. We're more masculine, or straight acting, to win more love.

The importance of boasting a visibly manly physique among gay men is also a reaction to the images of AIDS. While working out is part of living healthfully with HIV/AIDS, men of any serostatus want to appear strong and healthy, not frail and sickly.

Appearing fit and healthy is not a bad thing. Guys that are in shape deserve credit for the hard work they put into their bodies. It takes a lot of self-discipline. What motivates many, however, isn't their health. To compensate, albeit superficially, is why many men go to the gym. The fact is that if you don't look a certain way, you'll get far less attention from certain segments of the gay community.

Since several things add to the pressure to look masculine, i.e., to be straight acting, in the gay community, there's a lot of heavy lifting going on and a lot of posing. A strong masculine appearance may be emphasized to compensate for an inner sense of inferiority or weakness.

Except, the tendency of focusing mostly on the physical and superficial leads us to sexualize and objectify one other. In the search for true love, this is like looking to buy hardware at the bakery. Sex all by itself isn't fulfilling to the heart. We're using the wrong organ.

To compound matters, sex isn't such an easy issue for gay men. The freedom of sexual liberation—the very thing gay men founded their identity on with great pride—has become contaminated and restrained by the HIV/AIDS crisis. Sexual expression is supposed to be a joyful thing. It's the birthing of life. It's to be celebrated. But not so for gay men in the face of the AIDS plague. We have to physically (with condoms) and emotionally guard against one another while we get it on. In spite of advances in drug treatments for men living with HIV/AIDS, our unconscious mind can still equate having sex with possible danger to our life. Having sex poses a risk. We may think and fear in the back of our minds, "If I have sex with you, you may infect me or reinfect me with something that may hurt me." How can we emotionally let go, open up, and make love to one another fully this way? How can we celebrate who we are in a spirit of unity when the threat of a long-term disease like HIV/AIDS comes between us? No wonder we put our "gayness" at a distance and prefer personal ads that read "straight acting only." Indeed, the fear of HIV/AIDS helps to keep our straight-acting walls up. This profile read:

Total Top. I don't suck. I don't get fucked. Be a bottom, but not the fem type.

How intimate can we really get with each other through such defenses? It's hard to come face-to-face and wrestle with issues surrounding our gayness, masculinity, intimacy, mortality—all at once. Antigay demonstration signs often read "God hates fags." The ugly notions that "being gay is wrong and HIV/AIDS is an I-told-you-so from God" and that we're all "going to Hell" are out there. It's easy to understand how we may want to run away from it all. If I'm reminded I'm gay every time I see you, or I'm reminded of HIV/AIDS every time I play with you, it's easier to keep these challenging realities at arm's length. Quick sex can be a function of "Hurry up and get this over with. I don't want to deal with things for too long." If I can't cope, how can I be in a relationship with you? I may be able to en-gage for a short enough time to have sex with you, but can I really commit to something more for the long haul? Such "dis-tancing" makes it hard to form deep, lasting relationships with other gay men. Given such pressure, trauma, and anxiety, some Neg guys can feel uneasy about Poz guys. Some Poz guys may feel dissed by Neg guys. It can be hard to cross the Poz-Neg divide. HIV-discrimination in our own community underscores straight acting and draws another line in the sand.

Who needs more separation? The AIDS tragedy has hit gay men hard enough, leaving a hole in our ghettos and in our hearts. It's already as if we've been through a genocide.

To come together, breaking free from a sense of low self-worth, self-destructiveness, and loneliness, gay men need to stop and look inside themselves and others, not at the outside. We can go beyond the superficial and the purely physical, to fill our inti-macy needs. The gay gym culture's youthful, athletic, strong image serves the straight-acting role all too well. The bear image, a subgroup of gay men who are often older-looking, with beards or goatees, who typically have a masculine appearance, hairy chest and body, plus a stocky or heavyset build, is another straight-acting aesthetic (albeit more healthily freeing than the perfect body image). There's also men that get off on macho uniforms, leather, S&M gear, and more. Whatever our scene, we have to move beyond physical expectations of how manly we're supposed to appear and move past looking at each other as pieces of meat.

Many men remain emotionally unavailable for deep intimacy. This can seem like the norm for gay men rather than the exception. There's a myth that a gay relationship that lasts two months is equal to a straight relationship that lasts two years. Loneliness prevails in such an intimacy-phobic atmosphere. Brad, a cynically comical man I treat, said this about his gay dating frustrations:

> *I'm the Bermuda Triangle of dating. Whenever I have a nice date with a guy, he disappears, never to be seen or heard from again.*

A sex poll in the *Advocate* found that gay men are six times as likely as lesbians "to visit bathhouses, sex clubs, sex parties, or back rooms." Forty-three percent of men admitted they had visited such venues, while a quarter of guys admitted they have sex in such locales occasionally or frequently. Since many guys may not divulge this type of personal information, the numbers may be higher. Recall that most gay men say that they want a satisfying monogamous relationship. While men may have the ability to keep sex and emotion separate, we may also tend to take the easy way out and sexualize one another as objects for our own pleasure, rather than focusing on building emotional intimacy. Sexual conquest is studly male behavior. Emotional intimacy between men is harder and more "taboo." I overheard a guy say to his friend on his cell,

I met the love of my life. He's rich, ripped, and hung.

We need more substance to truly nourish and sustain one another.

Emotional matters of the heart get left out of our encounters. After all, those sensitive things are for women. "Real" men are emotionally tough. I saw an advertisement for "quick and easy local hookups." Have we reduced sex to something like buying fast food from the dollar menu at McDonald's? This online profile read more like a Jiffy Lube sign: *Looking to be serviced. Quick in/out.*

Many online profiles are very specific about what they want in a man. It's "be this" and "have that," with all sorts of rules. There are even warnings like "If you don't have it, don't bother" or clarifications like, "If I don't respond, I'm not interested." Online dating is becoming more like online shopping—I want this, in this size, in this color, and I want it overnight. It seems as though gay matchmaking has fallen more into the realm of consumerism and that the personal is going out of the personals. We've come to objectify one another like merchandise. Sean told me about a guy at his gym. He said:

I see him all the time. But I'm not attracted to him. So I don't pay any attention to him. He's like a piece of furniture.

We can disregard one another so easily based on nothing but sex appeal. We may reduce a person to his screen name, stats, preferences, or a body part. One can be discarded swiftly like a piece of trash if "it's" not what we're looking for.

In the heart of Chelsea on Eighth Avenue there are two porn stores on opposite sides of the street with large storefront windows. They usually have some bizarre, frightening sexual display with mannequins, erotic devices, and S&M and other exotic regalia. It's good we can show our gay pride like that. But what message does it send to the gay-naive passersby about the priorities of our community? We put sex out front on display and keep our "relationships" hidden out back in the peep booths. You can find one there almost anytime for $1 every three minutes. I hear there are often waiting lines.

It would seem that we prioritize sex over getting to know someone and making relationships. This leaves little room for emotional intimacy in our encounters. It makes it hard to find something more than surface. We keep ourselves emotionally unavailable for gay intimacy and then complain that we're alone. Glen told me:

> I went to the gay center and no one was talking. Everyone was logged on to Manhunt.net.

Toby told me,

> I went for bodywork and had sex with this hot guy. Afterward, I told him I wanted to cuddle. He said, "You need to find a gay guy for that." I couldn't believe it!

I received these two letters:

Dear Angelo,
I've been out for five years and still can't seem to form a lasting friendship with another gay man. Every time I try to make a friend, he either wants to have sex or nothing at all. I don't

*want a friendship with sexual undertones, just a true friend
that doesn't have a hidden agenda.
Signed, Friendless*

*Dear Angelo,
What do you think of friends-with-benefits? I have been "see-
ing" someone for three months when his "needs" come up.
But little by little, I am getting emotionally attached to him. But
I don't think he wants a relationship.
Signed, Hopeful Romantic*

Brad the comedian said:

*I went on a great date last night, but I'll never see him again.
After I talked about my interest in a relationship he said "the
f-word"—friends.*

I would say the vast majority of men-seeking-men personal
ads emphasize physical aspects and come across as looking for
sex or "friendship," not romance. We put our male image out
front, not our emotions, as this random sample of gay personal
lines shows:

discreet masc lkng for similar
lkng for a real man
straight guy for discreet action
lkng for masc men only
man2man—operative word "man"
masc/musc vgl jock
no fems
regular guy seeking same
love a masc man
masculine-voiced men only

normal bi-dude exploring
straight acting, straight appearing for same

We're saying, "Yes I'm gay, but I'm still a man. So, I'm better than a fag, I'm more desirable." It can be hard to meet guys for a relationship with all this male posturing going on. Earl says with a sense of humor:

I'm told to look at being single and dating as a positive experience. It's positively dreadful. I went to a popular coffee bar, a supposedly hot meeting spot, and no one even made eye contact, let alone talked. A room full of guys and everyone's peeled to their iPod, laptop, paper, magazine, or has their face drowned in an oversized drink before noon. But whenever someone new walks in the door, everyone looks. I yell, "you better enjoy it." They don't know it, but that's the only look they'll get.

More than half of us can't seem to hitch a guy for anything long-lasting and of much depth. And if we do finally meet someone nice, his intimacy fears may suddenly turn him into Linda Blair in *The Exorcist*. It's not a pretty picture.

I get many letters about the "Jekyll and Hyde" behavior of many gay men in the face of intimacy. When we've been hurt and fear rejection, we can mistrust people. We can feel pushed and pulled by two instincts. The need to approach people for love, and the need to withdraw from people to stay safe. This makes finding relationship hard, and can keep us in the middle with no one. Past experience of abandonment can make further loss too excruciating to even imagine, shutting us down, leaving a hole inside.

Shutting down our hearts to guard our vulnerabilty (a "real man" or straight-acting trait in reaction to the hurt of social trauma, as well as interpersonal hurt), is the biggest reason why many of us find ourselves alone in the gay community. But there's a high price to pay for such protective freedom. At some point, we have to open up, allowing someone to stick around and love us. Holding on to a "queen of hearts" is a good idea. Instead of freaking out when we find intimacy, we can have the courage to stand our ground, facing male intimacy fears head-on.

Unfortunately, lots of gay men flee from emotional intimacy instead. Since this is such a widespread issue and so important to mend in order to find true love, I share three letters with replies.

Dear Angelo,
I met and started dating a great guy about six months ago. I met his parents, he met mine, we met all of each other's friends, etc. Then just shy of the six-month date, we had a great evening together and it ended with him breaking up with me. No more than two days after the breakup he was saying that he changed his mind. I took him back. Then, two weeks later, he left for the store and never came back. I have watched close friends push others away like love was a sort of disease to avoid. This has left me a bit skeptical about gay relationships. It's next to impossible to find someone. I'm afraid it's too risky to try again.
Signed, Just One More Try

Dear Just One More Try,
It's not too risky to try again. In fact, you must try.

When we open our hearts, we are at our most vulnerable. After we've been very hurt in the past, many of us put ourselves in a fortress. This is fine for self-protection. But Kay Redfield Jamison, author of *An Unquiet Mind*, says the struggle is to build our walls high enough to protect us from more hurt, yet still low enough to allow others to come over them. If we don't get the height right, we will remain safe, but alone, in a self-constructed prison.

It's strange that we fear love, but nevertheless it remains true. It is possible to find someone good and we must continue to try, not close down. My advice is—Get back out there! You can be a wise judge of character by putting your best thinking with your best feeling. It's like going for a swim in the ocean. There are sharks in the water, but there are dolphins too. You can swim with the dolphins, but unfortunately, there's just one ocean. So you have to avoid the sharks while you find the dolphins.

All the Best, Angelo.

Dear Angelo,
There seems to be a gay game I call "come here, go away."
Gay life is tough enough as it is, why are guys so afraid of
getting closer, especially at the bars?
Signed, Hot and Cold

Dear Hot and Cold,
Most guys at the bar are interested in coming out, fraternal bonding, being noticed, the music, partying, and the hunt for sex. It's not the ideal environment to form deep, meaningful relationships. Having said that, intimacy is a problem for men in general, not just gay bar patrons. Men are raised to be tough guys. Somehow, we are all supposed to be the contented Marlboro man, scoring often, but ultimately alone on the range. We're in part socialized to be independent, swallow our feelings, compete, fight, and work. Many men end up having trouble creating noncompetitive emotional relationships that are egalitarian. Not wanting to be smothered, we may become commitment-phobic.

Gay men are men and do not escape. Only, unlike our straight brothers, we have no females to guide our relationships on emotional matters. All we have are the masculine role models that we were raised with. Also, we're too busy worrying about coming out to get the same level of dating experience as straights do in adolescence. Later, as adults, we can find ourselves playing catch-up, fumbling around without a clue.

So, when another man gives you the signal, "come here," and you do, it's understandable that he can become frightened and either shut down, or run the other way. We then receive the opposite message, "go away." There are countless reasons for this. Here are just six possibilities.

1. You're in a bar. Some guys in a bar can be "crazy," drunk, stoned, or high—out of it.
2. The dude may be closeted or newly out. He can be inhibited if he's uncomfortable with his gayness. Just stepping into a gay bar makes a man one down. He may act macho or uninterested to make up for the fact that he's even there. Maybe he's got low esteem.
3. He may not know how he feels.
4. Some guys may play games because of their insecurities. They may be flirting from a distance in order to puff up their egos. They're not wanting or expecting a real encounter. Maybe he's got a boyfriend.
5. Some men may be shy and unsure about how to respond.
6. Other men may be trying to protect their heart. Many men at my Successful Gay Dating workshops express that they've been so burned in the past, they'd rather not respond or call guys back than risk being hurt again. They can't take another disappointment. So they reject before they're rejected.

Reaching out is "risky business." Once we make contact, we can make like a turtle, going back into our shells for protection, despite desiring intimacy. Hence, all the mixed messages. My advice—Don't get sucked into someone else's drama. Believe in yourself. Keep putting yourself out there and move on to the next one.

All the Best, Angelo.

Dear Angelo,
I am a thirty-three-year-old gay man who was in a relationship that suddenly went bad. All the signs were good. We discussed everything openly, including our affection for one another. Quite literally, one day the guy was talking about how much he wanted to see me and the next day he vanished. It's hard for me to believe and he has really hurt me. I was starting to have deep feelings for him when he just vanished. It took me so long to be open to him only to let him go. How can I love again?
Signed, Disappearing Act

Dear Disappearing Act,
I am sorry you were hurt by someone who may be afraid of real intimacy. Ironically, some people run away from love to protect themselves from more pain. For in love we become vulnerable and risk being hurt. But the bittersweet truth of love is that it inherently involves some degree of risk because we have to trust to love.

People can only control whether they're trustworthy. Whether or not we trust people is up to us. Deciding to trust someone involves balancing your life experience with their character, reputation, and track record with you. Yet in the end, all trusting has an element of risk. It requires great faith in the person you are trusting. This is particularly true for fidelity. That may be why it is referred to as being faithful. Ultimately, trust is a precious and beautiful gift of faith that we give another person. It is the foundation of any relationship. Without it, a partner is likely to feel suffocated.

We have to have faith in people, letting them go every day, trusting them. We cannot keep an eye on someone 24/7. We can't own them or control them. Each day we release them freely. We hope that they decide to return to us each day. The best relationships are those where both people are there because they really want to be. Would you really want anything less?

When you're ready, my wish for you is to give the gift of trust again, opening yourself up. It's love we need and love that heals us.

All the Best, Angelo.

It may seem impossible to find love with all the compensating we've touched upon. But I know it's absolutely possible. It just takes a little extra understanding and effort to beat the system. Next, in the last two chapters, I'll tell you exactly how you can win, but first let's just deal with those attitude queens.

Superiority Complex

Other gay men develop a superiority complex, or act "better than" others to overcome feeling "less than." These might be the type of guys who worship their appearance, their possessions, and their accomplishments. They can think they're too good for anyone else. This was described to me once as the "I'm a bitch to mask my insecurities" complex. These types come across as arrogant, and others may not find them likable. I overheard two guys at one of my workshops. One asked, "Why is it that the hottest men are the most fucked up?" The other replied, "I guess the last thing to go on psychotics is their looks."

But these guys deserve compassion. They are actually harboring deep insecurity, not vanity. They may feel so flawed inside that they strive for perfection—to be a cut above the rest of us. Typically they're straight acting since it's "better." Alan, in his interview, said:

> *When I check some guys out they try and act straight like "Who are you looking at?"—and I know they're gay.*

Recall from earlier in this chapter that when two gay men encounter each other, inadequacies about their sexuality and manhood get triggered. Unfortunately, when they encounter other gay men they like, their own sense of inadequacy as men can cause them to act arrogant, aloof, and uninterested, the very opposite of how they may feel. This can be a defensive maneuver, allowing them to avoid feeling their shame. Embracing our gay brothers requires that we stow our gay baggage. Since this can be challenging, we may defensively put ourselves above them, snubbing them instead.

Brad, the humorous man I treat, said bitterly at the start of his therapy:

> *I hate the words "gay community" because there is no damn "community." I have never felt more isolated since I came out. This isn't a lovingly supportive social network by any means. It's one giant piranha tank.*

Superior types can become elitist and self-absorbed as a defense, but they too can feel disconnected. Underneath their arrogance, there might be a love-call masquerading as standoffishness. They may protect their vulnerability by pushing everyone away. They might fool themselves into thinking no one is good enough for them, so they can be left alone in safety. No matter the reason, Brad told me how he deals with these superior types:

I get rejected by a lot of the superior types. They'll take one look at me and say they don't feel any spark. So now I carry a blow-torch.

Jim, an Ask Angelo subscriber, doesn't find attitude appealing for any reason:

I think a lot of hot guys don't say "hi" back because they just think everyone wants to get in their pants. They can't imagine someone is just being nice and saying "hi." What egos. Who wants such conceited control queens anyway!

It is sad that some of us can become suspicious of others because they're being nice. This is twisted thought and it's a good example of stinking thinking.

What's commonly referred to as "attitude" is a big part of the superiority complex. This comes across as "nasty" or "aloof." It's like a "Don't even think you have a chance with me" pose. The best-looking ones can be the worst offenders. Maybe they were manipulated for their looks in the past. It's scary enough as it is to open up, be vulnerable, and risk more hurt.

Nevertheless, Jeff described attitude this way in an interview: *Attitude is just plain bitchy.*

I informally asked about one hundred gay men what percentage of gay men they thought have attitude. The top three answers were: *70 percent, most, all.*

Attitude is a personal pet peeve of Joel's. It makes him angry:

Whenever anyone approaches me, I am pleasant. I always smile and say "hello" even to an unattractive ninety-year-old admirer. There's just no excuse for being rude. And I'm not gross or ninety! So what's up with these jerk-off guys who can't say "hi" back to me?

I received this letter from a guy who gets down about attitude:

> Dear Angelo,
> I've been going to the same gym five times a week for over a year. I try to say "hello" to people I see each time. Why is it that after a few weeks, or even months, they still can't say "hi" first? I'm tired of doing all the work. This sucks. What gives?
> Signed, Why Bother Anymore

Attitude can hurt others and affect them in a profound way. Being sensitive, gay men can take rejection to heart and close down. Brett said during our interview:

> *I'm tired of the guys who are too full of themselves. I give up. I don't even go out and try anymore.*

As we discussed, attitude can be a way we protect ourselves. Knowing hardship, prejudice, discrimination, and the pain of rejection, we don't like to risk more. Attitude can be a preemptive strike to reject others first before they can reject us. In being unfriendly, we don't have to risk opening up and possibly being rejected again. This is a position of power, coming from a place inside that feels powerless. It shifts our self-esteem from "I'm less than you" (inferiority) to "I'm better than you." Recall Dr. Terrence Real's coping mechanism of elation in chapter 5.

While the general idea of "the narcissist" may help us here, I'm not saying all guys with attitude are narcissists. But, the narcissist is a seemingly arrogant god of perfection outside, who is really a wounded boy inside. A narcissist doesn't feel you or have empathy. He's a person obsessed with his outside image and superiority. He believes he is superior. He needs to be adored because he can't face his pain inside. Your adoration of him allows him to feel good about himself to avoid his inner wound of inadequacy.

Far from having a healthy self-esteem, many exclusive "A-Lister" types believe they're so fabulous to make up for their feeling quite flawed. So some straight-acting guys with attitude may have a superiority complex. They have a remarkable way of projecting their sense of inferiority so you feel inadequate instead of them. You might feel insignificant, as if you were an ant, around them. They may only prefer to keep the company of other A-Listers, or guys with inferiority complexes who worship them. They can get off on rejection because it makes them feel "better than" instead of "less than." The last thing we want to do is compliment and affirm this type of guy, but that's exactly what they need most.

It saddens me that I get so many letters from gay men about loneliness, in part because we have so much attitude with one another. In the spirit of Agape's Dr. Beckwith, you can "change your 'tude, dude." Attitude is a waste of energy. Kindness is our essential nature. It takes far less energy and it's far more rewarding to be kind. Songwriter Eden Ahbez writes, "the greatest thing you'll ever learn is just to love and be loved in return." Loving kindness is a better way for us to connect. It creates more community. We can break through the psychological defenses and compensations that drive phony, superficial, and unfriendly behavior. In spite of any negativity you have received or may receive out there, continue to be friendly to other gay men. Like attracts like, and you will soon stumble upon good guys like yourself.

For instance, several months later, Brad, the cynical comic, was joyfully exploring, experimenting, finding his place in the gay community, and dating. It wasn't easy. In therapy, he invested time, money, and effort in himself. It may be time for you, too, to turn within and do some soul-searching.

Looking outside of yourself, like to any mainstream gay rag, may leave you feeling worse. You may get the feeling that gay life is one big happy party and you're missing it. There is often an overemphasis on the gay scene—partying and getting off— for the superior A-List crowd. These magazines are readily and widely available. Practically every city has one and they're picked up like gay bibles. Weekly circulations for some can be over 100,000 copies. They help set the standard for what's seen as "in" and what's "out" for the community. This is where many budding gay youth and closeted men will get their information first.

Is this the dimension of gay life that we really want them to see? Does this reflect the reality of our lives? Is there anything more substantial than sex, drugs, and what the DJ is playing? Like the Wendy's commercial says, "Where's the beef?" By painting on a superhappy face, we're making up for the reality that being gay is no picnic. The inflated images in these magazines try to sell a powerful message to everyone that gay life is fun, friendly, and sexy. But it backfires. Many outsiders look at the images in these magazines and then see them as shallow, dirty rags that reinforce their stereotypes of us as hedonistic floozies. This is our fault for overemphasizing sex and partying.

While it's important to express ourselves as we are, some of us have a need to put it all out there at times—one big "fuck you" to society. The media tends to pick out and feature the extremes of our behavior, which aren't always the most flattering. This leaves our community looking scandalous and stereotypical. It's an unfair portrayal, but it's also partly our fault when we choose to spotlight sex, substance abuse, and cross dressing. So to a large extent, our own media is also responsible. Many of the images we use in our media perpetuate the stereotypes of us.

Alongside the stereotypical images, our media also endorse the superior image of the "real man." Everyone pictured appears flawless. Images of sexy, masculine, young, good-looking, nearly naked, hard-bodied, smooth, hung guys is what you'll see most of. Some of the photos are so revealing that it's unclear if you're looking at a porno mag or a popular gay magazine. They've really become one and the same, except for exposed genitalia. Despite airbrushing, cutting and pasting, and other slick photo tricks, we actually get hypnotized into thinking that everyone looks that perfect. The "super-man" images in these publications reflect our real-life concern with straight-acting appearances. We like to reveal our masculinity for all to see. To honor our male identity, we feel a need to bare our manliness to the culture that tells us we're not "real" men.

So we're drawn to the gay publications for their visual images of superior masculine specimens. It's like the fascination with Hollywood celebrities. How do they look? What's the latest style? What do they do? Where do they hang out? Who's in and who's out? We all want to know. We're all concerned about them—because they seem to have it so good. They're the popular kids at school. The in-crowd. The big boys. We want to be like them. It's the prom king we may never have had. We want superior perfection to make up for feeling "less than." By showing everyone "super-man" images, we're compensating to make up for the fact that we are really seen as feminine and weak. We're like two-year-olds obsessed with the pretty packaging, forgetting that the present is inside.

Unfortunately, the select and often computer-enhanced images become the yardstick we measure ourselves against. If you don't look that way, you may think you might as well hang it up. If you don't fit in, you may feel like you're missing out on all the friends, fun, and sex. You imagine everyone is having a great time, but maybe you're not. You may think something's wrong with you, or that things would be different if only you were somehow better in some way. So we can strive even harder to perfect a certain aesthetic, especially as we age. Awesome bodies, trendy hair, designer clothes, big titles, expensive things, and the list goes on. We strive to be superior, the cream of the crop.

But the bar is set so high, that few can make the cut. Mr. Unrealistic Expectations makes a lot of lonely hearts. No one can be perfect like these images. David wrote in to Ask Angelo to express how he feels:

> I did not win the genetic lottery, so I'm not perfect like all the guys we see in the gay community—the perfectly chiseled twink—all cheekbones, eight-pack abs, chest, and a 9" dick, along with the military hair, blue or green eyes, and perfect teeth. My self-esteem is very low. It's hard enough to be gay, but then when we are shown images of these perfect guys—and the old motif that the beautiful only hang with the beautiful—reminds me why I never go out anymore. Essentially, I know I just need to "get over this," but it is way hard when I see these perfect bodies being paraded around. The subconscious message says, "if you don't look like this, well then, you might as well just think about buying a cat." But pussies do nothing for me.

Since we're judged for being gay, and since we can't change being gay—our inside, we conform on the outside to fit in. This pressures a lot of guys to plug into the gay "mainstream"—a "mini-me" of the American mainstream. If you don't fit the mold, you can be rejected. We judge one another harshly. We forget that we were all rejected from the mainstream in the first place for not fitting in. Such a cutthroat physical climate can make gay men feel terrible about themselves, especially when they flip through one of these magazines. We can end up feeling worse about ourselves, because we fall short of the inflated images that were designed to make us feel better in the first place.

That brings us back full circle to the inferiority complex. We perpetuate these perfect images, and happy, carefree party times, to make up for the underlying truths of our painful reality—that we have a sense of shame and inadequacy, and it's not always fun to be gay—it's stressful.

No matter what we're doing—carrying out an inferiority complex, overcompensation, or superiority complex, we're masking our pain, hurting ourselves and each other.

You may wish to take a moment to ask yourself the following questions. What do I do most to perpetuate straight acting? Is there one thing I can do differently?

We can change our course by looking on the inside, not the outside. Now let's move ahead with solutions and dating advice.

7

Solutions

How Gay Men Can OPT OUT, Triumph, and Thrive

> *"In the depths of winter I finally learned there was in me an invincible summer."*
>
> —Albert Camus

In this chapter, we will discuss exactly how you can create the change you want in your life. I provide six concrete steps for you to OPT OUT of masculinity, lots of keys to be comfortable in your own skin, and many tips to meet more men. But we need to lay some groundwork first.

We all have a personal narrative, a life story we tell ourselves about who we are. In the wisdom of Agape's Dr. Michael Bernard Beckwith, whose teachings in part about love and authenticity that I have adapted for some of this chapter, you can triumph over life's challenges by shifting your attention away from fixing what you think is inherently wrong with you. Instead, place your attention on showing the world what's absolutely right about you.

There is no point in trying to be something you're not. The "inauthenticity" of straight acting can be sensed. Human beings are remarkable creatures, and can detect phoniness. But you don't have to be fake. It's unattractive, and besides, you're all right.

There's nothing to alter. There's no part of you that needs censoring to get love.

You may feel like there is. It can feel like we're all "yucky" at times. It's easy to overlook all the good things about ourselves when we zoom in on all the negative aspects of being a gay man. But if we imagine that all the negativity we feel is just a big, black storm cloud overhead, we can imagine the storm cloud blowing away, revealing the sun. You can conquer a problem more easily if you see it as an outside enemy, not as part of you. You can see yourself as separate from your pain and suffering. Those don't define you. You're much greater than they are.

It doesn't matter how the world views you. It's how you view yourself that matters. So zoom out on yourself. You can step into an authentic existence by not holding back and simply being the terrific gay man you are.

"Sounds great," you may be saying, "but how does that translate into getting a date on Friday?" Well, you have to ditch the "real man" to attract the right man. When you follow the prevailing social attitudes of what it means to be a man, you limit how much you can be yourself. You also limit how much others can be themselves around you. In contrast, authenticity creates harmony in your relationships. Authentic thinking is the most powerfully attractive thing you can do. Redefining manhood for yourself makes you an authentic thinker.

You don't have to be like the "real man," because that's how you're supposed to be. It doesn't have to be business as usual for you. You can buck the system. You can take your attention off fear and break free from "real man" ideology by focusing on being yourself. Everyone else may be following the status quo, clinging to the set of expectations about manhood that they were born into. But you don't have to be a follower.

You can be brave and overcome the male taboo that says men aren't supposed to get emotionally intimate with one another. It takes a strong man to stand first in line and not fall prey to the widespread opinions of what makes a man a man. It takes courage to travel beyond the horizon. But you can be an ambassador, representing a new idea of manhood in a foreign land. You have to be a special man to redefine manhood, swim against the tide, be different, stand out, and not fit in. But you are special. You're probably out. You made it this far not being a crowd pleaser—standing up for your individuality—didn't you? From facing social adversity, gay men are tough and resilient like those GI Billy dolls.

As gay men, we can use our fortitude, resourcefulness, and determination as a super glue that sticks us together, rather than treating each other badly, which is a bomb that blows us apart. Our bond, from the shared struggle we face, puts us in a position to experience very deep feelings of intimacy with one another. Right here and now we can commit ourselves to lower our shields of masculinity. We can aim for each other's hearts to get the intimacy we yearn for, instead of engaging in self-destructive behavior from the lack thereof. We can build man-to-man relationships that are examples of true love and devotion to the world by breaking the rules of the man code and subscribing to our own definition of manhood. The way to relationship isn't about being straight acting. It's about being you—the unique gay man you are.

One person can make a difference—Thomas Jefferson wrote the Declaration of Independence, thus defining a new, free nation, Susan B. Anthony fought for the rights of women, and Martin Luther King, Jr. led the African-American civil rights movement. Communal change happens one person at a time. Major world change has always stemmed from just a handful of people.

Today, it can start with you. Personal change spreads to those around you and can grow into a larger movement of social change one individual at a time. When you're "real," one gay man will admire you and emulate you, another will him, and so on and so forth. Once the idea of authenticity reaches a critical mass, it spontaneously spreads through the entire community by "downloading" itself into expression in the lives of gay men everywhere. This strategy of social change was made popular by the story of "The Hundredth Monkey," first told by Lyall Watson in *Lifetide*. He said, "It may be that when enough of us hold something to be true, it becomes true for everyone." In this spirit, I invite you to venture out with me on a pioneering voyage of self-exploration where you can discover the truth—that you're fine just as you are.

Many gay men would be more than willing to go on this journey, breaking all the barriers of masculinity, if they were certain they'd find true love. But many Romeos don't even bother to start packing for the trip because they're convinced that gay romance is dead.

Perhaps no one knows better the pain of planning his whole weekend around a trip to the food mart, spending a holiday alone, or being so starved for touch that even an accidental brush from a stranger feels arousing. Perhaps no one knows more the feeling day after day of not getting any voice mail from that special one, of having no one to call, no table for two, and not having anyone to talk to besides his hairdresser. Perhaps no one knows better the anguish of thinking he doesn't measure up and everyone else seems to be prettier, more successful, and happier.

Perhaps you're tired of gazing outside a window at all the fabulousness passing by, thinking that everyone seems to have some magic that works in their lives and you don't. Resigning yourself to loneliness and hopelessness, perhaps you're tired of even trying anymore. Maybe you see yourself in a state of perpetual single-hood. But I positively know that it's possible to meet more men, develop intimacy, and find gay romance by being your authentic self.

Gay intimacy and romance are not dead or impossible to achieve. The longing is there and many gay men are fed up with the straight-acting game that gets in the way. Philip, a self-identified straight-acting guy, confided in me:

Being hot and masculine is a kind of trap. Sure I get lots of attention, but it's all for sex. A relationship isn't shagging for twenty minutes while your roommate's away. I want something deeper, but having "feelings" scares guys away. It gets pretty lonely at times.

Straight acting makes finding a meaningful, lasting gay relationship more challenging. We have to stop separating ourselves into butch and fem camps and accept one another fully without any facades—as the gay men we are. That is how we can come together.

You can put a new face on manhood by summoning up your strength and bravery to represent the man you are, rather than presenting the man others expect you to be. It's our unique, authentic self that matters. In finding your "voice" and expressing yourself as the gay man you are, you will be happier and get more of what you want in your life, including attracting other men to you. It's like the message in the movie *Field of Dreams*—build it and they will come—Build your platform—that is, your authentic self—and they will come. Men love men who exude confidence. Once you're comfortable in your own skin, men will flock to you. You can also allow others to be themselves around you—everyone's free from judgment. Now that's attractive!

It can be hard to free yourself when other people's opinions about gay men help shape who you are. When we are discriminated against, we can learn how to accommodate other people in order to get the love we need. We give away our power. We become Transformers or Shape-Shifters and people-please. We lose our authentic self, trying so hard to win everyone over. After all, we may think, "They won't love me as I really am." But as long as you're maintaining a life to please other people, you're lifeless—dead to yourself.

It's not an easy thing to reveal our deepest selves. Given all the hardship we've experienced as gay men, it's easy to understand how we may feel flawed and be quite sensitive to rejection if we show people who we really are inside. Many of us are afraid of being judged. We already know what that's like from the rejection we face—even from our own kind. We may believe that no one would accept us if we let them see the real us, the us that's underneath the butched-up images we present—the very masculine guy who "happens" to be gay. We may think, "if they really knew me and learned my secrets, they would see how awful, weak, effeminate, or unmanly I really am and they wouldn't like me." We may reject others first in a preemptive strike. You can surmount these "insecurities" by befriending yourself.

The challenge is to turn within, get reconnected to yourself, and rediscover your true inner "voice." You can begin an archeological excavation, digging deep inside, unearthing your authentic nature. There is something more to come forward in you—the full expression of the gay man you are. But he can't have a new beginning unless you're willing to leave old ways of being behind. You can "molt" your old "skin" and make way for new growth. You can make it a priority to start fresh and begin anew right now.

If you're not yet convinced, ask yourself what's important in your life. In the end, the year you were born, a dash, and the year you die will be engraved on your tombstone. But it's all in the dash. It's what you did with the time that you had that will matter most.

I can assure you that it's not the sex, the parties, the drugs, or the music. It's not your body, wardrobe, money, title, car, or other external things that people will remember most about you. It won't be your life partner, your friends, or another person. What they will remember most is how YOU touched them. It's your intimate relationships that make life meaningful.

Thus, the meaning of life is in you. It's in how much you are able to give and receive love. Take your attention off what others expect of you, the scene, appearances, a boyfriend, hassles, bills, the things you want, your career, and place your attention on your most intimate relationship, the one you have with yourself. To discover contentment, you have to turn within and make peace with your inner man.

It is a wise endeavor to look inside and meet yourself. It's a worthwhile investment that pays priceless returns. What is your happiness worth? What's the cost of your troubles? The enduring journey within is challenging and not at all for the faint of heart. But I know of no more valuable commitment in life. No one is grown up. We are only growing up. While it can be painful at times, finding your way home (to yourself) is the only way to your heart, to others, and a joy-filled life. I promise you that there is no cold, dark shadow where there isn't also warm, bright sun. Nothing and no one outside of you can take this road—only you can.

On our road to selfhood, we may need to call upon the wise and unwounded part of us. The part of us that is still pure and magical. The part that is still trusting, emotionally open, feeling, and creative. It's this innocent and childlike part of ourselves that can help lead us to the truth of who we are.

The trek can't be accomplished halfheartedly. If you really want something valuable, you have to put out the effort to get it. For instance, many men put their trust and confidence in my education, training, and experience to guide them on this sometimes perilous road. I know the woods well. I have walked the walk. They invest in themselves with the hopes of getting what they want. The ones who just come to therapy now and then, or simply show up to treatment, don't make it. It's the ones who consistently put the tools I give them into practice, living the advice each day, that succeed.

So make your personal transformation a top priority. Life itself is a constant process of change—evolution. So it makes sense to move in the same direction. You can turn your life around by putting this book into action. Pave your new path to manhood. I witness brave men doing it every day, and you're no different.

It's simply too stressful and confusing to continue to be relatively straight acting with this person and "gayer" with that person. The "real man" is not a singular fixed idea that applies to everyone. It's just one perspective. You can be a rebel, taking back your power. When you can be authentically you with one person, and yourself with another person, and another, both here and there, you can be free and peaceful. Nothing else matters if you're not right with yourself. In the words of Iyanla Vanzant of *Starting Over*, you can "walk in your own majesty"—very attractive!

Remember the first time you jumped off the high dive? Take a deep breath and leap off the edge. Yes, you can do this! Don't let fear hold you back.

In an interview for *notesfromhollywood.com*, I was asked how I help people be authentic. You may be wondering the same thing. To best answer this, I asked the interviewer, and I now ask you, to imagine a stream. The stream has been dammed up in places with logs and boulders. These are impeding the flow of the stream. While blocked, the stream will continue to flow no matter what gets in its way. But there's some rough water where the logs and boulders are under the surface. This is where the turmoil is. If the debris causing the troubled water is removed, the water calms and the stream returns to its natural smooth flow.

We all have an innate healing capacity within. I help people remove the troubling blocks to themselves, so they can return to their natural flow of being. Once they're reconnected with their self, they intuitively know what they need to do.

Sometimes we're not tuned into our authentic self, or we're out of step with our inner "voice." Think of masculinity as a sort of block to your authentic self. Masculinity is about adhering to a prescribed set of expectations that have been put on you by others. We act like the men we think we have to be. But that's someone else's point of view. You don't have to live someone else's life. Truth is, both masculine and feminine qualities exist in all of us. Recall that the ones we choose to express have very little to do with our genetics, and a lot to do with the norms of the culture we live within. We are taught which qualities to express and which ones to inhibit, based on our biology. You can let go of the man others taught you to be, and give yourself permission to be the man you are.

Some gay men avoid self-evaluation and simply imitate the stereotypical queen. Most of us however, do the opposite. We turn down the signals of gayness, because it's equated with femininity, and conform to masculinity to blend as much as possible. This makes life much easier. It's comfortable, like an old sweater.

But it's sticking to the familiar like cling wrap that creates the problem. The goal is to remove the masculine facade and be yourself. It's not about being either masculine or gay. It's about being both gay and masculine. There's an important difference between being gay and masculine, and being straight acting. The former doesn't "censor" "gayness" for approval like the latter does. You can be as manly a gay guy as you want. There's nothing wrong with that if that's you. The problem is in diminishing your gayness, using masculinity as a facade, and discriminating against other gay men who don't "supplement" their gayness with "traditional" masculinity.

Straight-acting guys may say they're turned off by "Marys," but it's really the "Mary" inside of them that repulses them. They're uncomfortable with the "gayness" or "effeminacy" inside. Having been hurt, they reject their inner "sissy" by turning down their gayness and amplifying their masculinity to feel more "adequate." Until they complete their walk of shame, they may feel "insecure" and compensate for their gayness with their manhood.

In just a bit, I'm going to give you practical suggestions to trash shame, uncovering the true, confident man within you. He's probably been hurt and may have fled deep inside for protection. He might be hiding in exile, but you can find him again. I absolutely know that together we can embark on a rescue mission to find, embrace, and save your lost hurting self. You may have to get rid of some static on the line to hear him more clearly. The source of much of that static is coming from the culture outside of you. Everyone's telling you that you have to be someone other than you are. You can lose yourself in meeting others' expectations of you. But don't let anyone else (homophobes), anything else (the "real man" image) or any circumstance (being gay) define who you are. Let nothing that homophobia has done to you over time define you. Your negative experiences of being a gay man in the world don't make you less of a person. Things can be better than they have been. You were unhurt first. Despite unfairness and discrimination, you have to stand on your own two feet and accept responsibility and take control of your life—right now. As you become more connected to the man inside of you, befriending that wounded, frightened man under the straight-acting "tough guise," you will free yourself up. And as you're more at liberty to be yourself, you will discover the right solutions to your problems and experience more joy, more love, less stress, and a greater sense of peace.

Following the path inside reconnects you to your natural state of joy—your true cheerfulness, or gayness, which is unequivocally beautiful just as it is—whether it's feminine or not. When we discover ourselves, accept ourselves, and trust in ourselves enough to be who we really are, we become our own master and gain riches. In order to do this, we have to come from our hearts rather than a place of showmanship—masculinity. Yep, you can do it. How do I know? Because I've done it myself.

I am going to share with you how I came to do the work I do, because I know that if I was able to come out from behind the false front of masculinity to be more myself, so can you. Being myself turned my life around. The more masculinity I "traded" to be the gay man I was, the better my life got. My hope is that my story inspires you to do the same. *Notesfrom hollywood.com* reported that my life has many elements of a riveting movie at a gay film festival. Perhaps, it continues, my "story is your story."

I can best describe what I do by sharing a defining period in my life that was challenging. When I was seventeen, a number of things collided to make for a very difficult time. I broke generations of silence and became a truth teller. I was a survivor of childhood abuse. At that time, I didn't get the support I needed from my family—working class, traditional Italian, macho, Roman Catholic. For my own healing and well-being, I had to disconnect from much of my family. On top of this, I had a face full of cystic acne, was struggling terribly with the conflict of coming out, and was silently in love with my best male friend. My family didn't reject me for being gay, but the acceptance of it was first expressed in silence. My beloved stopped being my best friend after I told him I loved him. Even though I was an altar boy and aspired to be a priest, my gayness was not embraced by my church either. I was angry at God for letting all of this happen to me. I felt hopeless back then.

I soothed my painful feelings with addictive behaviors. I ran away to Rhode Island for college. I was completely closeted and homophobic. I got points on campus because I made it public information that I was uncomfortable with my obviously gay roommate who consequently moved out of our dorm room. I didn't want anyone to think I was gay because I was his friend. The truth is that I was secretly attracted to him. My charade succeeded. I was invited to join the most popular jock fraternity on campus. I accepted. I wanted to fit in and be straight. But my guilt about my ex-roommate haunted me. I confided in my best female friend, Kelly, about it. Kelly later became an official little sister of my fraternity.

My nickname in the fraternity became ALF. I thought it meant "Alien Life Form" after the TV show *ALF*, which was popular then. After all, I was smart like ALF, and they did call me a freak for being able to party hard and still be a straight-A pharmacy student. A freak is sort of like an alien. Plus I always felt alien, like I was from another planet. So I convinced myself that their naming me ALF was insightful and endearing. Those guys!

But I later found out that ALF was an acronym for "Another Little Faggot." Somehow they got my number. Kelly had told them my secret. Even though I was accepted and popular in spite of it, I couldn't handle them knowing. I was humiliated to have my manly cover blown and I felt betrayed. I changed schools and ran away to Boston. Before I left, I found and apologized to my old dorm roommate. But it was too little, too late. He understandably resented me.

I had so much shame for being gay. Terrified, I cut off all ties, including old high school pals, lest they find out the truth about me, too. In Boston, I remained closeted to nearly every-

one. I made a handful of new gay friends in a secret compart-
mentalized gay life.

When I turned twenty-one, a partner of mine, Rod, gave me
a great gift. He connected my childhood abuse with the great
turmoil in my life. He actually said, "Do you think that your
abuse has anything to do with why you're so fucked up?" He
didn't hold back any punches. After I was aware of the link, I
read about abuse and its effects in *Victims No Longer (Second
Edition): The Classic Guide for Men Recovering from Sexual Child
Abuse,* by Mike Lew. I went to see him for counseling and made
friends with other survivors. More and more I began to recon-
nect with myself to think clearer, like myself, take better care of
myself, like my life, other people, and the spirit of life itself. I
began to change my ideas about what it meant to be gay and
what it meant to be a man. I began to come out more and accept myself as the man I was. As I grew away from abuse in my
life overall, my relationship with Rod came to an end. I renewed
healthier relationships with my immediate family.

A few years later, I met a guy named Barry with whom I fell
deeply in love, but it lasted just a few months. He distanced after
I posted love notes all over his house. He said he needed more
space because I was suffocating and codependent. I probably was.
I was so desperate for love. But I was shattered, nevertheless. I
couldn't handle the rejection. To avoid more hurt, I would end
up keeping myself alone, wandering in the desert—my heart sealed
off—for the next ten years. I focused on my recovery, working on
abuse issues and my sexuality. I gradually accepted myself more
and kept coming into my own—slowly.

It was toward the end of that healing time that I decided to
cash out of my unhappy life as a pharmacist in Boston. I had a
six-figure plus salary, a penthouse, BMW, growing stock portfo-
lio, and I was just turning thirty. But a pharmacist wasn't the
kind of medicine man or tribal shaman I desired to be anymore.

Something was missing. It was my life purpose. I wanted to devote my life to my passion—assisting other gay men who had the misfortune of experiencing alienation, mistreatment, or abuse growing up. I wanted to help other men share from their hearts about their burdens, to learn about the devastating impact homophobia had on their lives, and to get through to the other side. I wanted to do my part to help alleviate gay men's suffering.

I started over. I did what it took to reinvent myself. I went back to graduate school for counseling psychology and clinical practice. Wanting to utilize my medical background, I specialized in health psychology, which focuses on the biological, psychological, and social factors influencing illness and wellness. From there, I narrowed it down to men's psychology. I further refined it to gender and sexuality. I finally settled in to the area of GLBT issues.

When I graduated for my second profession, I gave myself a gift. I took two years to travel much of the world, which included spending a special summer in Provincetown, MA. I learned from many cultures and people from all walks of life. It helped me be a more well-rounded therapist. Toward the end of that time, I met Carlos, the man of my dreams. We would forge a three-and-a-half-year love relationship.

Meanwhile, between 2000 and 2002, huge losses in the stock market left me unexpectedly broke. Like so many others before me, I made my way to Los Angeles with just a suitcase and the hope of being a star. I wanted to be a star therapist, but Dr. Phil already owned my spot. Then I tried to be a therapist to the stars. But that didn't work, either. Feeling defeated, I just started putting myself out there for what I actually was—"The Gay Man's Therapist."

I was frightened. It felt like too huge a risk to toss off the mask of masculinity for good. But things started working for me. I got affiliated with the LA Gay & Lesbian Center, the Los Angeles Gender Center (LAGC), earned my therapist's license in CA, was invited to interview with *notesfromhollywood.com*, and launched *askangelo.com*—all for my greater vision to unfold. I soon landed my first Ask Angelo column at *westhollywood.com* and then *gay wired.com* network (now here! Interactive Media) and their international magazine *Gay Monkey* (now *here! magazine*), and *edgenewyork.com* network came next. So much more came my way from being authentically me, not less, as I had feared.

I started out doing free workshops to promote my practice. I offered a free therapy session for those at the workshop. But nobody signed up for my free sessions. I couldn't figure out why. I thought I was doing everything perfectly. With only a handful of private practice clients, I needed more to make ends meet and I wanted to help more people.

Then something happened to me. The love of my life, my partner of three and a half years, Carlos, unexpectedly dumped me over the phone on the Fourth of July, deserted me, and never once looked back. As you recall from chapter 1, the grief brought me to my knees for a long while. I was extremely vulnerable during that time, but I still had work. People were depending on me to help them. So, no matter how I felt personally, I wanted to be there for them. That change of focus helped me get through things.

There was a big shift in my work at that time. I was raw. I was me with no "makeup." Before, I presented the perfect image of "The Gay Man's Therapist." I was leading workshops, giving good information, being professional, and presenting myself as the gay man's expert. But now, I shared relevant tidbits about my life. In my workshop about dating, I said, "Being alone can be hard at times. The thought of dating in your thirties can be really difficult. It's hard to meet somebody out there. I know what it's like." I would even tell a personal story that jived with the experiences of the men in the room.

What was different? I was Angelo, the gay professional. Before, I was hiding Angelo. I felt I had to be perfect and strong as "The Gay MAN'S Therapist" or people wouldn't find me credible. I feared people wouldn't come to see me if they didn't think I was perfect, if they saw me as flawed, weak, or too flamboyant. Well, the opposite thing happened.

I keep appropriate professional boundaries to maintain a therapeutic context—but as I showed people that I was human, they began to connect with me. Men started signing up like crazy for my free sessions. My practice became busy virtually overnight.

I've learned over time that the more I use my self as an instrument to help others, people can connect with me as a human being, and my professional message becomes even more powerful. When I got that, I got a thriving private practice.

My column got better and spread like wildfire over the Web. Some columns were translated into Chinese. *Askangelo.com* is now visited by people from over one hundred countries and ranks highly among the world's most visited Web sites, according to Amazon's *Alexa.com*.

It seems counterintuitive, but the more "big gay Angelo" I was, the more success I had. Although, as you know from chapter 1, I wasn't happy at all in West Hollywood.

I practiced what I preached, using what I learned. Happiness is not about the trappings of masculinity—wealth, material things, titles, muscles, substances, egos, attitude, hot lovers, or anything outside of us. Contentment comes from being ourselves and following our hearts.

So, to honor myself, I followed my own advice. I gave up my California life, successful LA private practice, and a chance to lead the LAGC, and moved back to the east coast where it felt more like home. My life is about my passion—my work and my message. I try my best to be love and accept love—ultimately those are the most important things to me. I trust that if I do these things, then everything else follows. I had no guarantee I'd make it in the Big Apple. I took another risk. I believed in myself.

The first roommate I moved in with in NYC was a total stranger to me. Rents are so high there, that this is not an uncommon experience. Despite a thorough telephone interview from LA, he ended up going on a crystal meth binge within several months of me moving in. He suffered a psychosis with hallucinations, paranoia, and suicidal intent when he used. I intervened the best I could to help him. But he didn't want help. He didn't even want to live. For my own safety, I moved my things into storage. With a budding New York City private practice and an upcoming invitation to appear on *Montel* as a mental health expert, I checked into a hotel until I landed my own lease, a difficult feat in the city. But when all was said and done, I secured my lease, made it to *Montel*, and in less than a year rebuilt my private practice in Chelsea to the same level as it was in West Hollywood. Soon after, I surpassed it. Tragically, I later heard that my ex-roommate hung himself.

This relocation experience reminds me that while nothing comes easy, we must choose life, believing things can get better. Albert Einstein said, "The most important question any human being can ask themselves is 'Is this a friendly Universe?'" We all have a choice to answer "yes" or "no." A choice that determines the course of our lives, since our thoughts (expectations) shape our experience. Our answer must be "yes!" We all face existential dilemmas regarding our mortality, freedom, isolation, and meaning-making. But we must believe in the preciousness of life. You can turn your life around and triumph as a gay man in the world. You can thrive and sustain satisfying relationships, starting right here and now. It doesn't matter what others' picure of you is. What matters is the picture you have of yourself.

Today, I continue to provide safe support and tools that gay men can use to explore their situation in the scheme of things. I assist individuals, couples, and groups in lessening their troubles through *askangelo.com*, Ask Angelo advice, teleseminars, podcasts, writing articles, speaking, leading groups, workshops, retreats, and private practice. My clients' concerns include anxiousness, feeling down, empty, or lonely, substance abuse, sexual compulsivity, codependency, childhood wounds or abuse, loss, living with HIV, coming out, relationships, and more.

I witness the changes people make—the metamorphoses—with reverence. When a man takes a step outside the comfort circle where he's lived his whole life—and transforms himself from a caterpillar to a butterfly and soars to places he never thought he could go—that's what it's all about. You, too, can grow to be more of the person you want to be.

It makes sense that I mistook my work for that of a priest, medicine man, or pharmacist. I was on the right path toward being a therapist all along. My difficult past has groomed me to be a better therapist and to help others.

I absolutely know this—to be happy, you have to turn within, strip yourself to the bare bones, follow your heart, and rebuild an authentic life. Like the phoenix, you are strong enough to recreate yourself from your own ashes if you must. Unlike Humpty Dumpty, you can put yourself back together again. If I can do it, you can. I'm not special. I have great faith in you.

The more you're yourself, the more things will work for you and the more men will want to meet you. You can apply this message to men and dating. It's no different than the story of me doing it in my work. I applied it to dating too and my dating life has turned around. I'm busy cultivating new fulfilling relationships.

Now, you're ready for six secrets to help you break down masculinity, be more yourself, and move closer to more guys. Then, I have lots of dating tips. The acronym for the six secrets is OPT OUT. You can use the six secret strategies to OPT OUT of masculinity, befriend the man within, and manifest more gay relationship in your life.

To OPT OUT means to adopt a new paradigm, a new ideology. This isn't the same as living in a make-believe world. It's creating a new reference point for manhood so we can see "a brave new world." If you place a mirror in the middle of a fish bowl and put a fish in on one side, it will still see a whole bowl because of the reflection. But because it can't go there (it bumps into the mirror), it gets conditioned to swim in just half the bowl. Funny thing is, if you remove the mirror, the fish will stay confined to its small space. It's robbed of its freedom because of its limited view. Don't rob yourself of living in a "whole new world." There's a lot of space for you to expand into once you leave the constricting paradigm of the "real man" behind.

OPT OUT has six dimensions:

Openness
Pride
Transformation
Outness
Uprooting
Togetherness

You have the power to OPT OUT of masculinity, thus making a better life, by redefining manhood and being yourself. Being gay doesn't equal being less masculine, so there's no part of you to restrain. Here are the six secret steps for embracing your authentic self.

Openness (OPT OUT)

This step is about having the emotional openness to decrease isolation and build gay relationships. As John Donne said, "No man is an island." We need relationships with other people. Being in relationship is biologically healthy for us. We are social beings. Relationships define us and help us grow.

Pointing out the good of being in relationship isn't meant to conspire with the bias in our culture to be coupled or married. We often hear "two halves make a whole." This is a message that supports the idea that we need someone else to complete us. In reality, a relationship doesn't necessarily bring us happiness. Couples can be miserable together and single men can be happy. A healthy relationship is created in the space where two whole or complete people overlap. We can never fill our inner voids with another person, making them our source. Instead, we can be our own source, filling our own empty spaces. Then we can choose to share our lives with others in a dynamic way.

It is a perfectly valid position to be happily self-sufficient until we meet that someone special, to have a relationship that's modeled on being nontraditional, or to not want a romantic relationship at all. Some men may consciously choose to stay single. If you're one of them, it doesn't necessarily mean you have an intimacy problem. There can be many healthy advantages to being single. But no one I know of wants to be lonely. We all need friends, at the very least. And for those of you who do want to share your lives with someone special, being single can suck. It can be a drag to be on your own. It can provoke anger and despair. So whether you desire a romantic relationship or not, openness is for you.

It can't hurt to open yourself up to being friendly, loving, and emotionally closer to men in your life. We must be men who use our hearts and feel. Because of the manner in which we've been socialized, a lot of men find it hard to talk about feelings due to a lack of emotional awareness. We can certainly feel, but we're often unable to label, explain, or understand our emotions because we haven't gotten the proper social support or "training." Men can un-numb, feel, and express our feelings, leaving our hearts open to love. I use the word "love" in the broadest sense. It's amazing how something so simple as love can be so very hard to come by.

Dear Angelo,
Every time I tell a great guy just how much I like him after a
fair number of dates, he just loses all interest, and, for lack of
better words, runs. How do I deal with this issue?
Signed, They Run

Dear They Run,
I recently had the unexpected opportunity to experience the self-less unconditional love of Amma at the Manhattan Center in NY. Amma is Sanskrit for "Mother." Many consider her to be divine or an enlightened being. Amma was giving her "darshan," another Sanskrit term describing an "audience with a sage." To Amma, "Love is the basis of the universe." As I witnessed her darshan, I became aware of the power of her mission. While her work is multifaceted, to put it simply—she is here to give love. Thousands of people took off their shoes, got to their knees, and waited hours for a love hug from Amma. Amma is estimated to have blessed and consoled more than 25 million people worldwide to date. Sleeping sometimes only two hours a day, she lives to serve through love.

It struck me that thousands of people all came to this one place over three days to receive pure love. To be held in a truly selfless, loving embrace. During my hug I certainly felt Amma's embodiment of unconditional love. It was moving, healing, and beautiful. Yet it was sad for me, too. Sad that so many people were there seeking this love. I found myself asking, "Why's it so hard for us to love each other?"

In my work with children, I observed how they make friends

so easily. "Hi, wanna come play and be my friend?" That's all it takes. It's a done deal. What happens to our openness as we grow older? How often have we wanted to walk over to someone and say, "Hi, wanna be my friend?" But we just don't. What stops us? Social rules? A line in the movie *Wedding Crashers* says it all—"They say we only use 10 percent of our minds. I think we only use 10 percent of our hearts." My advice to you today is to simply continue to love others. Continue to extend yourself and reach out. People do run away from love to protect themselves from more pain. For in love we become vulnerable and risk being hurt. But it's love that we need and love that will heal us. Your love offering can make a huge difference. It works. Just continue to be loving as an antidote to bitterness. By being love you will attract love.

All the Best, Angelo.

This may all seem like pie in the sky. You may be asking, "Well, how am I supposed to feel good, be open and friendly, Angelo, when I'm so pissed and bitter that I'm alone!" This is a good question and I've been in the rage and pain of it all myself at times. Sometimes it's hard to feel and be open when we've been disappointed and hurt by relationship. We may become so jaded that we don't even bother to try anymore. A lack of intimacy can even make us mean. Many of us may grow to be so bitter that we basically shut ourselves in the house, as far as our social life goes. It's like we've been mugged. Afraid to put ourselves out there, we bolt the windows, pull the shades, and triple lock the doors. We may live in a beautiful castle, but what good is it if we never lower the bridge over the moat? We can help free ourselves from isolation and guardedness if we recognize that what we imagine as outside is really inside.

Our thoughts create our experience of reality. What we experience in the world and with the people around us is a mirror reflecting what's inside us. Often the world we imagine out there isn't favorable, because for many of us, ugliness is part of what we feel inside. The world and everyone in it seems unsafe and feels dark because we've been hurt and we feel pain inside. Caring for others feels too risky. We feel vulnerable. Getting emotionally close to someone again brings up insecurities from past hurts. We may run from our own terror about being close to someone again. Since we need love so bad, we may express the opposite feelings of closedness, anger, and meanness as defenses. Plus, for men, it's considered a weakness if we're not in control of our emotions. So men can numb out their feelings to stay strong. Men often cover their deepest vulnerabilities with the "tough guise" of masculinity.

Stuffing our emotions is not the road to self-acceptance. Self-love means feeling our feelings and embracing all parts of ourselves—the strong parts we like and the weak parts we don't. Our "masculine" parts and "feminine" parts. The more fully we accept all of our parts, the more whole we can become.

Getting support from family, friends, the community, or professionals can help you identify and feel your feelings. You might also want to consider keeping a journal to help you explore and clarify your feelings. Take maybe twenty minutes a day for self-reflection. Simply write your thoughts as they come. First thoughts are best thoughts. You may want to answer some questions like these. What was your experience of your day? How have you been affected? What's happening inside of you? What are you feeling? Where in your body do you feel it most? Is there a thought that goes with the feeling? Did you learn any lesson today? You can also try to imagine your problem sitting next to you. Ask your problem what it wants you to do and write down what it says. Another idea is to capture it all in a poem. Or if you don't like to write, perhaps draw three pictures: you, you with your problem, and you with your problem solved.

Feeling is healing. Feeling does not mean you're a wimp. In fact, it shows that you're a strong man. Feeling the full weight of your feelings is hard and tough. Confronting your feelings takes strength and courage—things you already have as a gay man. You can gather the momentum to move forward, as this letter reveals:

Dear Angelo,
I am so fed up with gay life. I am stuck in a real rut. I don't even bother to go out anymore. What's the point? I'm so bitter and jaded and I'm only thirty-three. It seems impossible to meet someone for a relationship. I'm tired of all the attitude. What can I do?
Signed, Giving Up Hope

Dear Giving Up Hope,
It sounds like you're in a real deep funk. A good way to bust out of a funk is to start doing the opposite of what you'd normally do. This takes you out of your comfort zone into something new and exciting. This stimulates you back to life.

I gave that suggestion to a deeply depressed client of mine who lives in Chelsea, who was going through the same thing you are. He has a friend who'd been trying to get him to go out for a while. But he never went. One Saturday night he got into his robe as usual and went to bed at 10 PM—hating all gay men. He felt inferior, down, and hopeless. Five to ten years ago, he wouldn't have been caught dead being home on a Saturday night. He wanted sleep to take his troubles away—at least until morning. This was the negative pattern he'd gotten himself into. But one night, out of the blue, he "heard" my suggestion. He found his inner strength and forced himself to get out of bed, shower, dress, and call his friend. His friend took him to a few bars he'd never been to in a neighborhood in Queens—a twenty-five-minute train ride from Chelsea. This was something he wouldn't ordinarily do. He ended up having a fantastic time. This one affirming experience rejuvenated him back to life.

You may not live in New York City, but you can still do something different for yourself. Go to a different bar where you live, try another coffee shop, gym, or bookstore. Break away for a weekend and go somewhere new. Join a group, volunteer—just try some new stuff, present your best self, and reach out. Wherever you are, you can shake up your routine.

So get shaking, babe. Take new action and watch your reality change.

All the Best, Angelo.

My wish for you is that you throw open your shades and allow people to look into the windows of your soul. If you believe that people suck because of what you've been through, then you'll stay locked up inside. But if you can shift that idea to "the hell with everyone else's attitude, I'm going to open up and be friendly so I can meet someone nice," you might be more willing to venture out. As Anaïs Nin said, "And then the day came when the risk to remain tight in a bud was more painful than the risk it took to blossom." Be loving because you benefit. Feel because that's what makes life worth living.

You'll see that over time, others will respond positively to you and the ice around your heart will melt away. Being loving helps you get love. Don't stamp out your natural and fabulous "gay" expression, traits, or "tendencies." After all, to be "gay" means to be cheerful and have fun. These are attractive qualities. Enjoy your life. A state of playful joy attracts others. The mean face of masculinity repels. Forget about trying to get love from someone else. Instead, let love happen by staying open, not closed.

LA psychotherapist Dr. Leah Matson, clinical mentor, friend, and colleague, whose teachings in part helped inspire and inform some of this chapter, says staying open is the "yoga" of relationship. We have to stretch to position ourselves and it can be uncomfortable. But once we get into the right space, it feels really good to just flow through things as they come. To help stay emotionally open, you may want to try asking a yoga teacher about some basic yoga postures that open the chest and heart chakra. Postures like Cobra, Salutation, and Upward Facing Dog might be good ones to ask about. There are many other poses you can try, too, like Bow, Camel, Cow-face, Fish, Half-moon and Wheel.

We can't ever give up on love. It requires a certain stamina of character to keep putting yourself out there. In the search for love, we carry all of our hopes and all of our baggage. Love isn't just a bunch of roses. It's also the longing, jealousy, rage, boredom, despair, and more. But love is a worthwhile endeavor. The pitfalls make the rewards more ecstatic.

We can't let anger and hurt close us down and shut out love, because it is love that will heal us. By all means protect yourself, but always leave the door of your heart open to love—even if it's just a little.

In some of my workshops, I have people partner up and sit cross-legged, knee to knee. I ask them to place one hand over their heart and the other over their partner's heart (and hand). I then ask them to hold eye contact for several minutes. This exercise really disarms them. You may like to give it a try with someone.

We all have to be disarmed. Relationship-building can take time. We need to be patient with people. It may take several months or more of routine contact to go from a smile, to "hello," to conversation, to lunch, to sharing your deepest problems, and sustaining a relationship. You have to nurture relationship along. It's like cultivating a garden from the beginning, preparing the land, planting the seeds, watering, sunning, de-weeding—all the way to harvest.

In the spirit of beginning to move toward people, my wish for you is that you try this for yourself. As you're going about your ordinary day, notice the people in your path—especially the gay men! Smile, make eye contact, and say "hi" to as many folks as you can. Now, I don't want you to have expectations or to focus on their responses. Their reaction is not the point of this. This is for you. Your goal isn't about trying to get something from another person. It's about being loving and allowing love to unfold without blocking it. I simply want you to start acknowledging people who cross your path. That's it. Even if you're bitter, sad, or shy, just try to extend yourself a little in this way. All I ask is that you stay open to staying open. Interestingly, when we release having any expectations, we open a new space for something spontaneous to happen. You may be surprised at how much a smile and a nice attitude can bring you. People feel safe around and respond to an open heart, not an aloof one.

Masculinity calls for us to be unfriendly, cool, and distant. But would you rather be loved or feared? Give openness a try and see what happens. While it's counterintuitive from the viewpoint of a rough-and-tough masculinity, I bet you'll get much further being nice and sweet. Underneath the tough guise of masculinity that's put upon men, the essential nature of men is gentle, kind, sensitive, and loving. Remember that masculinity is about men impressing other men. Most guys will let their guard down if you do. When you put up your masculine shield, you take the offensive and that causes other guys to put up their masculine shields. You won't get far that way with another guy— at least emotionally. You might get sex, but that doesn't bring you love. So instead, when you're at that coffee house and you see a hot guy a few tables over—be friendly. With a "no attitude" approach, you will be well on your way to manifesting new possibilities for relationship. So take a chance, break the ice, and go talk to him.

Ignore the "voices" in your head that might be saying "be cool" or "you don't stand a chance." Don't listen to them. If you do, you might become shy, close up, and come off as having attitude or being aloof. Don't do that. Instead, even if you feel you don't, act "as if" you had confidence. The best thing is to be yourself. Have faith in who you are. Just go over and say "hi." Feel it out. Let the conversation flow. Trust yourself.

Go for it. You have nothing to lose and everything to gain. Relationship is what matters in life. What if he's your Mr. Right or turns out to be a great friend? You'll never know if you don't try. A single client of mine who's suffering from testicular cancer told me, "Angelo, if I regret anything, it's not taking more chances and approaching more guys. I've always been too afraid."

If you happen to get rejected, just remember that his reaction tells you about him. It's about what he wants or doesn't want. If it doesn't click, be thankful. You know he isn't a good match for you.

Even if you're open, you can't control how other people respond to you, but you can control how you think about and react to the situation. Remember, dating is like fishing. You have to keep baiting, throwing your hook out, and being patient to catch anything good. You may have to toss some "bad" catches back into the sea, but sooner or later you'll hook a good one to take home. Getting a quality man doesn't just happen. Dating requires focused effort, commitment, and the drive to keep putting yourself out there. Like they say, you have to kiss a lot of frogs to find your prince. Don't give up. Your match may be waiting just around the corner.

Draw upon that unwounded part of you that's unjaded, open, loving, and creative to help if you need to. Everyone else may be shut down, trying to stay strong in the name of masculinity, but that doesn't mean you have to be emotionally closed. Have pride in the magnificent person you are.

Pride (OPT OUT)

Being gay isn't a problem, but being OK with being gay can be a different story. However, we *can* feel proud to be gay. According to the Gallup News Service, "those under forty years old are widely tolerant" of gay rights, signaling that gay rights are more of a generational issue. A gay paradigm shift is in progress in America. Brad Pitt has taken the stand that he won't marry Angelina Jolie until gay marriage is made legal in America. Other allies like Madonna, Cyndi Lauper, and Margaret Cho have done a tremendous amount for our community. We can choose to focus on all those who support us rather than on those who don't. We have to keep the gay stigma in perspective. Everyone isn't against us. And we don't have to be against ourselves. As the song says, "What a Wonderful World" to embrace.

If someone rejects you for being gay or "too gay," it tells you something about them, not you. It says they have a need to label you for whatever reason they have. Whatever they think, whatever they reject you for, doesn't make you so. In the spirit of *It Wasn't Me,* by songwriter and singer Nancy Day, it isn't you and it's not your problem. It's them and it's their problem. So don't take it on. Don't be afraid to take pride in yourself. You don't have to hide any part of yourself away.

When we begin to stand bravely in self-love and appreciation for being gay men, all the negative things that our parents, society, and religion told us about being gay or "effeminate" men dissipate. The bad things that we've since come to believe about ourselves begin to break away. The "unacceptable" gay self that we've internalized, which was formed by the teachings of the external world, gets dispelled when we value ourselves and are rooted in the authenticity of who we are. Self-acceptance, peace, and joy replace it.

Yes, it's true that we have to love ourselves before we can

love others. It's not selfish to love yourself first. Selfish is thinking of yourself only and disregarding others. Self-love is meeting your own needs while considering the needs of others. In every airplane safety drill they tell you to put on your own oxygen mask before the kids'. You can't help the child if you're passed out. To help others, we have to help ourselves first. We have to nourish ourselves or we won't have any strength to give. Your car doesn't go far on empty. You have to fill the gas tank. You have to recharge. Melody Beattie, author of *Codependent No More*, says it's not selfless to put yourself last. It's self-destructive. So how do you fill up your tank? You guessed it: by loving yourself first.

But in order to love yourself, you have to accept yourself. So every day needs to be gay pride day. In the infinite wisdom of Aretha Franklin, I want you to fill yourself up with "a deeper love"—self-love. I want you to celebrate you. Cultivating an inner sense of positive self-esteem is crucial for men who are gay. Like creating relationships with others, a good relationship with yourself takes patience. The process is a bit like farming. It's a lot of work in the spring, and there's a bit of a wait, but when it's time, you get a big crop. I have a few fabulous keys for you to do this.

Self-esteem is built up by consistently behaving in accordance with your own conscience. It doesn't matter what everyone else is doing, thinking, and saying. What's right for you? The contrast of doing drugs on gay pride day speaks for itself. If you need something artificial to make you feel good about something or to have fun and celebrate, then you don't truly feel proud about it. Practice being comfortable in your own skin. If you feel like you're a mess, just act "as if" you had confidence. This is not to have attitude, or be arrogant or fake, but rather to push through and defeat your insecurities.

Men are constantly sizing themselves up compared with other

men. Since men are visual, gay men, like straight women, compete with each other by using their appearance to attract men. Perfect male images in the media become the ultimate benchmark that many of us measure ourselves against. With such impossible expectations, we can become competitive and obsessed with insecurities—am I thin enough? Ripped enough? Big enough? But this can lead to feeling constantly defeated.

Take special care not to compare one aspect of yourself to someone else's superstrength. For example, everyone envies Stephen Hawking's mind, but no one wants amyotrophic lateral sclerosis (ALS). We do not want to be him. We just want to have a part of him. This type of selective comparison is a form of distorted thinking. It's mental torture that leaves everyone feeling bad about themselves. Look at the big picture. Don't be so hard on yourself. Instead, take in the whole person, not just their strong points.

Now I know the reality that strutting along the gay beach is a game of sudden death. The gay beach is more like a fashion runway. We can feel the judgment as soon as we step foot on the sand, let alone strip down. But realize that a particular event can bring all the boys with awesome bodies together in a concentrated area at once, like flypaper, although I'm not implying muscle boys are like flies. So when you look around, it may seem like everyone else was made from a cookie cutter that was much better than yours. Resist focusing on persons you have selected as gods, and making the best part of them represent everybody. A very small percentage of the overall population actually has a seemingly perfect body. Remember the piecemeal thinking of selective comparison. Take in the whole crowd, not just the circuit boys. Everyone's human and has flaws. Don't abandon yourself and forget about the strengths you have that they don't.

This includes all your inside qualities that people can't see. We can learn a lot from many of our lesbian and straight sisters.

They seem to care much more about what's on the inside of a person than the outside. If you approach some of these gorgeous guys for what's on their inside and avoid objectifying and sexualizing them, you may be surprised how far you may actually get with them. Get to know and respect them for their person, not just their looks.

This looking-within approach also helps defeat our strong bias for youthful appearances, which can make aging a bitch for many gay men. Many maturing single gay men are terrified of being alone forever. They think getting older is a death sentence. Rafael said:

> If you're twenty-three, gorgeous, not fem, 5 percent body fat, 8"x6", you got it made. These guys instantly fit in and get whatever they want. It makes me sad that I'll never know what that's like. I never get sex and I have few gay friends. I'm really miserable. Why couldn't I just have been born like that? Gay years are like dog years and now I'm thirty-seven. I fear it's too late.

Even if you have a life partner, you may not escape the fear. Here's a letter with my reply:

Dear Angelo,
Getting older is rough—even with my life partner. I feel invisible to gay men now. I long for the yesteryears. What can I do to bring myself back to life?
Signed, Out To Pasture

Dear Out To Pasture,
Know that you are beautiful just as you are. Growing older can be difficult in gay life. But it's not aging itself that makes it so—it's our culture. Most cultures around the world revere their elders. As a result, they remain vital and strong through old age.

Unfortunately, in America, we fear death. To block it out, we discard our elders and prize youth. Gay culture turns up the volume on this one, especially since AIDS.

Much suffering comes when we resist what is. Accept and embrace the positive changes that come with age. You may be financially stable, comfortable in your own skin, and wise. Those are successful attractive qualities. Cherish the value of what you share with your partner. Socialize more with your peers. Take a gay cruise. Seek out groups like Senior Action in a Gay Environment (SAGE), Prime Timers, or those at your local GLBT center. Live in the moment, not the past. Look forward to the great times ahead, not back.

All the Best, Angelo.

My office is filled with guys who feel hopeless about aging. But my office is also filled with young, gorgeous guys who seem to have it all just like he describes. Physical beauty, popularity, abundant sex, parties, artificial substances, money, or material things don't bring happiness. The "gods" themselves tell me that it's all empty. They're tired of the same rat race that "older" men are tired of. They too are searching for something more meaningful—love. The grass isn't always greener. Drew said:

You have to look a certain way to make it. It's exhausting to be gay—not to mention expensive. You have to go to work, the gym, stay thin, tan, keep up with the right trends in clothes, accessories, hair, clubs—and I still can't find a relationship that lasts. Sure, sex is easy, but I can't meet anyone with substance. Sex isn't making love, and that's what I really want. Everything else seems empty.

Clearly, exteriors don't bring you lasting love and happiness. They can bring you more sex, but not love, and certainly not happiness. We can only rely on ourselves to make us happy—nothing outside of us. This isn't to say, don't strive for good things. It's just to point out that you have to look inside for happiness, not outside. To be happy, you have to love and respect who you are. You can be young, hot, and famous, have all the stuff in the world, yet feel lonely and unhappy. A healthy inside is what brings us happiness, and it's what allows us to enjoy all the exteriors. Plus, belief in yourself and self-pride are attractive. Your person is what brings you love, not youth, money, drugs, sex, or anything else.

Maybe all you do is try your best or constantly work out and you still feel like you're not hot enough. It's hard out there with all the pressure. Do you spend your time trying to figure out what guys want? Often we're hardest on ourselves by thinking we have some awful flaw. You may want to answer these four confidence-building questions to help boost your self-esteem:

1. Are there any parts of yourself of which you are critical?
2. What do you think of as your worst feature or quality?
3. If that aspect belonged to someone you love, how would you reassure them?
4. What's one step you can take toward accepting that aspect of yourself?

I would like you to name five reasons why someone is lucky to know you. Remember, you are your greatest asset.

You may also want to try repeating or recording my affirmation to build confidence.

I am a beautiful and magnificent person. There is no one like me. I am unique. I have special gifts to share. When someone rejects me, it's not about me. It's about them taking care of themselves. My imperfections make me wonderfully human. I am proud of who I am.

You can also try an Aikido technique. Aikido is a Japanese martial art. Masters use this strategy to take over a room with their presence. Try to imagine taking all of your insecurities and making them into a ball that you place beneath your navel. This spot is your center of power, solar plexus, or hara. When you turn your insecurities into a powerball, you're transforming disempowerment into empowerment. Make that spot your seat of strength. Walk proudly with confidence from that spot.

There's no reason not to be proud. Same-sex attraction is natural. Gayness is found throughout nature. Animals like apes, fruit flies, flamingos, and others can be gay. A full 8 percent of rams seek sex with other rams only. Reuters reported that the project leader of an exhibition documenting homosexual behavior among animals at the Oslo Natural History Museum states that "homosexuality has been observed for more than 1500 animal species and is well documented for 500 of them." Based on these findings, the museum concludes that "human homosexuality cannot be viewed as 'unnatural'" or a "crime against nature," since it's found across the animal kingdom.

Freud thought humans are bisexual. Alfred Kinsey concluded from his research on human sexuality that few people are either all straight or all gay. He believed that most people exist someplace along the continuum. In 1948, Kinsey wrote that nearly half of all men he surveyed reported a sexual experience with another male in their lifetime and 38 percent reported reaching the point of orgasm with another guy before age forty-five. Homosexuality has been found in all cultures across time. In the *Bible*, 1 Samuel, Jonathan and David were probably in love.

I'm not implying that everyone's gay or bisexual, but I am

suggesting that everyone isn't as polarized or fixed in their sexual orientation as we like to think. Human beings share the capacity for a range of sexual potential with other humans. Human sexuality is fluid, dynamic, and expansive rather than static, unchanging, and narrow. The "gay" or "effeminate" part of us, no matter how big or small it is, can get deeply repressed from centuries of religious teachings and social conforming. Since "gayness" isn't socially accepted, it's become a sort of latent sexual potential for most. This means it still potentially exists as a part of our sexuality for all men, but it remains undeveloped and hidden until personal and social circumstances are right for its development. If it were more socially acceptable to be with the same sex, then we would see more men openly exploring all the possibilities encompassed by the full range of their sexuality. It's the gay stigma that inhibits people, especially men, from doing so more openly.

Studies have shown that it's common for people to have same-sex thoughts, fantasies, or experiences—they just don't openly acknowledge it. It's adopting a gay identity that's less common, not same sex behavior itself. A New York City survey revealed that about one in ten self-identified straight men also reported having sex with another man in the previous year. This shows that a lot more men have sex with men than just the ones who say they're gay.

Perhaps gay-identified men are simply the ones with the strongest same-sex desires on the spectrum. So they are biologically compelled to express those desires. Men whose desires are not that strong may not choose to act on them, or they may deny them in fear, or hate or envy other men who do express them.

But those of us who aren't repressing that part of us—again, no matter where we are on the scale—can choose to feel good about our "gay" or "effeminate" part. This may take some doing, given homophobia, but I know it's possible and it's paramount.

While homophobia inhibits men from being their full "gay" selves, the surest way to end homophobia is to not "censor" our "gayness," i.e., to aspire to a place where we're not straight acting at all. A place where we hide no part of ourselves and pretend no more. In that place, the prevailing opinions that are different from our own have no dominion over us. It's where we give ourselves permission to be fully ourselves, recognizing the freedom of choice for others.

You can leave the closet of masculinity behind. As Glinda the Good Witch of the North sings, "Come out, come out, wherever you are" as the man you are. So you have some fear. So what? What's a little fear? Right?

Many famous quotations about "courage" capture the message that courage is not the absence of fear; it's moving forward in the face of fear. It's breaking through our worry, doubt, anger—anything that separates us—toward connection. And I know that there's a brave man inside of you. You can demonstrate courage and move ahead.

In the spirit of singer-songwriter Jimmy Cliff's words, we have many rivers to cross, but we survive because of our pride.

Transformation (OP*T* OUT)

We must change our negative beliefs that being gay is less manly.

A tenet of cognitive behavioral therapy is that you can feel better and change your life if you change what you believe and how you think. You can start by transforming your thinking about masculinity. We've come to internalize a bunch of lies about what it means to be a gay man. These negative perceptions have been "bestowed" on us by external systems like family, education, society, religion, and so on. These opinions can help determine our self-concept and life experience. But those beliefs are the expectations of the outside world. They're changeable! You don't have to let everyone else's highly-charged attitudes about gay men define your life. It's commonly said, what someone else thinks about you is none of your business. You don't need acceptance from another person. If you accept yourself, then others will accept you. And if they don't, you won't have to change because you accept yourself. Keep your power. Don't hand it to someone else.

It's not what other people believe about being a gay man that matters. It's what you believe. If I called you a green martian, would you think I was right? Of course not. You know it isn't true, so it has no power over you. What I think or say about you only has power over you if part of you believes it's true. Make up your own mind. Being a gay man doesn't mean you're less of a man and it isn't shameful. You can tell those homophobes what Glinda the Good Witch tells the Wicked Witch: "You have no power here, be gone before someone drops a house on you."

You don't have to wait for a social sanction in order to release your cultural expectations of what it means to be a man. Rely on yourself. Right now you can make a conscious choice not to conform to the rules of masculinity because they limit you. Don't change yourself to fit someone else's standards. You can define your own standards by changing masculinity to suit yourself. You can respond authentically in the world by not reacting like the crowd. Instead of acting how you're supposed to, do the right thing and be yourself.

The most closeted men I treat don't accept themselves as men because they're gay and they don't accept themselves as gay because they're men. While they'll tell you otherwise, it's not about what their parents, co-workers, neighbors, or society think anymore. It's about what they think. It's about a lack of self-acceptance. When you come to know their life stories, these men understandably have deep shame and fear about their sexuality, because they learned that being gay is very bad. Some may even exhibit paranoia about others knowing or finding out about them. This anxiety is actually a projection of their own inner shame about being gay onto others. While there are very real things to fear from the homophobic world outside, we can manifest negative outcomes in our lives by ingesting male dogma, as well as gay stigma, and digesting them as truths.

Instead, we have to challenge these demons, expel them from our minds, exorcize them from our bodies and vomit them out all over the ground. At some point you have to stop listening to what everyone else is saying about you and trust yourself. Don't let outside approval determine how you feel about yourself and how you live your life. Don't go on another day thinking that it's your fault that some of society doesn't get you as a gay man. Otherwise you may be left thinking and believing horrible things about yourself like Ralph. I asked Ralph to record his negative thoughts about himself. Such thoughts are automatic, running constantly like old tapes in our mind. Automatic thoughts make up our negative self-talk. Here are just ten of Ralph's:

From the way he looked at me, he must think I'm a jerk.
I must look so weird.
Who wants sensitivity and feelings in a guy?
I'm a freak, unlovable, subhuman.
I have nothing he'd be interested in me for.
Nobody wants my body. I'm old, fat, and ugly.
I'm so limited and socially awkward.
Poor, pathetic me, always trying and failing.
I should never have been born. I just don't belong. I should give up.
I'll probably be a suicide in my 70s.

Thoughts like Ralph's are deeply painful. It's hard to imagine positive things when we've had negative experiences and been told bad things about ourselves. We may not think things will ever improve, especially with a trauma history. We can imagine they may stay the same or get worse, but not better.

It's important to know that our thoughts are not absolute truths. Ralph's self-concept isn't true. I know that because I treated him. He's kind, likable, interesting, talented, driven, successful, attractive, and a good conversationalist. Ralph can learn to see himself more accurately, just as I see him, by changing his negative self-talk. We have to fix the self-defeating tape about ourselves by replacing it with a positive tape. For instance, if I think I'm worthless, I can write that negative thought down and then write at least five positive things that prove it untrue:

I'm not worthless because my plants, betta fish, and Teacup Yorkie depend on me to live.

I'm not worthless because people count on me in my work.

I'm not worthless because I help people.

I'm not worthless because I wrote this book.

I'm not worthless because I care about myself and there are people who care about me.

Try to consistently contradict each of your untrue negative self-statements with five true affirming thoughts—whether you actually believe them at this point or not. In time, you will believe them.

The nature of our experience in the world is that life responds to us largely by corresponding to whatever we're thinking. An easy way to understand this is to say that life matches what you're giving. It's like a good 401K fund. You've probably said this yourself many times with casual phrases like, "you get back what you put out" or "like attracts like." We can only receive what we give. If you're tuned in to AM radio, you get AM radio, instead of an MP3 file. If you're nasty, you get more aggravation. If you smile, you get easier times. This concept has profound implications.

Many gay men are living in the world feeling that life is punishing, cruel, and bad. That love is scant in a world dominated by hate, lack, and limitation. We live in a broader culture of violence, fear, and separateness. Many people are depressed in our Prozac Nation. We can feel disconnected, in spite of our technological advances. We're stressed and have little time to connect with one another while we serve materialism and our capitalist economy. American households now contain more TVs than people.

Gloomy Gus, an artist, shared his poem, *The Abyss*, with me:

I no longer desire to live;
I prefer to die.
The agony is so painful I can't even cry.
Why shed a tear if I have no fear?
Why travel without a destination?
I ask myself, who is behind this creation?
Is this madness or just a bad dream?
A different race, another team?
Why don't you answer me if you exist?
Can all of this be destroyed
With a simple gesture of a powerful fist?
Is this really our world,
Or nothing more than
The Abyss?

But this is only part of the whole truth. Life is also rewarding, good, and loving. It is giving and abundant. It works for us and not against us. Quantum theory has revealed that nothing is separate. The foundation of the cosmos is connectedness. We are all connected. We are all united as gay brothers. Our sexual difference is what makes us the same. We can create the life and relationships we want by changing our perspective on what it means to be a man who is gay.

We can stay stuck in old patterns if we act as if new people and situations are like the past. For instance, if you think people don't accept you because you're gay, then you may act stand-offish, angry, or quiet. People may sense that vibe and stay away from you. Then you might feel rejected. But people may not have approached you because you were acting "strange." It probably had nothing to do with you being gay. But "no one likes me because I'm unacceptable" can become a self-fulfilling prophecy if you attribute people shunning you to your belief that they don't like you because you're gay. Your sense of self projects outward so that your core negative belief about yourself is proved true. This negative experience has a basis in reality only because you project it. One popular twelve-step acronym that embodies this idea is FEAR: "False Expectations Appearing Real." This means that what we expect to be true will determine our experience.

Alternatively, you can manifest good outcomes. People will respond positively to you if you love yourself enough to be yourself—a nice, outgoing, approachable gay guy. You can change your experience if you change how you think. A very useful book that can help you change distorted thinking is *Feeling Good: The New Mood Therapy*, by Dr. David Burns.

As soon as your thinking matches positive thought, you'll get good things. You don't have to wait. You get the benefits of right thinking as soon as you do it. Take the law of buoyancy. If you throw a rock into the water, it sinks. If you build a ship, it floats. The water can't support the rock because it doesn't match the properties of the law of buoyancy. But the law is always there waiting to float something as soon as its properties are matched. It just takes awareness.

Awareness is a key component of making transformation and breaking the chains of traditional masculinity. Awareness of confining cultural expectations leads to new choices, which leads to new action, which ends in change. You may think adhering to the code of masculinity protects you, but it traps you. You can be the firewall that blocks the part of masculinity that says "real" men don't love men, look gay, act gay, talk gay, and so on. Realize that being a "real man" means being the gay man you are. If you're masculine, that's fine, but don't try to be more masculine to compensate for feeling unmanly because you're gay, and don't judge other men who aren't masculine. Accept your "gayness" as it is. Accept others' "gayness," however they express it. Once you accept "gayness" fully in yourself and others, you'll stop worrying about rejection and grow happier.

We can learn a lot from stereotypically "feminine" men. They are able to be who they are without any pretense. They can do something most guys can't. They can cross the gender line and come out from behind the screen of the "real man" in order to be themselves. This doesn't mean you have to be effeminate if you're not. It means you can be who you are without squashing your gayness, and without discriminating against those who are effeminate. If you know you're a man, you're a man—period— no matter how "feminine" you are or aren't.

My specialized work with transgender people can help us here. Some people are born with a female body but identify as male. They think of themselves as men whether or not they have a penis. Similarly, some people are born male-bodied and identify as female. They don't think of themselves as men, even though they have a penis.

Some men dress in women's clothing or cross-dress. When dressed, they gain access to their feminine gender. Dressing is not about changing sexes for this kind of cross-dresser. These men have a part of them that is female-gendered. It's a bit stronger than a man just having a feminine side. They relish being in their female role for a period of time. It's not a sexual fetish for these guys. For them dressing is largely about escaping the pressures of the masculine role for a bit. It's about fun, recreation, relaxing, letting loose, and being sensual. It's easier to relate, to be sensitive, feel, cry, and see their inner beauty. While dressed, they can do whatever they wish without worrying about their masculinity. These men actually become their female selves for a while, but they're still men. In fact, they identify as straight men.

Cross-dressers aren't to be confused with drag queens. Drag queens are gay men who cross-dress. Both cross-dressers and drag queens cross-dress, but for very different reasons. In fact, lots of groups cross-dress. It's not the cross-dressing, but the reason for it that distinguishes them. While some drag queens later realize that they actually have gender issues, most drag queens cross-dress for fun, entertainment, work, or to express the feminine side of their manhood. Drag queens are gay men expressing their feminine side. For a drag queen it's more of an act or persona, as opposed to a gender issue, like it is for a cross-dresser.

All gay men can redefine masculinity. Don't worry! I'm not going to tell you that you have to change sexes, cross-dress, or become a drag queen if you have no desire to do so. Just recognize that men and women are not opposites. It's not an either-or world. It's a both-and world.

Jung said that there are masculine and feminine aspects in each of us that represent preexisting thought patterns in our minds. This simply means that we all come equipped with both masculine and feminine qualities to some degree. Jung called these thought forms archetypes. He called the male archetype "the animus" and the female archetype "the anima." Jung believed that self-actualization was in part achievable by integrating these two archetypes in one's personality. You may want to try the following exercise.

Imagine yourself as androgynous. What characteristics do you have that are stereotypically feminine? What characteristics do you have that are stereotypically masculine? Do you see both of these dimensions as the man that you are?

It takes a tough, strong, and powerful man to exhibit fluid, flexible, and well-rounded qualities that are both masculine and feminine—human qualities. This also means accepting other people just as they are. You can't do that if you're straight acting or if you're telling others that they have to be a certain way— "no fems," "straight acting only," "masculine/muscular"—to be with you. No matter what mix of masculine and feminine qualities you have, how can you be the gay man you are?

Transforming into your own man takes courage and ongoing commitment. You can move forward continuously in spite of inner voices of fear and doomsday prophecies. If you stay subscribed to the male gender role out of fear, becoming its slave, you will be miserably chained and bound by the shackles of masculinity. You'll be living your life for other people. As long as you stay in fear of being all of who you are, you will be restrained. Alternatively, you can move forward.

If I were chasing you with a gun and I suddenly stopped, sat down, cracked a Corona with lime and lit a cigarette, what would you do? You would probably keep running, not sure when it's safe to stop. Well, it's time for you to stop running now. Running from all of the hopes, dreams, expectations, obligations that others have imposed on you. Running from the fear that they won't like you as you are—that they'll reject you for what you are. You can interrupt the traditional patterns of society regarding manhood that you have followed all your life and allow your true nature to come forth. It's time to be who you are, right here and now. If someone rejects you, it doesn't say anything about you. It tells you what kind of person they are.

The truth is that you can experience freedom from gender limitations at this very moment. You can be the person you are on the inside, on the outside, and be happy. You must be authentic. Who cares what others think? You can rest easy in your own seat of power, not living a life based on the expectations of those around you. This is so freeing and so much less stressful than pretending. Being authentic has a ripple effect by impacting everyone around you and around them and so on—the social ramifications are tremendously powerful. A transformation toward authenticity only brings you more relationship, not less.

Outness (OPT OUT)

Since being authentic means being yourself, you have to be out to be authentic. You're probably out already. But even if you're out of the gay closet, you may not be out of the closet of masculinity. If you're still turning down your "gayness" and turning up your masculinity, you're probably still carrying some emotional shame about being gay. We saw in chapter 6 that there's a relationship between how much shame you carry about being "unmanly" and to what degree you use masculinity as a "cover." Until we complete our walk of shame, our gay relationships are affected because they trigger our unresolved shame. The overall satisfaction you have in your gay relationships is directly related to how far you're able to let go of expectations around masculinity.

How safely you think you can express yourself openly as a gay man, rather than a "real man," directly impacts the quantity and quality of your same-sex relationships. You can't have lasting, intimate relationships with other men if your homophobic guard is up. Internalized homophobia is at the core of why it can be so hard to meet a man for something more. You can't connect emotionally to another man if you're defensively wearing masculine armor to safeguard your manhood, because you think being gay is less masculine. How closely you hold your masculine shield is directly proportional to how far you're able to develop meaningful and lasting same-sex partnerships. The closer you hold the "real man" shield, the less intimate you can be with another man. The further away the shield, the further you can go. A hard exterior isn't that porous to emotional intimacy with other men. We have to take off the straight-acting covering that keeps us from piercing one another's hearts. Consider this letter and my reply:

Dear Angelo,
I was closeted for a long time. I have never been in a real relationship. No one that I am attracted to seems to be attracted to me. The clincher is that I seem to only be attracted to straight men. You could put one hundred guys in a room and one straight guy and I will find the straight guy and end up liking him. What is that? The long-term depression has got me contemplating on giving up on life, not suicide, but just giving up mentally and emotionally. Now that I'm out, I can't find anyone, and I'm tired of trying.
Signed, Straight-Loving Gay

Dear Straight-Loving Gay,
An attraction only to straight men can be a creative way that you have to keep yourself from being hurt in relationship. While pining over someone you can't have is painful, you know he's straight. Therefore you also know that nothing romantic will happen. So it's safe to put all of your feelings and energy toward him because it's just a fantasy. It's actually brilliant. You can meet your need to love, but you don't have to be vulnerable and he

can't burn you. If a gay man were emotionally available to you, it might be too frightening for you to experience this level of vulnerability and intimacy up close. Perhaps you're not comfortable in your own skin being gay and liking straight men is a way to push your gayness away. A gay relationship based on mutual love and respect forces a man to deal with his gayness, and being part of a male couple makes it easier for others to identify us as gay. Being in a gay relationship means we have to be comfortable with our sexuality.

So while many gay men may prefer masculine men because they think it's attractive, liking only straight men can be a manifestation of internalized homophobia. It's a way to deal with the shame of being gay.

Don't give up. Forget about getting a man for now. Turn your attention to you. Concentrate on being comfortable with yourself. Then the right men will come.

All the Best, Angelo.

Simply outing ourselves isn't enough. It doesn't stop there. Coming out is a lifelong struggle to decrease shame and increase self-acceptance. Each day you have to work toward ridding yourself of more shame and ultimately being completely comfortable in your own skin. This is hard work to do in a predominantly antigay culture. Internalized shame can be so deeply painful that confronting the issue can feel overwhelmingly terrifying. The No. 1 reason the gay men I treat drop out of treatment is to avoid the powerful feelings of rage and utter despair that confronting the shame can bring.

You don't have to be more out today because I say so. I respect that this is a highly personal choice. You have to decide to do it in your own time, at your own pace, and in your own way. But I work to free us all from the horrible ongoing fear, humiliation, and shame of being gay. So I can't support keeping gay "discreet" to any extent because I think that would support the idea that there's something wrong about it. Instead, I want to give you this message—unless you're in danger, there's no reason to keep any part of your magnificent self hidden anytime, anywhere. To find the right man, we have to leave the "real man" behind. We have to continuously work toward the place where we fully reveal ourselves and where we allow others to fully reveal themselves. That is how we can get the intimacy we crave. "Straight acting only, no trolls, fats, or fems" doesn't do it. We have to accept and appreciate one another exactly as the men we are.

You may not know who you are, since you're so used to people-pleasing. But I have a bunch of ideas to help you find out. You may want to try some, or all of them, for yourself.

Try looking in a mirror, deeply into your eyes. What makes you feel good about yourself? Which of your qualities make you proud? In my workshops, I do an exercise where everyone has another person tape a blank paper to their back. Then, everyone walks around in a silent meditation with the paper on their back. Their aim is to partner with everybody in the room. When partnered, they look into each other's eyes and write the quality their partner exudes most on their (the partner's) back. In the end, everyone is left with a list of their most amazing attributes. It's important to believe these wonderful things are true about you. Some people hang their list where they can see it every day. This doesn't have to be a group activity. It can be done one-on-one, too. Maybe you can ask several people to do this for you.

In the mirror, you can also answer, "What's important to you? What do you think about various issues? To what extent does how you feel about something or what you say depend on other people's opinions?"

Maybe you can make a list of your values. Acting in accordance with your own beliefs and feelings builds your identity and esteem. When you know where you stand, you can tell others what you like and don't like. Telling people what you authentically think and feel in the moment allows them to adjust their behavior in relationship to you. This is how congruency builds a sense of self.

You can also identify things you like to do. If you don't know what activities bring you joy, try new things. Get out and about, experience a breadth of new activities. That will help you learn what you like and don't like. It can help to rate the activity on an enjoyment scale of zero (worst) to ten (best) both before you try it and after you do it. I might give skateboarding a three before, but an eight after. This helps you know yourself better.

As each one of us discovers, befriends, and shares ourselves, we become free. So how do you overcome the fear to be your own man? Separating from the masses isn't easy. Know that the "gayness" you are in touch with is normal, and that everyone else who doesn't think so is out of touch. There is nothing wrong or bad about you. It's the limiting, judgmental paradigms about what makes a man a man that are wrong. Know that your life gets better as you act like yourself. There are consequences to face and sacrifices to make, but it's better to deal with them than to stay locked in the small cell of masculinity. Recall that courage is going forward in spite of fear.

Besides, there's nothing to be ashamed of. "Flamboyant" gays are true pioneers. They are the agents of change and true heroes for the freedoms we enjoy today. According to David Carter, author of *Stonewall: The Riots That Sparked the Gay Revolution*, they were the ones "who fought the hardest, showed the most courage, and took the most injuries" during the Stonewall riots. We can all learn how to be ourselves from them.

Maybe they get so much flack, even from their own kind, because other men resent them. Perhaps the feminine man is despised because he can do something most men can't. He can stand up and be himself, tearing down the masculine facade. He doesn't sacrifice himself on the altar of masculinity. This takes a lot of strength and these men deserve nothing but respect. There is a big upside to this kind of bravery and boldness in putting yourself way out there.

Just as straight-acting gays resent the queens, it's conceivable that straight men are envious of gay men in general. They may resent us for "gender trading." This could explain in part their hostility toward us. They may be stuck in the prison of masculinity. Relatively speaking, we have a freedom they don't. By coming out, we escape the confining straitjacket, creating movement by saying "no" to the pressure of masculinity and expressing the "feminine" part of ourselves. Instead, they can remain terrified of their "feminine," "sensitive" parts, locking them away until they marry or mature. Meanwhile, they may stay overly attached to their masculine identity, not trespassing on such uncharted, protected territory.

When we're straight acting, we buy into that fear. When we unmute our "gayness," we're free to express ourselves as we are—whatever that "looks" like—"masculine" or "feminine." It's paramount that we're ourselves, to change the tide of insidious homophobia that threatens to drown out who we are.

Do you remember the first image you saw of a gay person on TV? The first time you read something about gay people? Did you agree with what was being portrayed or said about you? Probably not. Nevertheless, the gay images people see in the mass media can determine their overall feelings and thoughts about you and your gay compatriots.

Sally, a straight woman who lives in a rural town, explained, "When I think of gays, I think of zany guys in pink underwear, doing hair, decorating, throwing parades, having sex in the streets and looking for kids, because that's what I see on TV." What people see or read influences how they perceive and treat gay people—which makes the images and portrayals we see in mass media that much more powerful.

When we're out as gay men, we run the risk of losing our identity and being overpowered by the gay stereotypes that are propelled in the media. Everyone's got their preconceived notions of what a gay person is, so we get plugged right into that image, regardless of what we're really like. We can be reduced to a stereotype instead of a person.

We're no longer "the truck driver," "the neighbor," or "governor." We're "the gay truck driver," the "gay neighbor," or "gay ex-governor." We can even be reduced to just "gay." Stereotypes miss the human element. No one really knows exactly what a gay person is—except for a gay person.

You might want to take a break and write a short script to defeat stereotypes. The story could be about a man who challenges society's gender norms and how he triumphs after some initial adversity. There may be a message in your story that guides you toward healing and wholeness for yourself. How does your script compare to your own life story? How similar are you to the main character in your script? What can you learn from him? How can you rewrite a better ending for your real-life story?

Our unique life experiences as gay people open the door to the truth of our lives to all the people who hear them. When we open up, we become real people with real stories who share in the common human experience. Our differences fade and our likenesses prevail. We are more understood and welcomed. Accurate images of us as men who are gay shatter stereotypes. Without the human element, we are objectified and dehumanized as "the other," and prejudice and discrimination can thrive. We are misunderstood, feared, judged, and rejected. Research has shown that knowing someone gay eradicates homophobia.

So it is up to each one of us to put a face on "gayness" and set the record straight by being ourselves and educating those around us—family, friends, colleagues, society—about what being gay is and isn't. The gay community needs to have more credible poster boys for the general public to see than gorgeous twenty-something cover boys. We have a responsibility to let ourselves be seen as the diverse gay family members, friends, co-workers, and neighbors we are, to insure respect and equal rights. So put a face on "gayness" by taking off the false face of straight-acting masculinity and be fully who you are. As each one of us shares our essential nature, someone gets to know us for who we really are, and stereotypes decrease, one person at a time. A powerful ripple effect happens and things spread. Remember Rosa Parks? Being your own individual and taking a stand makes a difference. Don't hide behind straight-acting conformity.

Yes, it is risky. We may fear rejection by those we love. Living your truth is a tough road to travel. But living that truth is the road to inner peace and happiness, and it's the path to creating a new gay-affirming world. The best way to beat stereotypes is to become a real person by expressing yourself authentically as you are.

You'll be up against many popular images of gays: *Queer as Folk, Will & Grace, The L Word, Queer Eye for the Straight Guy, Noah's Ark, Brokeback Mountain,* Ellen, Rosie O'Donnell, Sir Elton John, the Village People, Erasure, George Michael, k.d. Lang, Melissa Etheridge, Rufus Wainwright, Lance Bass—just to name a few. It's very positive and quite wonderful that we can finally see ourselves reflected in the world. This is crucial for enhancing our self-esteem, which has been so eroded by the gay stigma. For far too long there were no positive images of us. We could only look to so-called sinful, dirty porn clouded in shame and secrecy to find images of men together. Elsewhere we saw images of gays who were insane, sick, bad, and wrong for committing illegal acts. Thank goodness times have changed. But Hollywood has its limitations.

I don't think people really want to watch the pain of our truth. Albeit a different time, when *Ellen* was a comedy show about real gay issues, it was cancelled. Now that Ellen has the persona of a daytime talk-show host who's fully out on *The Ellen DeGeneres Show*, but—unlike Rosie, formerly on *The View*—doesn't make her gayness a focus, *Ellen*'s a huge success. Now Ellen is awesome. Her character started it all by coming out on a prime-time sitcom. Our community owes a great deal to Ellen. She's a heroine. Today on *The Ellen DeGeneres Show*, she dresses "masculine," doesn't ever dodge being lesbian, and advocates for us if the gay subject should come up. She keeps her partner visible in public. I have nothing but admiration and respect for Ellen.

But I'm also curious. Overall, does Ellen's persona lean a bit toward straight acting on *The Ellen DeGeneres Show*? I mean, is the Ellen persona fostering more acceptance of gays in middle America by being a "normal," "good gay" who's just like them, or is it conforming by toning down, i.e., normalizing gayness to be just like everyone else? Does it take a little of both, being two sides of the same coin? Perhaps she's just being herself? Does it make you a "bad gay" if you're "oh so gay" without any muting like Rosie was on *The View*? This discussion isn't about who's a "better gay," Rosie or Ellen. It's about asking the question: Where does one draw the line to authenticity—if there is one?

The reality is, if something's too gay-focused, it runs the risk of not getting the majority of mainstream viewers. People like to watch gay characters to laugh and be entertained, not to learn about our plights or suffering. They enjoy our talent, but they don't necessarily want to see or hear about our "sex" lives. Some don't want "it" "in their face."

Yes, many shows are sure to include the flamboyant, lispy, finger snapping, swishy, fashion queen who decorates, cuts hair, and throws dinner parties. While this character is familiar, I don't think he reflects how most gay men are, or furthers our fight for equal civil rights. The fact that he's always good for a laugh tells us how low he is. He may make people comfortable enough to let him make them over, but perhaps not enough for votes to let his love relationship be recognized. Being gay in real life isn't always about fun. Many of us are coping with living and working in a straight world. We suffer and behave accordingly—with great discretion.

But being "normal," straight-acting, "good" gays doesn't advance us either if we sell out, stamping out our uniqueness. To fit in, even years before the Holocaust, some Jews of Europe passed as gentiles to escape anti-Semitism and have easier times. Today, some African-Americans may try to be more "white" to escape racism, while some Asian-Americans may try to Westernize their features. I'm sure we'd all agree that's wrong. Every "group" deserves social acceptance for the distinctiveness of its members, not because they are clones of the most influential one.

Well, straight acting is wrong, too. Gay men in America are straight acting to make their lives easier in a climate of antigay hate. We have to stop homogenizing ourselves by being straight acting. Sure, there are universal aspects of love, friendship, self-acceptance, and struggle that gay men share with everyone else. Emphasizing the commonalities of the baseline human experience helps others affirm us. This is an acceptable use of normalizing ourselves, as Ellen and Rosie do. The key difference is not selling out at the same time by diminishing our unique appearance, behavior, voice, or experience as a gay person—which isn't the same as everyone else's. Like Ellen or Rosie, we retain our uniqueness. We are men, but we're men who are gay. We can't be subjugated by the dominance of the "real man." This doesn't mean you have to be feminine. It means don't mute your gayness and blast your manhood. We deserve the respect to be accepted as the people we are without having to change anything about ourselves to blend in.

So how can you have others understand who you really are and accept you when you'll be competing with all the gay images out there? An effective way to educate straight people about being gay is to turn their perspective around with questions like: What made you straight? Then share your experience regarding how you're the same as, but different from, popular gay images, and how being gay has been hard for you because of stereotypes.

The trick is not to give up. I have seen people turn 360 degrees and do amazing healing work. I recall a client, Jill, who was an ex-nun. Jill disowned her lesbian daughter for many years on religious grounds. But the daughter challenged her mother's ideology and never gave up. Jill eventually renounced her Church and renewed her relationship with her daughter. At that time, Jill was diagnosed with an aggressive form of leukemia. She later made her transition from cancer peacefully with her daughter right by her side.

It takes time to change traditional beliefs about gays. But most people will come around and discard their prejudices once they know, hear, and see the truth from a man who's gay—you! You'll free a mind and you'll free up yourself.

Meanwhile, we have to stop self-destructing from our shame about not being masculine enough.

Uprooting (OPT OUT)

You have to uproot addictive behavior because it disconnects you from yourself. You have to be able to stay present with yourself and sit with your own feelings before you can expect another man to stick around.

While vices help take us away from pressure, where's the line between what's "healthy" and what's "a problem?" Using alcohol, drugs, sex, and such are not behaviors unique to gay men, but how much "fun" is too much? Whatever your vice is, if it's causing problems in your life, you have to uproot it. Self-destructive behaviors can stop once you tackle the underlying emotional issues that drive them.

It's hard to kick a habit. Every year, one-third of all Americans make a New Year's resolution. Most of them will have broken it by Valentine's Day. We make promises to lose weight, quit smoking, work less, etc. Try as we might, however, it is really hard to change our behavior. We comfort and soothe ourselves with "bad" habits like overeating, not exercising, smoking, drinking, drugs, sexual compulsion, unsafe sex, porn, overshopping—the list goes on. We pleasure ourselves with the "naughty" stuff. Who really wants to decrease pleasure by doing more "good," "healthy" stuff? Unfortunately, most of us will die from health-related illnesses resulting from our poor habits. So why isn't that enough to stop us in our tracks and frighten us into changing?

We do "bad" things to ourselves to relieve unpleasant feelings that are happening in our lives right now. Living longer seems so far away when we are looking for an immediate fix to feel good. If whatever we're doing is also physically addictive, then we get hooked twice as hard. We're actually trying to love ourselves by self-medicating our pain.

However, our choices can end up hurting us. Almost anything can be used in a self-destructive way and become harmful if it's overdone. Anything can be an addiction if it's being used routinely as an escape from life, if we can't stop it on our own, and if it's causing problems in our life. But we have to come out of denial to recognize that. Life can be scary all by itself. It isn't easy. It's tough to stop a comforting habit and face life as it is without any anesthesia. Tough, but not impossible.

The first step may be to surrender, giving up control, acknowleging you have a problem. If you're juggling a substance-abuse problem, get yourself into recovery. Confiding in your physician, a mental health professional, or someone at a community center is a good place to start. There are also twelve-step programs that are free and easily accessible. Twelve-step members are concerned with their own recovery as well as supporting others in recovery. Alcoholics Anonymous (AA), Crystal Meth Anonymous (CMA) and Sexual Compulsives Anonymous (SCA) are just a few of the many support groups out there. Usually there's at least one meeting on something somewhere in your area each day. You can get instant support from other people dealing with the same issues you are. You can make new friends at just one meeting. Check out a twelve-step meeting today and see if it's right for you.

An unexamined life of addiction and self-destruction will get the better of you. The gay scene will eventually take its toll. The friends you had in the scene may not be the kind of friends who are there for you when the chips are down. Many of these scene-based relationships are fleeting and disingenuous. This is because the big secret behind all the party pals is addiction. We can't build real relationships with each other through the fog of a substance. The connections are with the substance and not to the people. When the party's over and the stash is gone, everyone disappears through the veil. Martin said:

> *When I dropped out of "the scene," guess how many "friends" came with me—zero. Zip! Months have passed. Sure, they call you: "let's go out." You go, drink a lot, do your bumps, dance in your circle of ten. But none of these friends call to ask things like, "Where've you been?" "How are you?" "Is everything all right?" or to say, "I miss you." I'm thankful to have had those experiences and those friendships at that time in my life. It gives me more security today knowing that I'm not missing out on anything and why I don't want to be a part of "the scene" anymore. The friendships I built in "the scene" have all but disappeared, and I realize that I have more quality and depth in my friendships outside of "the scene" today.*

The NYPD periodically closes popular Manhattan gay clubs because undercover sting operations often find illegal drugs on the premises. Not to mention the paradox of AIDS service organizations benefiting from the proceeds of events that are actually massive drug parties where unsafe sex is likely to follow. I was stunned to see a NY gay event advertised as "Booty Bump." A booty bump is when you put a bump-size of drugs up your anus. Party promotion glamorizes drug use and normalizes it as OK. Isn't everyone doing it? A little partying doesn't hurt, right? Wrong.

The way to beat addiction is to get support and confront your feelings, not numb out. You heal when you feel. It's a wise endeavor to work through your issues head-on. You can cope and overcome hardship. You're a survivor. You've already beat the odds. You have what it takes inside of you—a willingness to change things and triumph. I know that because you're reading this book. You can turn around all the lies you've been fed about what being a gay man means. But first, you have to look at your situation, square in the eye. Like Abbey Mallard in *Chicken Little* says, stop messing around and deal with the problem.

Much of recovery is grief work. To accept ourselves, we have to mentally and emotionally work through the trauma that comes with being a gay man in America. We can erase the brainwash of masculinity—the lie that gay men aren't "real men"—that gets broadcast loud and clear. Dr. Terrence Real says that unresolved trauma and subsequent shame can lead to hidden depression. Men usually mask depression by engaging in risk-taking behavior or doing "bad" things. This is an effort to dodge falling hopelessly into a black hole of despair. But Dr. Real reveals that it's only after a man deals openly with his trauma, shame, and depression that he can be free.

To recover, we have to fully take the brunt of shame, anxiety, despair, rage, and other difficult and profoundly uncomfortable feelings. Then we can triumph. Deep pain can't be shrugged off or masked by a false front of strength like straight-acting masculinity. We need to identify and express our feelings fully with support. It's only by moving toward our pain that we can heal it, moving on to create a better life for ourselves. We can choose to embrace and surrender to our pain, not avoid it. We won't get stuck in it. We won't live it. We can work through it and move forward to a better place. Any addict in long-term recovery will tell you their first year was hell, but they'll also tell you they would never trade their sobriety today. William Styron, author of *Darkness Visible*, says the reward for suffering depression's agony is a renewed capacity for serenity, joy, and love that's rich and enduring. Like any investment, getting a big return on recovery requires an initial expenditure. The cost is the pain of our feelings.

Recovery comes from the depths of our being, the bottom of our soul. It taps into the core of who we are, our bedrock. Feeling our feelings requires raw exposure, extraordinary vulnerability, or what Jung referred to as "legitimate suffering." We can either "F*#! Everything And Run" or "Face Everything And Recover," two more meanings of the twelve-step acronym FEAR. I have done my fair share of feeling work.

Recovery from many wounds has brought me some of the most incredible emotional pain I've ever known. But facing this pain head on is the most wonderful thing I have ever done for myself, growing through it in order to move forward to the other side. My pain has great meaning for me, as it has helped me to be a good therapist, giving me the know-how to tenderly usher others through the process. Pain isn't the enemy. The fear of passing through it is. That's what keeps you stuck, hurting. I believe you can stand your pain. I have great faith in you, after all, it's only your pain, and you can tolerate it to free yourself from it. Victor Frankl—psychiatrist and Holocaust survivor, said. *"For tears bore witness that a man had the greatest of courage, the courage to suffer."*

Inner child work can be an important part of this process. In *Homecoming: Reclaiming and Championing Your Inner Child*, John Bradshaw writes about healing our wounded inner child. Our inner child is the part of us that is the forgotten, hurt child of the past who continues to live on somewhere inside of us. He's most often the one who needs tending to. He's the holder of many of our most troublesome feelings.

In my work, I often ask men to do some of Bradshaw's exercises as part of their healing. I ask them to imagine and communicate with their child within. Through visualization and letter-writing, they can refather themselves by fathering their inner child. This can be powerfully healing. It may be by fathering ourselves that we can finally grow up.

TJ, who looks like an all-American jock today, wrote this letter from his adult self to the hurt boy he was back in time:

Dear Little TJ,

I know that you may not want to tell me about your troubles, but I think you may be having a difficult time. I think you're having a hard time growing up because other kids and adults make fun of you for being different, effeminate, unathletic, or just not like them. Remember that I am here for you. I can be your friend and will be your friend regardless of what you look like, how you dress, how well you play sports, whether you are masculine or feminine, or whether you like girls or boys. You are a smart, fun-loving, and tender person. You have a lot to offer other people, and you make a great friend. I know you are concerned that your parents, especially your mom, will see you as tarnished (you were always the good one in her eyes, unlike your sister) if they find out that you are not liked by the

other kids, or that you like boys. But I know that regardless of how hard they can be on you, or how much they might be hurt, or how embarrassed they may be to have a gay son, that deep down they will love you and hopefully will come around to respect you for you. In the meantime, while you wait to tell them until you are stronger, you can be open and be yourself with me. I can teach you to be stronger and make your life better in these areas. I know the other kids at school and I am not going to tell you everything is going to be OK. You are different and may not be liked by those people. But they are limited in their view. They are conditioned to dislike you because you are different. But remember, there are people like you, including myself, and people who see your uniqueness and will like you. The world is not full of those bullies you meet every day. One day, you will look back, as I do, and be thankful for who you are and that you did not end up like them. They may be having their fun now, but your enjoyment will increase later in life. As for now, focus on what you want to be and take steps to get there each day. I can help you get to where you want to be. Let's continue to talk and be friends.
Big TJ

Fede works in a gym. He, too, was teased as a kid for being effeminate. He wrote this letter from his inner child to himself:

Dear Big Fede,
Don't worry too much. I'm surrounded by tough girlfriends who protect me.
Little Fede

Juan wrote a letter to his actual father (deceased) from his inner child:

Dear Dad,

I feel weird writing you this letter because we don't have the kind of relationship where we can speak openly. However, I have nobody else to turn to that I can trust. I have this problem at school where I get picked on constantly because I'm so quiet and shy. I know why, though. I feel ashamed of who I am and I feel I'm not worthy of interacting with the kids because of a secret that I keep with me. I don't want to tell you what it is because I fear you won't love me anymore and because you'll be disappointed in me. I don't like bringing attention to myself because of my secret. Basically, I feel very alone and without friends. I don't like the way it feels. I feel like I don't belong. Because of this loneliness, as an adult I often turn to other things to make me happy, like food, sex, alcohol, and drugs. I know none of these things are good for me, but I can't help doing them because they're my only escape. I don't know if there's anything you can do, but I just need to have someone understand and support me.
Your Son, Juan

I recommended he go to the cemetery to share the letter with his dad.

Maybe you would like to write some letters yourself? Start by finding a special time and place for reflection. Find pictures of yourself at times you were hurting. Work with one picture at a time. Take a few moments to really look at a picture. Pull yourself back in time and remember yourself at that age. What was life like for you then? Coloring, painting, or doing arts and crafts can also help you reach your inner child. As the adult you are today, write a letter to your inner child from the perspective of giving him what he needed most from a sane adult back then. If you don't like writing, you can also try imagining cradling your inner child or imagine holding your son's hand. If he were going through what you are, how would you make this child feel safe and reassure him?

You can also reverse the process. If your inner child wants a chance to be heard, give him permission to express himself. What does your inner child want to say? What does he need from you, the adult caretaker? Try writing a letter from him in your non-dominant hand, drawing a picture or playing. Maybe have your hands "talk" with puppets.

As for what to do with all the letters, I recommend making a scrapbook of them. If they contain goals, I recommend addressing them to yourself and having someone else send them to you in several months. If you're more tech-oriented, send yourself an e-mail, but wait a few months before opening it.

These exercises can bring up powerful emotions. It's important to recall that feeling is healing. If you feel like crying, despair, rage, panic, terror, or something else, realize that your present life isn't falling apart. You're releasing powerful pent-up emotions from the past. It's a good thing. Stuck emotion is a primary factor that can contribute to psychological and physical dis-ease. We need to let it out and let it go. So don't be afraid to express yourself. Try not to hold it back.

You might want to try a short exercise to help you move through your feelings from the inner-child work. Shamans and other indigenous healers have been using breathwork and dance for millennia to loosen up thoughts and feelings that keep us stuck in anxiety, fear, depression, anger, and illness. Such mind-body work can transform emotions like worry, sadness, anger, and dis-ease into healing. Knowledge of this work is fine, but you have to actively participate in it to really benefit. You may feel foolish at first, but it's exhilarating in the end.

First try breathing rapidly in through the nose and out through the mouth as you flap your arms and raise your knees—dancing in place like a chicken. Go on for about three minutes. Next, put on some upbeat music. Shake, jerk, and jump around in a wild frenzy as you scream. Go on for about five minutes. Immediately follow this with a slower melody and free flow. Let your body go and sway effortlessly to the melody. Try to go for another five minutes. Finally, sit down cross-legged or lie down. Close your eyes and turn within. Meet yourself. Place your hand over your belly button. With each in-breath, push your hand out with your belly. With each out-breath pull your hand in. Minimize any movement in your upper chest. Belly-breathe deeply for three minutes to calm yourself.

Other options and forms of bodywork you can try are exercising, focused breathwork, yoga, Tai Chi, chakra-work, acupuncture, massage, and laughter to help release emotion. You can express any feeling by drawing it with coloring pencils, crayons, or paints, too. The result can be an image that's distinct, amorphous, or something in between.

For anger, you may want to try some anger-work. Outlets that release anger like stomping, hitting a mattress with a plastic bat, screaming into a pillow, or boxing can be helpful. Anger in particular is a feeling that has to be worked out bodily. Physical exercise like walking, strength training, or aerobics also works well. You can also write down the name, or get a picture, of who or what hurt you. Throw darts at it, burn it, tear it up, squish it, or toss it in the trash. You don't have to feel angry before you do any of this. Doing it will bring up the anger and vent it.

Observe your feeling experience. Give yourself permission to grieve. Understand that you may feel hurt and sad for a time. It can help to share what's happening and lean on a supportive friend, family member, or other trusted ally. Don't go it alone. Reach out.

It can be exhausting to process this kind of information. Listen to your body. Get plenty of rest, nutrition, and support. Avoid addictive and other risk-taking coping behavior. Remember to be gentle with yourself and take good care of yourself.

We can't do this work if we continue to numb out our feelings with addictions. It doesn't have to be New Year's to create change. You can do it today. Looking at yourself brings fulfilling rewards. Recovery has countless benefits, including fewer troubles, more solutions, less stress, fewer feelings of being "stuck," along with movement, increased peace, wholeness, joy, love, greatly enhanced relationships, and much much more.

As I mentioned with Transformation, awareness is an important first step toward change. For instance, if a guy finds himself involved with alcoholic men over and over, he can't break free from that dysfunctional relationship pattern until he's aware of how he's been affected as an adult by his father's drinking in childhood.

Awareness by itself isn't enough, however, to create a change. A person may be aware that he has to lose fifteen pounds, quit smoking, or meditate every day, but that's not good enough to actually lose the weight, to be smoke free, or experience peace. In order to lose fifteen pounds, stop smoking, or feel relaxed, he has to put a great deal of effort into making it happen. He has to take new action—exercise, quit smoking, sit (meditate). This is where most people fall short. Awareness without taking right action is like wishful thinking.

More people don't change because it's hard. It requires sacrifice. It also leads us into new, unfamiliar territory, which may feel strange and scary. But you can do it. We've established that by being a gay man in a heterosexist culture, you've already proven you're resilient. You have the courage it takes.

So, my take home tip is—in order to change something you're already aware of, you have to put in the effort to step outside your comfort zone, make new choices, and actually do things differently this time. Also, building a support network is a vital part of initiating and maintaining this process.

Try out my Eight Steps to Recover the Man Within.

Step One: This is the precontemplation stage. It's simply doing an inventory of all the possibilities. Think of changing something concrete that will have a positive impact on your life—you want something that will have meaningful consequences in your day-to-day life. Go with the specific over the general. So "I can choose not to use crystal today" is better than "I want to get sober."

Step Two: Choose a specific, measurable behavior you feel confident you can change. It's important to have realistic goals. Far too often, people set goals for themselves they have no way of reaching. They set themselves up to fail. Unless you're an alcoholic, "I want to have no more than two drinks when I'm out on Saturday night" is better than absolutes like "I will stop drinking forever." Make a list of pros and cons for changing that behavior. Do the same for not changing it. Use the pros of changing it and the cons of not changing it to motivate you. Reading information, or going to a lecture to get educated about what you're changing, can also be motivating. You might want to try writing your goal or intention on a piece of paper. Say, "I am drug free." Write what you're giving up on another piece of paper. Say, "Cocaine." Release the habit by burning the latter, tearing it to shreds, crumbling it up into a ball or throwing it in the garbage.

Step Three: Plan it out. Rash, hasty decisions or going cold turkey are not the best approaches. Build up your determination by planning ahead. First, make a commitment to change by setting a start date and preparing ahead of time. For example, if you want to have safe sex, plan to have condoms and lube on hand. Avoid using mind-altering substances that might affect your judgement during sex. Rearrange routines like the places you go (sex club), times you go there (4 AM), who you hang with (sketchy night owls) and what you do (party).

Step Four: Baby steps. Break things down into small, manageable periods of time. Think of recovery as a road trip from California to New York. You couldn't drive it straight through, could you? You'd have to break it up into parts. Imagine each step is a mile. A popular twelve-step slogan we all know is "one day at a time." Take that first step by taking one small action. Stop thinking about it and in the spirit of Nike "just do it," making the commitment to change real. If you want to know your HIV status, find out where you can get tested today. The next step would be to go get tested tomorrow.

Step Five: Get support while you feel your feelings. Join a twelve-step group, call a hotline, get a buddy or sponsor, inform your partner, friends, or family, get a life coach, a therapist, go to a clinic, etc. Whatever you do, don't do it alone. Share your story with helpful others. Those who talk about their secrets have better outcomes. If you use professional assistance, it doesn't mean anything is wrong with you. Therapy is a tool for improving the quality of your life. If you broke a bone, you'd go to a medical doctor. If your car's broken, you'd go to a mechanic. If the drain's broken, you'd call the plumber. It makes good sense to ask for help from those best suited to give it. Therapists are "experts" in life. The right relationship makes a difference. Seeking it shows strength, not weakness.

Step Six: Substitution. One of the best ways to change an old habit is to replace it with a healthier one. Start a project you've been putting off, rather than surfing porn for hours.

Put a carrot stick in your mouth instead of a blunt. Go for a run instead of shopping. Dr. Maxwell Maltz is credited for the Twenty-One-Day Habit Theory that says if you repeat something each and every day for twenty-one days, you'll make a new habit. There's a space between the impulse to do your old habit and the compulsion to carry it out. Interrupt the addiction cycle by filling that space with a healthier choice.

Step Seven: Maintenance. Measure how you're doing. Charts, journals, calendars, and post-its are great tools for keeping track of your progress both before you do it (reminding you to do it) and after you do it (checking off that you did it). Motivational sayings or pictures also help. Put these things out in the open where you see them several times a day. Keep it up for as long as it takes, whether it's twenty-one days or a lifetime! Good maintenance prevents relapse.

Step Eight: Prepare for the possibility of relapse. It's probable. Change is a process, not an event. It often takes many tries to change something permanently. It takes most people seven tries before they can finally quit smoking. Relapse is not failure. It is a tool you use to figure out where you went wrong this time, so you can keep it in check next time. If you fall off the horse, don't stop riding. Get right back on, knowing not to take the same path, ending up stronger and better prepared! Make the right choice each time, keeping perspective on what will best serve you over the longer haul. Ask yourself: What choice will lead to my greater happiness or higher purpose overall?

Well, that's it for my Eight Steps to Recover the Man Within. Being able to look authentically at the man in the mirror with no impediments, will enable you to build the strong, lasting bridges of love you want to other men.

Togetherness (OPT OU*T*)

The gay community is a celebration of diversity. The rainbow flag is our symbol. It stands for unity in diversity. Our difference is what unites us. But we're anything but fully united. Is our symbol a joke?

There's a talented gay volleyball league that's quite serious about its sport. I have treated some guys who came to see me because they didn't make the cut. The men I saw didn't even bother to try out for the play divisions. They went to try out for the recreational divisions with the simple hope of joining something fun, being part of a team, and meeting new gay friends. Instead, they were devastatingly rejected by gay volleyball "captains" in a high school gym for not playing well enough for their recreational divisions. Nightmare! It was like high school gym class all over again. Except now, some former members of the high school "out" crowd have deemed themselves the popular "in" crowd, by selecting a new "out" crowd from their own ranks. I don't say this to slander this particular volleyball league. I don't know the details and I'm sure they're good people with organizational limits on the number of men they can take. I'm using this example because it really captures a pervasively rejecting dynamic that plays out among gay men in many venues. It's a group dynamic that's reinjurious instead of welcoming. We go home to our gay brothers with open arms and get the door slammed in our faces because we're not athletic enough, not good-looking enough, not rich enough, etc. This awakens old feelings of inadequacy as men. There are few gay places we can go to feel welcomed and lovingly embraced by other gay men.

We can't continue to exclude one another, especially our brothers who may not choose to be as masculine. It might help to realize that it's the "flamboyant" guys who are free. Maybe the "effeminate" guys aren't the ones with the issue. A man's revulsion to other men who are "feminine," or not masculine enough, is the product of the way he's been socialized. When we see a "flamboyant" guy, our mind immediately reminds us of how men are supposed to be in our culture. When we ridicule, snub, or reject "effeminate" men, we are simply reinforcing what we learned from society—that it's not OK for a man to be "feminine." When we reject them, we may be giving them a dose of what we got. Our reaction to "effeminate" men can reflect our own shame about our own "sissyness" inside. If we're not comfortable with it in ourselves, we may certainly despise it in others.

We project our shame onto someone else. We may in fact be tossing our own ball of shame to those "Marys" when we mistreat them. Rejecting other "obvious" "fairies" reinforces our sense of belonging to the "Real Men's Club," allowing us to avoid our own shame. We can sell each other out to fit in. So, we see again that it's shame that comes between gay men, blocking their connections.

Sometimes if we know another guy is gay, we may even deliberately avoid him, reject him, or mistreat him. We may "read" him with cattiness. I overheard a gay man say to his friend—"I guess she lost her Prada glasses when she got dressed tonight"— about the new guy who arrived at the party. This isn't quite the same as "Hi, I'm Steve, welcome to the party. Why don't you join us?" Some of us even turn on one another. There's too much to risk in opening up, exposing ourselves and being vulnerable. It's scary. So we may retreat, disconnect, or lash out instead.

Obviously we don't always treat each other very well. There is too much divisiveness, disconnection, and loneliness in our community. I get lots of letters asking either "How can I meet more gay friends?" or "Where can I meet gay friends?" This is an important need. Having gay friends boosts our self-esteem. Relationships are healing. We see ourselves reflected in others.

We share our life experiences with mutual understanding. It's validating and affirms who we are. But outside of the scene and the Internet, meeting gay men for friendship or romance can be challenging. This is especially true for gay guys who aren't interested in the scene, who are in recovery, or for gay couples and families.

Often, gay men know how to connect for sex, but not on deeper levels. As men, we often don't know how to relate to each other emotionally. If two "lost," emotionally numb guys fall in love, they may not know how to find themselves, each other, or work through their feelings together. This makes it hard for many gay men to successfully build emotional intimacy. Most guys tell me they don't feel there's anywhere to find this kind of connection. Truth is—there isn't much. It can be frustrating.

Our community needs to create more venues for men to meet men in drug- and alcohol-free, friendly atmospheres that don't revolve around sex. It takes great courage for gay men to come together and be present with other gay men in the absence of alcohol, drugs, sex, or other substitutes for love, in order to unite and connect meaningfully—heart to heart and soul to soul. Nothing seems more important.

I create such an atmosphere in my groups, workshops, and retreats, but together we have the strength to make this practice more widespread. We're behind Hollywood, Broadway, fashion, beauty, design, and more! We are inventive and creative. We need to build Gay Relationship Centers that bring men together and help them build intimacy. We have to begin mentoring our own. This vision isn't an "impossible dream." It can unfold.

We know that male taboos break down and lose their power in times of crisis. In extreme circumstances, men are forced to discard the man code and surrender emotional control. In the shared experience of an intense and challenging situation, men can develop unparalleled commitment to each other. When this happens, love and devotion are created between men that are absolutely beautiful. The Greeks believed that love between men was the purest form of love. The male bond can last lifelong. Men can stick together—will even die for each other. War heroes make a beautiful example of this kind of love and honor.

Gay men go through the adversity of being gay together. We share a bond of resiliency from this crisis we all go through. We can call upon ourselves to use our shared experience to create incredible relationships with one another that serve as models of lasting love and devotion for everyone.

No longer can we discriminate against less masculine men—gay or straight. We must stay open, accept each other as we are, and unite. We have to focus on getting emotional intimacy from one another—not just sex. We can create more gay role models for support, guidance, education, and courage. We can educate by teaching gay history and guiding gay youth. We have the strength necessary to create an affirming support system for gay relationship, so we can enjoy living in an emotionally nourishing community of like-minded people.

Right now, unfortunately, there's no particular place to go where all this is waiting. I tell my clients, if you want this to happen you have to go out and make it happen. Here's how I suggest the men I treat do that.

Don't try to twist yourself into a pretzel to meet the guys you're looking for. Base it on you instead. The best strategy is to get involved in something that interests you, meets regularly, like weekly, biweekly, or monthly, and has a high potential for social contact with other gay men. Perhaps join an organization to be a big brother to a gay youth, volunteer for Gay and Lesbian Alliance Against Defamation (GLAAD), attend gay game night, or play gay softball. Pick activities, social groups, or organizations that you're passionate about—or start your own. Some ideas: check out volunteering with your local Human Rights

Campaign (HRC) chapter, AIDS service organization, PFLAG, or GLBT center. If you like to hike, get walking on a popular trail. If you love to exercise, join a class at the gym. You might enjoy a freeing gay nudist weekend. If you connect through meditation or prayer, explore a spiritual community or gay-friendly church. Join a support group or recovery program if you need to. Choose things for their intrinsic value. Ask, "What would I like to do?" and go do it, not "Where is everyone hanging out tonight?" You don't want to end up having your name engraved on a stool at the local gay bar. Think along the lines of an "activity," not a "place." You know what to do for you.

A rule of thumb that I have is to try something new out about three times to give it a fair chance. If you like it, stick with it, and if not, give it up and try something else. Try a bunch of things, anyway. The idea is that, by doing what you love, you'll encounter like-minded people with similar interests doing the same thing. This provides a common ground—which is a great starting point for relationship.

When we engage in things we like to do, we're a part of something larger than ourselves. That fills our life with meaning and makes us happier, which makes people want to be around us. You are much more likely to gel with someone you're doing an activity with, since the focus isn't on meeting people. Going to a gay fund-raiser, or joining a team that delivers meals to people living with AIDS, are activities that trump going to a speed-dating event. The ice is naturally broken, so meeting happens more naturally during a shared activity. You could easily "bump into" others who cross your path. Take the opportunity to make small talk with the persons you resonate with. Be friendly, yet assertive. You can simply say, "Hi, isn't this fun?" That can lead to a more personal icebreaker like, "Hi, I'm _____, what's your name?" This can lead to more interaction and eventually an invitation. You could later say, "Would you like to join me for a bite to eat after?" or "Would you like to exchange numbers?"

Stay open to what the image of a friend or date might be for you. Avoid rigid thinking: "I only hang out with gorgeous redheads who are six feet tall, with green eyes, and quarter-inch moles on their lower left chin." The nicest person could be different. You could miss out by having such specific standards. Remember, people can have friends. Someone you meet could also invite you to a party where you will be introduced to other people that suit you more. A sort of ripple effect can happen.

Even if you don't click with someone, you'll be spending time doing something you care about, so all is not lost. Until you meet someone, center on you—what you enjoy and things you care about. Here's a letter with my reply:

Dear Angelo,
I have everything except a lover. I feel so alone. This is a big enough problem to eclipse everything else, keeping me down most of the time. Any suggestions?
Signed, Please Send Me Someone to Love

Dear Please Send Me Someone to Love,
Often we look at what we want and don't have. Try instead to give thanks for all that you do have in your life. Practicing gratitude changes our perspective, upleveling our mood from lack, limitation, hopelessness, and depression to abundance, prosperity, hope, and contentment. For instance, a client of mine told me that he had about twenty people call to wish him a Happy Thanksgiving holiday. Unfortunately, the one guy he most wanted to hear from didn't call. He spent the whole session lamenting about this. I suggested that he focus on the twenty people who did call, rather than the one who didn't.

We all want to be loved. It's fine and beautiful that you desire this. But please don't let not having a love ruin the rest of your life. Getting down won't attract more love to you. In childhood, we whine to tell our caretakers that something's wrong so we can get our needs met. But this strategy doesn't work as well when we're grown. When we get down we may still be trying to call others to our aid by signaling that something's wrong. But a depressed mood can actually push people away in adulthood.

Instead of being down for not having love, try sending out more love. Change your state of mind from getting to giving. Why be miserable any longer? You're the one who suffers most. Give yourself more love by living your life with the same zest and fulfillment as if you already had that true love. I know it can be hard to cultivate overall happiness when you're single, especially around the holidays. But having an air of confidence and contentment is exactly what will attract more love to you, including that special one. Be your own man until the right man comes. Think in terms of your interests, rather than places. I don't think there is any single place to meet Mr. Right. You can meet him anywhere at any moment. I tell my clients to go about their lives doing things that interest them, which also have the potential for meeting men.

I had a client who took my advice and joined a gym, took Latin dancing classes, participated in a spiritual community, played in a pool league—among other things that interested him. He chose things that were either gay-oriented or gay-affirmative. It wasn't long before he was going on dates and making new friends, to boot.

I think there are three key ingredients: (1) get involved in a variety of things that you really like to do; (2) choose things that meet regularly for a period of time, preferably weekly; (3) and pick things that'll have gay men in them. Equally important is putting yourself out there with confidence by introducing yourself to others as you go about these activities. Keep a pleasant demeanor, stay open, and give it time (be patient). Then sit back and watch all that comes your way.

In spite of this external truth, you have to check in with your inner truth, too. Turn within and ask yourself if you're really in the right space for a relationship. I know there have been times in my life when I haven't gotten a single date in a year. And there have been other times when I had several dates in a week. The difference was in what was happening in me and not in anything outside of me. We communicate so much information nonverbally. Human beings are very perceptive creatures. We can pick up on each other's emotional availability quite easily—without sharing a word. So make sure you're doing your inner work, too.

In short, strike a balance between confidently putting yourself out there and doing your work on the inner. This is a winning combo that's sure to bring you more love.

All the Best, Angelo.

Building community is a worthwhile goal. Separateness doesn't have to be part of the picture for gay men. There are two types of hallucinations. One type is when we see something that isn't there. A less common type of hallucination is when we don't see something that is there. We have to see that we are all united by our gayness. Moreover, we are all united in our humanity. Change is coming if we can work together. Gay rights is not a struggle for just gays. It's a fight for all Americans about preserving the constitutional right for personal freedom and justice. We don't have to hate the haters. Society and straights aren't the enemy. It's old paradigms and outdated ways of thinking. We can use our anger constructively to change things, instead of being combative or self-destructive. But we can't be apathetic.

We need each other now more than ever. The battle of gay marriage reveals the truth. We are fighting a cultural war in our own country. An article title, "Gays face same enemy as Jews in '30's: hatred" in the *Miami Herald*, by Pulitzer Prize–winning commentator Leonard Pitts Jr., says it all.

It's such a bittersweet time for gays. While the fight for gay rights has grown more visible, the conservative backlash has grown more acrimonious. The more they see us, the more they protest. The future for gay rights certainly seems bright, but also uncertain. As we rub up against the mainstream, the line gets blurred between a bold desire for equality and a complacent desire to blend in. We may demand equal rights, but not demonstrate the resolve to get them. As a movement, we can be too unassertive, apologetic, and politically correct. We can't afford to just give the gay civil rights movement lip service. As a community, for the benefit of us all, we have to come together, hold people accountable for antigay sentiment, and show up for each other.

The best revenge for the hell gay men have been put through is to get out there and forge a fabulous life. Go for the best in yourself and have no guilt about it. We may think that being happy lets everyone who hurt us off the hook. At least if they can see we're miserable, they'll know how much they've made us suffer. Maybe we have a rescue fantasy. But we're the ones who are suffering most if we're wary, straight acting, sad, lonely, angry, and miserable. Use this book to explore your situation in the scheme of things, replace stuckness with movement, deprivation with options, and alienation with belonging.

Your potential is limitless. Quantum physics has shown that the universe is a fabric of possibility. When you look through a microscope, you'll discover that nothing is solid, or fixed. Everything is made up of atoms which are made up of space. We can reduce everything to smaller and smaller particles that just have more and more space emergent from a pool of endless potentiality. You have infinite space. You are bound by nothing. A limited idea like the "real man" can't stop you from unfolding and out-picturing the real you.

Subatomic particles have also been shown to change their behavior when they're being observed. It's like—"hey, someone's watching me, so I'll respond." This implies that you have the power to affect whatever you put your attention on. Your thoughts are incredibly powerful. In *What The Bleep Do We Know!?*, Dr. Emoto speaks about his proof that thoughts, feelings, and intentions affect physical reality. His research shows that water reflects the energy of the vibration it receives. When the molecules of water receive good thoughts, feelings, and intentions like a thank-you, love, and classical music, they form beautiful crystals when frozen. When the molecules of water receive bad thoughts, feelings, and intentions like I hate you, anger, and war, they look ugly. Our bodies are roughly 70 percent water. The movie asks rhetorically, "If thoughts can do that to water, imagine what they can do to us?" Can you imagine how the energy of positive thinking can change you? Put your attention on being the man you are with optimism and see what effect authenticity and right thinking have. Erasmus said, "It is the chiefest point of happiness that one is willing to be what one is." And Camus said, "What is happiness except the simple harmony between you and the life you lead?" Amazing men are waiting to respond.

So what are you still sitting there for? In the spirit of Unity New York's gay-affirmative senior minister Paul Tenaglia, "Get off your affirmations." Make this book come alive by putting its words into action. If you want to meet men, you can't afford to hide away. Unless you're in danger, I encourage you never to "hide" or subdue the gay man you are to any extent. Take your attention off fear and put it on revealing your full nature. You hurt no one else by being your full self. Yes, others may get upset, but you rob no one else by expressing yourself. Others will have their thoughts and feelings about you, but that has nothing to do with you. It's just their opinion, their expectations, and bondage to the "real man" image. Let them own that. Realize that there is nothing shameful about being a gay man. Snap a rubber band on your wrist every time you forget that reality. Until you're fully you, you keep yourself and everyone else living a lie. You stifle all that your life and the world can be— including full of love.

Oh, there is one more thing. I've included a bonus chapter packed with dating/relationship advice. How good is that? It's made up of several quick tips lists and twenty-five Ask Angelo letters. It's a pleasure hearing from you via *askangelo.com*.

Enjoy finding true love!

8

Quick Tips for Gay Dating/Relationships

Get Into the Know with Ask Angelo

> *"Know Thyself."*
>
> —Thales

Now, it's on to some dating/relationship advice, helping us come together for true love.

Whether you're single and don't want to be, just want more action, or to be closer to the man you're with, the straight-acting thing can get tired. "Straight-Acting, Straight-Appearing Only," "Masc/Musc," "Discreet," "No Fats, No Fems" are all too familiar. Attitudes like this don't make it easy for us to form relationships. You might want to try a different approach.

I want to share my Ten Quick Tips to Find True Love to show you how being your own man can really work. The more you're yourself, the more you'll attract someone. So forget dating tips that tell you how to change yourself to hitch a man. If you're not yourself, then your soul mate, the man who's looking for you, won't recognize you. Your catch is out there. While you can't control who takes, or doesn't take, the bait, my ten quick tips give you the best tool—yourself—to increase the chances that the right guy will. So be your own man, and the right man will come. You'll be a man magnet.

This isn't the same as being passive. Dating isn't something that just happens to you, especially if you're sitting home isolated. Dating requires focused effort, commitment, and stamina. Use my Ten Quick Tips to Find True Love to help you put yourself out there. You may have to get up and dust yourself off many times. But you can keep stepping back up to home plate, taking another swing.

The ten quick tips can be your set of keys to unlock new revolving doors, leading to your Mr. Right or Mr. Right now. Each begins with the letter F for fabulous, because you're so fab!

1. *Focus.* Each day, turn within and meet yourself. Exercising your mind strengthens it, just like a muscle. Have a daily centering practice. Recall that anything can be centering as long as you're practicing mindfulness. Being grounded in the present moment connects you to your source—you. Your real self shines through. When we are relaxed and authentic, people are drawn to us. Take someone like His Holiness the Fourteenth Dalai Lama of Tibet and author of *The Art of Happiness.* He exudes the message "Welcome." He pulls us toward him with his energy. We want to move closer. We want to be near him. Being centered attracts others to us. Try to take at least ten to fifteen minutes with my visualization below to experience groundedness for yourself. You might want to record it as well or visit *askangelo.com* for a download.

   Find a special place where you'll be safe and undisturbed. Allow yourself to get into a comfortable position. There is no right or wrong way to do this. It's simply time for you to be with yourself. Rate your level of anxiety from one (calmest) to ten (most stressed). Now let that number fade away. Know that there's so much solid support underneath your body, that all you need to do is just rest, just lean, allowing the full weight of your body to be completely upheld. Close your eyes and turn within.

Meet yourself. Take deep breaths in and out. Focus your attention on the rhythm of your breathing. Try to catch a glimpse of that space between each in- and out-breath. Good. Imagine your body is like a tall glass, and that your breath flows like a liquid. A beautiful, warm, peaceful color pours into you with each in-breath. It fills every space in your body. This calming, nourishing light infuses every cell with health, healing, and vitality. It relaxes the tightness in each and every muscle it touches. It begins to pool in your toes. It rises slowly to your ankles, knees, your hips, your torso. The light wraps your heart like a cozy blanket. It's well-beingness, goodness, and love that surrounds, softens, and balances your heart. It's comforting, nurturing, soothing, and safe. Nothing can hurt you now. Allow any cynicism and guardedness around your heart to melt away. The light rises to soften your shoulders, lowering them. It drains down and flows out the tips of your fingers. It moves up your neck, to your face. Relaxing your jaw, lips, nose, your eyes (we try so hard to see everything), ears, your brow. Now it fills you up to the top of your head. You begin to overflow in all directions like a glass that's too full. Imagine morphing into one big beautiful ball of light, shining brilliantly like a huge star, lighting up the entire universe, dwarfing everything else with your light—all wonderful glowing you. Now see yourself surrounded by this color—mellow, glimmering, perfect, harmonious. Give yourself a smile. Send yourself love and self-acceptance. Now imagine a bunch of balloons right in front of your lips. Imagine a different color breath flowing out of you with each exhale, carrying all the stress, strain, and tension from you. Push the balloons away higher and higher, farther and farther, smaller and smaller. Release all the worry, doubt, fear, struggle, and strife, the things you long for, the things you're crying over, the toxic poison—let it all go. Breathe it out. Are you still trying to hold on to it all? Surrender. Give it all up right here and now.

Unload, download, delete, purge, burn all unnecessary files. Breathe it all out. Good. Keep blowing the balloons so far away from you that you can hardly see them. Let them drift away. Send them off, up into the sky. You are tranquil now. Count backward slowly from ten to zero. Go deeper into relaxation with each number until you reach zero. Then, sit with yourself for a few moments. When you're ready, bring your attention back to those pauses between the in-breath and the out-breath. Rate your level of anxiety again from one to ten. What do you notice? Open your eyes.

2. *Figure it out.* Make a list of what you're looking for so you can better attract the right types of men, creating the relationships you want. Your list can be made up of both outer and inner qualities. Brainstorm first. Write down everything and anything. Then systematically narrow your list to what's absolutely essential. You could eventually whittle it down to a top-ten list. What you realize is that this list is a mirror of you. It reflects your desires. It isn't a picture of someone else. Be those qualities yourself. Since like attracts like, the kind of men you desire will fly to you like a boomerang. The list can also be used as a tool to gauge commonalities and red flags. Try to think of your list as a starting point, rather than a set of expectations to rule men out. You may also use the list to establish clarity for yourself. Your top-ten list list can help point you in the right direction regarding what you want with him. No one likes feeling the uncomfortable ambiguity and confusion that can come with not knowing if someone wants sex, dating, or friendship. If you know what you want with a particular kind of man, you can better put it out there and get it.

3. *Finesse.* Men are visual. They can feel aroused by what they see. You don't have to look like Ricky Martin, but do look

your personal best. It says, "I care about myself." Good grooming is also a sign of general stability and sanity. A fresh glow of esteem is attractive. A few small things can help give you that extra spark like teeth whitening, good skin care, a slight tan, having style, and such. It's not about superficiality or impressing. It's about making a good impression. You may want to consider what's stopping you from being your personal best, perhaps reviewing the confidence-building exercise in the pride section of chapter 7. Remind yourself that your imperfections make you uniquely beautiful. Your "one" will like all the quirky things about you. In the end, just remember not to be fooled by a dude's appearance. It's not what's on the outside that really matters. It's what's on the inside that counts.

4. *Fun*. A first date is not the time to talk about how much your ex screwed you over. Take a positive approach. Humor's good. Compliments are, too. Keep it light and on the short side the first time. Maybe up to a couple of hours if it goes well. Do something new that will be a fun experience for the two of you. Don't be shallow, but focus on just having a gay ol' time rather than "interviewing" your date. I recommend holding off on sex the first time you meet. Maybe wait a few dates. You may want to avoid one of those marathon dates where you spend twelve hours together, spill your whole life story and have sex three times. It can be too much too fast. Those intense encounters usually peter out relatively quickly. A relationship isn't made like instant oatmeal. Simply having fun will draw him back like a magnet for that second date.

5. *Fearlessness*. Even if you don't, act "as if" you have confidence. Men love this. Don't let fear of rejection stop you. If I hate liver and refused to eat the one you cooked for me, would you think that was about you? Of course not: I hate

liver! That's about me, my likes and dislikes, my preferences. If someone doesn't like the way you look, it's the same thing. It's about them! Rejection is about someone else getting what they want. Don't take rejection personally. The person simply isn't a good match for you. You're still beautiful. You're a prince with a glass slipper just searching for the right fit. Rejection is a four letter word—Next! Get right back on the horse and try again with some other hottie. Move on. Continue to hit on all the hot guys you like. Even if 999 of them turn out to be just pretty packages with junk inside, number 1000 could be the one. It's all research—a numbers game. Everyone has a chance to win, but you'll never get your Mr. 1000 if you stop trying at number eleven. Resist getting discouraged, feeling insecure, defeated, and giving up.

6. *Forget attitude.* Confidence is hot, arrogance isn't. As we've discussed in the section on openness in chapter 7, be inviting and nice, not aloof. Have a warm, open heart. People will feel safe and respond to that over a "tough guise." You may wish to revisit the section on openness to review the know-how. But one new thing to add here is to be aware of the nonverbal signals you're giving off. Up to 80 percent of our "messages" are transmitted very quickly, without a word, through body language. Only about 10 percent of our communication is conveyed through words. Make sure you're giving off the right vibe.

7. *Frequent.* Don't be a wallflower. Do things of interest to you that meet regularly and attract the type of guys you want to meet. You may want to refer to the discussion in chapter 7 on togetherness for the how-to. Recall asking "What do I do?" not "Where do I go?" If I'm interested in relaxation and want to meet warm-hearted guys, then I may want to

join a gay group that meets weekly, like a volunteer team, gay choir, poetry group, meditation, or chant circle.

8. *Free your mind.* Think outside the box. Observe the subtle signs. Look for social cues that say "I'm interested." Try staying open to someone different from your top-ten list. Sometimes someone good is right in front of you. There's a joke about a man in a flood. He climbs to the peak of his roof for safety as the water rises. A swimmer comes by, a guy in a boat, then a helicopter pilot—all to rescue him. But he doesn't go with any of them. He exclaims to each of the rescuers, "Go on, God will save me." He stays behind and drowns. When he comes before God, he asks, "Lord, why didn't you save me?" God replies, "What do you mean? I sent you a swimmer, a guy in a boat, and a helicopter pilot!"

9. *Fine.* Yes, you are fine. Believe in you. Share all the special inner and outer qualities you bring to the table. You have to highlight, profile, or "sell" yourself to date. Forget about the fatal flaw you think you have. Use your strengths. How come someone is missing out if they're not with you? Tell us! Cockiness, exaggeration, and lying aren't alluring, but confidence is.

10. *First (pickup) lines.* Have them ready, but not scripted. You have to leave room for wit and spontaneity. Just be you and it will all come out fine. You might want to try making eye contact, smiling, and saying "Hi, my name is _____." Repeat his name after he says it. Sync it all with a friendly handshake and that'll do it.

You will not be left out of love! So give it a shot. What have you got to lose? Go get 'em, tiger! You're where the party's at.

If you use my Ten Quick Tips to Find True Love, you will pull them in. But be prudent. Sometimes we can get blindsided by someone who's way hot. Here are my Seven Speedy Tips to Spot a Player before things get too serious. Do go in with an open heart, but be sure to read his signs clearly and obey them. Don't overlook:

1. *Secrets.* This is the elusive one who is vague about his life. Yes, mystery can be attractive and self-disclosure takes time, but too much mystery spells trouble. He may be hiding something you'd want to know.
2. *Lies.* Watch for inconsistencies. Is his profile different from the way he really is? Or last week he said one thing and this week it's another story? Or he forgot what he told you a few days ago? This is rarely a good sign. It goes to character. The last thing you want is someone deceptive or untrustworthy to mangle your heart.
3. *No follow through.* Canceling dates at the last minute, no-shows, tardiness, promised calls at seven o'clock that never come. When this happens, run the other way. You deserve nothing less than respect and courtesy about changes in plans. It takes less than a minute to make a call and say "I can't make it," and it says a lot. If he consistently doesn't do this, you need to read between the lines—it's all about him. It's called the Me-Me-Me-Me-Me personality! The message is that you're not a priority to him. No matter how busy we are, when we want to be with someone we make time.
4. *When sex is the focus* and it's always at your place, a hotel, or some other hot spot. Sex on the spinning laundry machine is wild fun, but when you never get invited to his place or asked to dinner, you need to be concerned. And if he's only available on certain days to be with you, you're probably not the only one in his Rolodex.
5. *When he looks* at everything that walks by, if he seems to know everyone, or calls you the wrong name, then maybe there are

too many notches in his bedpost. Wandering eyes is perhaps the worst offender. No, he's not shy. It spells disinterest and blatant disrespect. If this happens, excuse yourself, get up, and leave. You deserve to be the focus of his attention. You want someone who wants to be with YOU just because you're wonderful. "Feeling you" has to be a two-way street.

6. *Phrases like "Take me out,"* "Buy me a drink," and "I have no money" are definite tellers. This includes getting stuck with the tab. Is it "costing" him anything to be in relationship with you? Do you get gifts? Does he take you out? Rub your shoulders? Does he go out of his way and sacrifice for you without you having to ask?

7. *A tiny cell phone* reveals a lot. If he's repeatedly on the cell during lunch or constantly checking his messages, it implies you're not important. Don't be a side dish. If he's more into his phone than you, tell him to put it on vibrate and stick it. Then go find yourself a piece of filet mignon.

When you click with a Mr. Right or Mr. Right Now, things can get wild fast. Here are my Ten Fast Tips on Safe Sex for the heat of the moment. Avoid mixing sex with:

1. *Alcohol.* Drinking lowers inhibitions, so you may do things you wouldn't, if sober. Drinking in excess clouds your decision-making, making it easier to get caught up in the heat of the moment. Drink in moderation, so you can still think clearly.

2. *Drugs.* Illicit substance use also alters your mind. You simply cannot make good decisions when you're using. Try to do it sober, staying in tune with yourself and your partner during sex.

3. *Loneliness.* It's easy to let your guard down if you think sex is the only way to get the affection that you need. You may compromise your health by barebacking to please or feel close to your partner. You don't have to subscribe to a feel-

ing of desperation inside or his "put out or get out" mentality. Call a friend for a hug instead, or join a support group or organization.

4. *Depression*. Self-destructive behavior like unsafe sex may serve to confirm a hidden belief that you're not valuable or lovable. Not protecting yourself may be a cry for help. You may be saying, "I don't care," in the heat of the moment, but that's your depression talking. You may be trying to counteract the anguish of depression with the raw pleasure of unprotected sex. Perhaps you don't even want sex. Maybe you just want to be held like you were precious. Shoot for intimacy instead of sex. Talk with a trusted friend or professional.

5. *Silence*. "If I pretend HIV doesn't exist and don't talk about it, then there's no problem." My advice is to talk, talk, talk, talk, talk about sex—before, during, and after you have it—clearly, openly, and honestly.

6. *Assumptions*. "He looks healthy, so he must be negative." "If he were positive, he'd surely tell me." Don't assume anything. Seek clarity by asking questions.

7. *Poor Judgment*. This is living for the moment. "The hell with everything. He's my fantasy." "He's so hot, I'll do whatever he wants." He may not be trustworthy, or he maybe taking advantage of, or manipulating you, for his own gratification. Trusting someone requires getting to know him better. Get the information you need about him up front to make sound choices.

8. *Wrong Information*. "The new HIV meds are as good as a cure." "If I'm the top, I'm totally safe." "It can't ever happen to me." Dispel myth, hearsay, and false ideas. Get current accurate information.

9. *Being Macho*. "Real men don't use condoms." "It doesn't feel as good with a condom." Yet another reason to ditch the "real man."

10. *Being Unprepared.* "I don't have any condoms or water-based lube." Think it through. Plan ahead. Be prepared.

Having sex too quickly can create the illusion of intimacy. After an orgasm, our ego boundaries can "dissolve" for a short time and we might feel "united" with the person we're with. This is lust, infatuation, passion, even desperation, but not love. Emotional closeness comes from knowing someone's person, not just their body. Sex can be the easy way out. Intimacy is much harder to achieve. Sex can be fleeting. It's over within a few minutes to a few hours. Words don't have to be spoken during sex. You don't even have to know the person's name. It can be impersonal. Intimacy isn't required for sex. Intimacy means allowing yourself to be fully available as you are to another person. It's sharing your whole self. It's being yourself without any facades. Remember that unless you allow yourself to be fully yourself with a man—that is, showing both your more masculine and feminine sides—and unless you allow him to be fully himself with you, you really won't be able to build emotional intimacy together. For something meaningful, I obviously recommend building an intimacy base along with sex. Having said that, I don't discourage sex for its own sake, as long as you're aware it won't bring you love all by itself, and as long as you keep it safe.

But if you want things to last, you'll eventually have to go beyond the surface. Here are my Ten Sizzling Secrets to Have Him Stick Around:

1. *Daily Maintenance.* Now, I know it's tempting to want to keep things light. But the No. 1 secret is that any lasting, quality relationship doesn't just happen. It takes continuous work and effort. Think devotion, responsibility, and commitment. You have to maintain a relationship if you want it to last, like you would maintain a car, home, plant, or pet. The

following secret steps are specific examples of daily maintenance.

2. *Open Two-Way Communication.* I tell my couples, "talk-talk-
talk-talk-talk." Talking is your best friend. It works in two
directions. Think versatile. A big one in this department is
not to assume your lover knows you. He's not a gifted psy-
chic who can read your mind. You have to tell him who you
are and how you operate. That way he can adjust his behavior and move closer to you. Maybe you're the kind of person
who needs to hear "I love you" five times a day. But your
partner doesn't say it because no one said it in his family. He
shows you his love by sending you flowers. But you're aller-
gic to flowers. You break out in hives. You're getting the picture. Clear communication can help you avoid a lot of mis-
understandings and unnecessary hurt feelings.

3. *Try Not to Have Expectations.* This goes in tandem with
open, two-way communication. Expectations can be bad for
relationships. Maybe you pay the rent and expect him to help
around the house, but he doesn't take the initiative. So
resentment builds between you that culminates in intimate
partner violence. Or you expect him to initiate sex, but since
you never make a move, nothing ever happens because he
thinks you're not attracted to him. He cheats, you find out,
and the relationship ends. Make your desires very clear to
avoid trouble in paradise.

4. *Maintain Intimacy.* Ask him "What's new?" or "How was
your day?" Take the time each day to connect with him.
What are his struggles? What are his dreams? Do you know
his history? We all need to be fully seen and heard and to
know that someone will be there for us when the chips are
down. Keep the emotional connection alive. Take a nonsexual shower together and wash each other, play patty cakes,

thumb wrestle, tickle, routinely hold hands, hug, snuggle, kiss, caress, etc.

5. *Try to grasp his perspective* on things by listening. Really listen. In fact, make active listening an important component in all of these steps. Respect his point of view. Come from a place of curiosity and compassion, not judgment. If you disagree on something, find the common ground and work from there. It's not about two men competing—who's right or wrong. It's about understanding one another.

6. *Respect.* Conflict is unavoidable. To sail through it, try bringing things back to yourself. You can do this by using "I" statements that own your feelings. Don't attack the person. Share what you're feeling about a specific behavior. A general formula could be, "When you do X, I feel Y." Try prefacing it or ending it with a caring, affirmative statement. Consider that saying, "You're fat" is quite different from, "Although I'd like to, I have trouble feeling as sexual toward you as I once did when you eat a pint of Häagen-Dazs every night. And yes, I still love you." Or "You're a lazy slob" versus, "I know you care and that you'd never do anything to upset me on purpose, but when you leave the cap off the lube, I step on it in the morning and it makes a mess. I go ballistic because cleaning it up makes me late for work. How can we negotiate this?" This approach decreases defensiveness, helping a solution along.

7. *Compromise.* You will disagree. It's how you work it out that matters. Conflict is a part of every relationship. What's important is how we work through the conflict and move toward solutions without attacking the other person. Don't criticize him. Practice patience and forgiveness rather than nagging. Resentment and contempt can be death sentences for a relationship. If resolved properly, disagreement can

actually bring people closer together, rather than being divisive, because you know each other better in the end. Avoid trying to change him. Avoid losing your own identity, too. A couple is a whole unit that has two separate, albeit overlapping, parts. Remember your "I" statements and to communicate respectfully. I suggest trying my Firm Formula. This communication strategy can be used to resolve just about anything. It has six steps.

Step 1. Begin with a positive statement about how you feel about the person. Like, "I love you and I'm concerned about you."

Step 2. Next state your intentions about the relationship. Such as, "I really want this to work between us."

Step 3. Lay out the problem as you see it, using concrete examples of the person's behavior. For instance, "I think_____ because you do x, y, and z."

Step 4. Explain how the problem affects you and your relationship to the person. Like, "I feel x and it causes me to _____ (pull away from you)."

Step 5. Ask for what you need. Such as, "I need you to _____."

Step 6. Problem solve. For instance, "Are you willing to try a, b, and c with me?"

Now you're on your way to successful communicating!

8. *Appreciate* him for what he is. Remember what attracted you to him and why you love him. Focus on his good attributes. Give him compliments freely and often: "Honey, you've got great knees that drive me wild—you're so hot."

9. *Support and encourage* him about things that are important to him. Help him relax and unwind in a way he likes. Give

favors like a backrub or footrub. Make him dinner or do his laundry. Rent his favorite movie.

10. *Keep things fresh and fun.* Newness keeps the fires burning. Go out and experience novel things together. Practice spontaneity. Keep dating no matter how long you've been together. Take in a comedy show or a movie, go dancing, to a water park or amusement park, Rollerblade, etc. Romance him. Do dinner and the theater. Surprise him with flowers, chocolates, and presents—just because. Don't forget the bedroom. Spice it up with new positions, foods, fantasy, role plays, and accessories.

That's it for my tips lists. Next, I hope you enjoy browsing through some Ask Angelo letters, finding many that suit your needs. All my best to you, Angelo.

Dear Angelo,
Why do so many gay men find it hard to get over past relationships? I have seen many gay friends be destroyed and deeply hurt by past relationships and some of them weren't even good ones. My friend is still pining over someone who treated him like dirt.
Signed, Straight Ally

Dear Straight Ally,
First off, thanks for your letter. We need more of you. As far as your question goes, for a person who has been thirsty in the desert for years, love is like water. They want to hold on to every drop for as long as they can. They know what it's like when it's all dry out there.

Most gay men are wounded from never getting the love they needed and deserved from family, friends, the world, or each other. So they may be starving, craving love. Who can blame them for clinging to love when they find it, not wanting to let it go? Even if the love was "bad," they may still hold on. Perhaps, listening to a beaten-down esteem, they may think that's all they deserve. But letting go is an important part of life. It's a worthwhile endeavor to learn how to surrender. We won't have room for our true partner to come into our hearts until we clean out old loves. Releasing a person requires a period of actively grieving. Most of us avoid this loss. Holding on to a past love can give us an external focus. We're able to avoid feeling the pain inside.

We can choose to let go of someone, having faith that there will be someone else. A new, better love will show up. We can't doubt it. Meanwhile, we have to fill our pain and emptiness with ourselves, not another person.

All the Best, Angelo.

Dear Angelo,
I feel like I'm not good enough for most of the guys out there.
I like this guy at the local gay pub. He's twenty-eight. I'd ask
him out, but I feel like a loser. I'm afraid I'm ugly and all
washed-up. Is there any hope for me besides plastic surgery?
Signed, Washed-Up

Dear Washed-Up,
Whether you are gorgeous or not, there will always be one person who will be blinded by your shining beauty. Of course you can help Mother Nature along with a fabulous upgrade to first class: quality product, grooming, some new threads, and a pleasant disposition. In the end, it doesn't matter if you're really nice-looking, young and sassy, or not. What matters is that you think you are.

You can look in the mirror and see a new man. Someone you like. Someone who has confidence. I've seen regular-looking guys pick up on gorgeous ones because they know how to work what they've got. And I've seen gorgeous guys go home alone. So go over to that crush. I bet he'd love someone to grab his hand and say with charming confidence, "Buy you a drink?"

All the Best, Angelo.

Dear Angelo,
I'm single and met a guy online. How do I go about asking him to meet me for real?
Signed, Real Time

Dear Real Time,
The important thing overall is to be aware of your own expectations. Don't set yourself up to meet the perfect love of your life like Cinderella. Keep an open mind. Few people will be exactly like they look or state in their profile. Try not to get too disappointed. Leave a little "wiggle" room.

Make the first encounter brief. It's just an introduction, not a date, marriage proposal, or U-Haul contract. Suggest meeting in a popular, public place like Starbucks. Somewhere like that is safe, easy to find, easy to leave, and not easy for the drama queens to make a scene. Make it a half-hour meeting unless he's not what he said. Then it's perfectly fine to respectfully say so and exit: "I'm looking for a workout partner. I don't recognize you as the athletic guy in the picture. This isn't a match for me, sorry." If it goes well, resist pouring your soul out for three hours! Instead, schedule a second, longer, meeting or set up a date. To build a foundation of greater intimacy, try not to have sex the first few meetings unless you're just looking to hook up. Hookup surveillance can take just five minutes. If you're interested, be sure to talk about HIV status, avoid drugs and alcohol, and play safe. A good line if you're not interested can be just "Sorry guy, not a match." In the context of strictly sexual sites, the rest is understood and usually isn't taken personally.

Sexually speaking, many of us have very specific turn-ons we're looking for. We may try to plug others into those flawless pictures in our heads. We might criticize them when they don't meet our expectations. Remember, your desires are about you. They're not about deficiencies in the other person. Own your preferences in a way that doesn't put someone down, even if they misrepresent themselves. Try "Sorry, I liked the redhead in your profile," not, "See yah later, you bleached-blond bimbo."

In general, try trashing attitude. It's not inviting. Download warmth and friendliness with other gay men. We're all in this together. Most important, be yourself and respect others. You'll get "hits" both online and off.

All the Best, Angelo.

Dear Angelo,
I am outgoing at work, but when I go to clubs I become very shy. How can I bring that outgoing person to the club?
Signed, Very Shy

Dear Very Shy,
You already have what it takes. Just transfer your strengths from work to the club. But to do this, you have to move outside your comfort zone at work.

Perhaps socializing at work is easier for you because you have to interact in order to do a good job and earn money. There are clearly defined roles at work, so it can be less personal. It's even encouraged to be insensitive in business. It's acceptable to be strong, aggressive, even ruthless to "make a killing." The person you are at work may not be the same person you are in your personal life.

Meeting gay guys in your private life can be scary. You are more vulnerable being seen as you, not your job title. It's not easy to put yourself out there. Outside of business, men have a lot of social barriers to break through to meet each other. Gay men have the help of strong attraction to assist them, but it can still be hard for us to break the ice. Approaching other gay men involves intense emotions, including anxiety and a sense of vulnerability.

To bust out, transfer the confidence you have at work to your social life. When you are at the club, call upon your strengths by acting "as if" you were at work. Simply integrate what you already do well at work, like being outgoing, into the club scene. Don't take the club too seriously. Just stick out your hand, smile warmly, and say charmingly, "Hi, I'm very shy." They'll be sure to love you.

All the Best, Angelo.

Dear Angelo,
This guy has a boyfriend. The other day we were hanging out and fooled around. He got into a fight with his BF about it, but they're still together. I don't want to be a home wrecker, but am still interested in this guy. What do I do?
Signed, Restless Home Wrecker

Dear Restless Home Wrecker,
It's frustrating to have a crush on someone who's taken. Ask him if he's in an open relationship. If so, it would be important to know how committed he is to his partner. Is he just looking for a fun hookup, or is he thinking of breaking it off? If it's for fun, don't have expectations for something more. If he's breaking up, will you be his rebound? Talk about things with him openly so you know where you stand.

We as gay men need to respect each other's relationships. If a guy says he has a BF, it's taken too often as meaningless data. Suddenly he becomes more desirable because we can't have him. Then it becomes about our egos trying to get him. We may think—if I can steal him, it proves I'm great. Our self-esteem gets a big boost. Well, if we truly felt good about ourselves, we wouldn't need to do this.

You probably don't want a guy who's cheating on his BF, either. Ask yourself—couldn't he do the same to you? What does this say about his character? Is this the kind of virtue you respect? Is this the type of person you want for a partner? Do you want to be betrayed, or feel second-best? Think of taming a wild horse. You may think you'll be that special one to tie him down. But stallions like to run wild. Respect yourself. Find a man who'll be there in the morning with 100 percent of the love you deserve.

All the Best, Angelo.

Dear Angelo,

I've been dating a guy I really like for about two months. The feelings are definitely mutual. The problem is, during the first few weeks the sex was really hot—and really versatile. But once our feelings started growing, he started insisting that he prefers to be only top. While he can get crabby about it, he's told me that I'm the first guy he's ever had feelings for, and before me his gay sex life was all just hookups. Do you have any insight into what might be happening?

Signed, Bottoms Up

Dear Bottoms Up,

We have three big clues as to what might be going on here. First, your sex life was versatile. Second, it switched abruptly when feelings emerged. Third, you're the first guy he's had feelings for. Now I'm not trying to be Nancy Drew, but it sounds like he may be feeling vulnerable and exposed—kind of like a crab that's been flipped on it's back. When we begin to fall for someone, it can be scary. We're emotionally naked and we risk being hurt. We do things to protect ourselves.

He may need to be the top to maintain a sense of dominance—power and control. If he's having issues with his sexuality, being the top may also be a way for him to maintain his manhood. Being the top for a while may help him to manage his emotions. Things can become balanced and versatile again once he feels emotionally safe enough in the relationship.

So ride him out if you can.

All the Best, Angelo.

Dear Angelo,
I've been dating this Neg guy for about four months. I'm in love. But I'm Poz and he doesn't know. I swear I've only had safe sex with him, but he's the bottom. What should I do?
Signed, Guilty

Dear Guilty,
Loving someone romantically involves our deepest experience of oneness. When we are in love, we are as close as we can be physically, emotionally, mentally, spiritually, and socially to anyone. Poz men aren't alone in not wanting to be rejected. Rejection from a love is a terribly painful feeling for anyone—a gut-wrenching pain. If we're facing challenges, emotionally wounded, or need more love in our life, this pain can be excruciating. We may do anything to avoid it. But you have to be courageous and not be afraid to tell him the truth.

Draw upon your love for him to respect him and tell him your HIV status. Trust that it will be as it is meant to be. He may be angry and feel betrayed. He may feel you've been dishonest and that he can't trust you. But in the spirit of colleague Kathryn Alice, author of *Love Will Find You,* if you're meant to be together, nothing can keep you apart. You'll work through it. It'll work out. No matter what. But if you're not meant to be together, it won't work out. No matter what. If he leaves, he wasn't your man. It's better for you. The next guy could be your soul mate. True love is when you're both there each day because you each want to be. So it's best to share what you need and want in your relationships up front.

Looking forward, it's a must to disclose your HIV status before becoming sexual—early on. There may be a legal obligation in some states to disclose. Get it out of the way. It lessens the worry about it. Don't you want someone to choose to be with you as you are? Would you want anything less? Share the truth. It shows you care about yourself and your partner.

All the Best, Angelo.

Dear Angelo,
I like a guy I see out. Three years have gone by and we're still playing games. I want to have someone, but I can't seem to do it. I become bored, scared, and too picky. If I choose just one guy, I think I'm missing out on fun or finding someone better. I'm forty-one and wondering how to get myself out of this adolescent phase.
Signed, Still Playing the Field

Dear Still Playing the Field,
Americans live in a death-fearing culture that prizes youth over old age. Gay culture intensifies this and it can discourage "maturity." The message portrayed in the gay media is "Stay young, hot, hard, and party."

During adolescence, bravado male teenagers normally focus on their appearance, being masculine, peers, cliques, competition, cruising, scoring, substance use, being carefree, idealistic, and sometimes mean-spirited. This may sound like some gay men you know. Adolescence is often closeted for gay men. We can miss out on dating, "sowing our oats," and other irresponsible fun at the appropriate time. So gay men often relive their "adolescence" in their adult years.

The essential developmental milestones of adolescence are separating from parents, creating identity, and developing intimacy. Growing up, accepting responsibility, achieving a solid sense of self, and developing the capacity for real intimacy can all be hard to achieve. Older mentors often guide youth into adulthood through hazardous rights of passage, like Gandalf did for Frodo in *Lord of the Rings.* But, unfortunately, there isn't a lot of mentoring between older and younger gays. The myths of the lecherous old man and the sugar daddy get in the way.

We can get lost without mentors, wives, or children to guide us. They can encourage us to grow up and be responsible. If our "parents" are our homophobic culture, gay men can rebel, disobeying the rules, going wild. But at the same time, we can long for our "parents'" steadfast love and acceptance. While jetting loose, we might really desire to be lassoed. While running free, we feel loved, knowing someone's there for us. It's like a toddler who darts away from his caretakers only to look back—just to make sure they're still there.

If you choose to settle down, loving one person in the now, you will reap far greater rewards than playing the field can ever bring.

All the Best, Angelo.

Dear Angelo,
I give everything to the man I love. I always put him first—even before myself. I drive two hours to see him. Twice I told him I loved him, and that's when everything fell apart. I just don't

know what I did wrong. After that, he said he wanted to date other people. I still buy him stuff, spending thousands of dollars on him. He calls me and texts me when he's lonely on his business trips. But he never just says he misses me or makes an effort to see me. It's so hard. I've turned to drinking, drugs, and antidepressants to be happy so I don't dwell on it. What can I do to save myself?
Signed, Falling Apart

Dear Falling Apart,
The best thing for you to do is reality-test. See the situation clearly as it is. Much suffering comes from resisting reality. This guy's a taker, not a giver. Save your money. Stop trying to "buy" his affection. He doesn't demonstrate the same feelings for you that you have for him. Realize that when he contacts you, it's because he's lonely. It's all about him. His calling or texting has nothing to do with you. You have to recognize that you're being used and let this one go.

It's time to put yourself first. Lay off the alcohol and drugs. They may offer you a reprieve, but they make things worse overall. Instead, face the truth and feel to heal. Get support. I know it hurts deeply, but avoiding it is far more dangerous than grieving it.

All the Best, Angelo.

Dear Angelo,
I've been seeing this guy for about two weeks. I don't really like him, but he really likes me. I don't want to hurt his feelings. I have a lot of anxiety over it. I want to break it off. What do I tell him?
Signed, Ax Man

Dear Ax Man,
I recommend you be straightforward and tell him exactly what

you want. You don't have to explain "why." All you need to do is
be clear in your communication about "what."

I wouldn't tell him by e-mail. Unless you feel unsafe, it's most
respectful to tell him in person rather than over the phone. Try
saying with a gentle tone, "It's not working for me and I need to
stop seeing you." In this case, don't sugarcoat it with, "We can
be friends" or "It's not you, it's me," because that would be disingenuous. You don't have to be harsh, you just have to be frank
and firm. Remember you can say anything to anyone—it's how
you say it that matters.

Don't worry. If you have good intentions overall, i.e. you're not
hurting him on purpose, he'll recoup. He's an adult who can take
care of himself. You don't have an obligation to take care of him.

All the Best, Angelo.

Dear Angelo,
I'm in my forties and am drawn to guys in their early twenties,
but it always ends up not working. How come I'm attracted to
guys half my age?
Signed, The Chicken Ranch

Dear The Chicken Ranch,
The obvious and simple answer is that youth represents virility,
which is attractive to men. The fountain of youth has been sought
for all time. But on a deeper level, perhaps you are trying to stay
young forever yourself by having young hotties by your side.

I'm also curious about what age was hardest for you coming
out? I bet it was your early twenties. Sometimes we unconsciously connect with certain types of people to heal ourselves.
By getting with younger guys, you may be attempting to heal the
part of yourself that was hurting at that age. When you were in
your early twenties, did you desire someone to befriend you,
mentor you into gay manhood (not in a sexual way), love you for

you, and do the things you do for these guys? Of course you did. We all needed this guidance at some point.

I recommend you focus on befriending your inner child. Your relationships might become more balanced or egalitarian.

All the Best, Angelo.

Dear Angelo,
I am a fifty-five-year-old guy who constantly gets hit on by younger guys. Some of them are so young they could be my son. Why is it the young guys hit on me? Am I sending some kind of wrong message? I don't want to be a sugar daddy.
Signed, I'm Not Your Sugar Daddy

Dear I'm Not Your Sugar Daddy,
Yes, some guys do deceive older men for money with greed masked as affection. But this can also be an unfair stereotype that keeps older and younger men apart.

Many young guys prefer older men. Maybe you're comfortable in your own skin. Men, especially if they're in their twenties, are attracted to confidence. This is when they're still trying to figure out life and who they are. They may be drawn to your stability, maturity, success, and wisdom. While you want an equal partner and not to be in the role of someone's father, we're all each other's teachers to some degree.

Don't presume. Get to know each guy. Judge their suitability to be with you on their individual merits.

All the Best, Angelo.

Dear Angelo,
I know this guy at work. I always catch him looking right at me as if he is waiting for me to say something. I wonder if he is gay or just friendly. I want to start a chat, but have no idea how to do that without coming on to him, yet I think that's

what he wants me to do. Neither of us is out at work. Do you
have any suggestions on how to break the ice?
Signed, 9 to 5

Dear 9 to 5,
Try to avoid guessing what he's thinking. Only mind readers can
do that. Here's what I suggest. Ignore the conversation in your
head. Stop talking to yourself and talk to him.

Next time you see him, take a deep breath, look him in the
eye, smile, reach out your hand, and say, "Hi, I'm 9 to 5." Just be
yourself. Go with the flow. If you're stumped, bring it back to
work—what you know you have in common. Get to know him as
a person first for a bit. Make the gay thing second and the sex
thing third. If you're not comfortable being direct with him, you
can float a gay feeler like—"So, what'd you think of *Brokeback
Mountain?*"

All the Best, Angelo.

Dear Angelo,
I met a guy who said he was too messed up to date seriously.
Two months later, he was doting all over me and telling me
how much he liked me, cooking me dinners, sending me off to
work with packed lunches, and constantly inviting me into his
close circle of friends. I reciprocated. Then he stopped it all.
Was I played by a serial dater?
Signed, Serial Dater Victim

Dear Serial Dater Victim,
I imagine this is confusing and quite disappointing for you. When
we are "falling" for a guy, we can overlook his flaws. Many of us
just want to get hitched so badly. We may ignore the red flags
and proceed anyway. This is understandably human. But your man
actually gave you a big flashing stop sign. He told you right off

the bat that "he was too messed up to date seriously." Would you really want someone who tells you they're unavailable up front?

Let me ask you. If you saw a warning sign on a cage in a pet store—I bite—would you disregard it and pet the cute little doggy inside anyway? Would you be upset if it bit you hard on the finger? While it is easier said than done in matters of the heart, my advice is to obey what the warning sign says. It's like seeing him on the beach in a thong—what you see is what you get.

All the Best, Angelo.

Dear Angelo,
I'm dating this guy and he wants to sleep with anyone he wants.
I don't think it's such a good idea. How do we navigate this?
Signed, Sexual Freedom

Dear Sexual Freedom,
This issue has to be talked about openly, honestly, and clearly. Consider my *Eight Quick Suggestions for an Open Relationship*. It's best if the two of you:

1. Equally agree that nonmonogamy is wanted. If one person wants it and one doesn't, it won't work well.
2. Use an open relationship to build upon an already healthy relationship, not salvage it. So many couples make the mistake of opening up their relationship in an attempt to fix it. This doesn't work. Your relationship has to be healthy enough to sustain the issues that arise from the freedom of an open relationship, like security, trust, and devotion. Successful couples who open up their relationship have their partner as their primary emotional commitment. They have a strong emotional foundation, making each other No. 1. There's usually a prohibition against outside romance and separation between love and sex.

3. "Play" in order to complement an already good enough sex life between you, not fix it. So many couples also make the mistake of opening up their relationship in an attempt to save their sex life. This doesn't work either. Your sex life has to be healthy enough to add other men into the mix. Other guys should supplement your sex life as a couple, not replace it.
4. Avoid possessiveness by creating the right balance of independence and together time.
5. Continue to commit to, be present for, romance, nourish, and nurture each other.
6. Mutually develop clear rules about "playing" and honor them honestly.
7. Set boundaries around "tricks" to avoid jealousy, especially around time and money.
8. Be honest and respectful of each other, taking your partner's feelings into account.

All the Best, Angelo.

Dear Angelo,
This is the first time I have ever approached this question with another person besides my partner. We have been together for six years and he is HIV-positive and I am HIV-negative. As time has passed, his sexual drive keeps going down. He has tried everything and he says he just doesn't feel anything. Do you know of any further steps to maybe help put a little spark back into the fire?
Regards, Always Looking to Keep the Fire

Dear Always Looking to Keep the Fire,
Thank you for the trust you are placing in me. It shines forth in your question how committed you are to keeping the passion alive between you and your partner. Romance in a relationship

normally ebbs and flows over time. Lust for a partner naturally decreases over the life of a relationship and as each person ages.

However, there is cutting-edge scientific research in *Why We Love: The Nature and Chemistry of Romantic Love* by anthropologist Helen Fisher, which shows that the best way to reignite romance with your partner and keep it burning is through novelty. The key is to keep doing new things together and having new experiences with each other. This increases a pleasure chemical in our brain called dopamine, which plays a huge role in the good feelings of romantic love and drives up lusty testosterone levels. So get the creative juices flowing and surprise your partner with spontaneous, caring, fun things to do and keep your romance red hot!

Yet, we have more chemistry to review. Decreases in testosterone from HIV and uncomfortable side effects of HIV medicines can put the brakes on lust and take anyone's mind off sex. Who would be in the mood if they were feeling drained, nauseous, cranky, and suffering from rashes, pains, diarrhea, or a bad headache? Be supportive of your partner's need to say when he is not in the mood for sex. He may have valid physical reasons. A physician's advice can help. A large part of his loss in sex drive can be psychological, too. Feeling down and nervous can be normal responses to the heavy pressures of living with HIV, including concerns about not wanting to infect you. His not feeling anything might be a sign of depression. You can suggest lovingly to your partner that he be evaluated for depression by a psychiatrist. Antidepressant treatment is available. Couples therapy could also be a wonderful way to try something new for you guys. Therapy is an educational tool for personal growth. It doesn't mean there's anything crazy about either of you or that your relationship is bad.

Continue to talk to your partner directly about things. Move toward him. Find out more what his inner world is like. Get your needs met, but remain open to the part your needs may be playing in this as well. Together you will find a solution that works best for your relationship.

All the Best, Angelo.

Dear Angelo,
I've been dating this guy for eighteen months. We have sex once every week on his water bed. How often should we be having sex?
Signed, The Dead Sea

Dear The Dead Sea,
I was not able to find any specific studies about how often gay men or gay couples have sex. Dr. Kinsey found that both men and women have sex an average of 2.8 times a week in their twenties, 2.2 times a week in their thirties, and once a week in their fifties. The numbers for gay men could be higher. According to a *Sex in America* survey of unmarried cohabitating couples, 36 percent of unmarried men and women have sex a few times per month, 40 percent a few times a week, and for 15 percent it's four or more times a week. The numbers for gay couples may be different. Age and length of time together play key roles. But I want to caution you about measuring your relationship against this data. Everyone has different sexual needs and desires. So every couple does, too.

There is a wide range of sexual activity among couples. How many times you have sex with your partner has little to do with the joy and fulfillment of your sex life as a couple. And the number of times you're having sex with your partner is right for the two of you if you're happy—no matter how much everyone else is doing it.

Is a healthy gay couple one that has sex daily? Twice a week?

Once a month? Can a celibate gay couple be healthy, too? Is monogamy the way to go for gay couples? Open relationships? Is just staying single better? It does take different strokes for different folks.

All the Best, Angelo.

Dear Angelo,
I met this really great guy, but I didn't think he was my type. Well, to make a long story short, he said I was the kind of guy he could have a long-term relationship with. We started dating. Since then, I fell for him, but I've discovered he likes to party. I have done my party time. But I don't want to lose him. What can I do?
Signed, My Frat Houser

Dear My Frat Houser,
It's hard when your partner behaves in a way that doesn't work for you. I would like you to do the following exercise with me to take "inventory" of your Mr. Right. You may be thinking, "that's dumb" or "I don't have time." But it's worthwhile to do this for yourself to know what you want in a partner so you can find the answer you seek. Find a quiet place to do this and try not to rush it.

Make a long list of all the things you want in an ideal partner. Then circle the things on your list that you must have in a man. Now put your list aside for a moment. We will come back to it. Next, make another list of things you like about your current partner. We'll call this "his list." Now refer back to your list, the one you put aside. Circle the items on "his list" that match the circled items on your list. Notice what's circled on both lists. Take a moment to have gratitude for all that is good in your relationship. Try not to take those for granted. Let him know how much you appreciate him for those things. Next go back to "his list." Add things you don't like about his behavior. Then put a square around the items on "his list" that are opposite of the circled items on your list. Those represent areas in which your partner lacks what you must have in a partner. In fact, in those areas he has the opposite qualities of what you need. Notice what these are. Which are nonnegotiable? Is partying one of them? Are there a lot more? What does this mean to you? What's the overall balance of matches to nonmatches? Give your partner a chance to do the same exercise. Then talk about possible solutions with each other. It's a balancing act.

The security of a relationship can protect us from the fear of being alone. But recognizing the difference between the picture of the relationship you have in your head with the one you actually got is important. Through this awareness exercise, my wish for you is that you become empowered to take action, creating the relationship you want.

All the Best, Angelo.

Dear Angelo,
I am a nineteen-year-old guy and have been dating a guy for almost seven months, and I am unsure now whether I want to be. I am madly in love with him. However, sometimes I lust after other beautiful guys. I am puzzled as to what to do.
Please help.
Signed, Betwixt Boy

Dear Betwixt Boy,
Having these different feelings can be confusing. I am going to break consensus thinking and say your feelings are perfectly normal. Try not to feel guilty.

Feelings of lust, romance, and commitment are powerful urges—but according to anthropologist Dr. Helen Fisher, they are independent ones. She says we all have the ability to lust after

someone in a video we're watching, while we're having a romantic affair with someone else at the office, while we're committed
in a long-term partnership with yet someone else at home. We
each have the potential to "love" three different people, in these
three different ways, all at the same time! In her book, *Why We
Love: The Nature and Chemistry of Romantic Love,* Dr. Fisher's
research shows that lust, romance, and commitment are three
distinct human drives hardwired into our brains. These basic
drives are as potent as hunger and direct our behavior for their
own purposes. Lust energizes gay men to get out and sample
men. Romantic love allows us to choose one man to focus on,
conserving our mating energy. Commitment allows us to feel
emotionally engaged with that man long enough to stick around
and help each other survive.

Interestingly, each drive influences the other. Romance, for
example, reportedly lasts for up to eighteen months–the exact
time you have been in your relationship! Dr. Fisher describes, as
commitment feelings like security, calmness, and unity increase
between a couple (after eighteen months), feelings of lust and
romance fall between them. This seems to be because lust and
romance give us energy to seek and choose a long-term partner.
Once we have that partner, we no longer have to woo them. But
the drives of lust and romance don't disappear. Thus, we begin
to desire others. For men, wanting someone other than their
partner enables them to spread their "seeds" quick and far. This
trait is very desirable from an evolutionary point of view to produce the most offspring. However, this isn't to be used as an
argument for or against monogamy, nor is it an attempt to excuse
infidelity or endorse polygamy. Biology isn't destiny.

We all may have a dual capacity for monogamy or not, but
monogamy boils down to choice. Fantasies may be human and
natural, as long as they remain thoughts and feelings. Acting on
them is another matter. We have individual values and will power.

While it can be hard, I have no doubt that men can override unfaithful drives for the sake of commitment, if they choose.

Whatever you decide, have clear, honest, respectful communication with your partner about it.

All the Best, Angelo.

Dear Angelo,
I've been dating this guy for nine months, but we became sex-less after six months. His love for porn has been stronger than his love for me ever since. I am overwhelmed and not sure if I want this.
Signed, DVD or Me?

Dear DVD or Me?,
I imagine it's painful to have this in your life. It can be hard to have a partner lusting after everything but you. I'm sorry you're going through this.

Every couple is different and will have sex differently. Porn and fantasy can complement a couple's already healthy sex life. But when you are replaced with porn and fantasy, that's another story. Giving complex reasons why this could be happening with your boyfriend would be speculative. So I would like to focus on you instead.

While it is tempting, don't ask, "Why is this happening?" Instead ask, "What can I learn from this situation?" In the midst of difficulty, it's kinda hard to think about going to school. We just want quick answers to take the hurt away! But asking, "What can I learn from this?" can be a great way to help you find answers that can get you "unstuck" and less overwhelmed. I have a bunch of questions for you to help get you moving. Just answering questions like these today will bring awareness, beginning to break old patterns. I'd like to see you have what you want.

When your boyfriend would rather masturbate to porn than

make love to you, how does that make you feel? How does it affect your relationship with him? Have you been able to talk with him about it? If so, how do you feel about his response? If not, what keeps you from telling him? What keeps you together? I wonder what you would like to have happen? What would life be like if that were to happen? What if that doesn't happen?

For more support, consider finding your own therapist, get into couples counseling, or join a support group to discuss the problems you are experiencing with your boyfriend. You can also encourage your boyfriend to seek his own counseling as well.

All the Best, Angelo.

Dear Angelo,
I've been happily dating a guy monogamously for four and a half months now. My boyfriend and I have a great sex life and I feel complete. However, I enjoy looking at porn, going to bookstores, playing with strangers, and cruising the locker room. I think he's suspicious. What do I do?
Signed, Hunter

Dear Hunter,
News flash! If you're honest with yourself, you know you're not in a monogamous relationship because you're playing with strangers. That's cheating. You're being dishonest with your partner and yourself. You're also putting your partner at risk if you're not playing safe. Your behavior isn't consistent with your statement that you're happy, great, and complete in your relationship. If so, unless you have a sexual addiction, why do you betray him?

You may want to reflect on the kind of relationship you really want. Maybe an open relationship is better for you. Level with your partner about what's been going. Tell him what your needs are. Is deceit what you want as the backdrop of your relationship?

All the Best, Angelo.

Dear Angelo,
I have met someone who lives two hours away. Do long-distance relationships ever work out?
Signed, Long-Distance Love

Dear Long-Distance Love,
Yes, a long-distance relationship can work out. In the movie *Cold Mountain,* Nicole Kidman's character holds a flaming torch for her beloved for years while he's away in the Civil War. Love and devotion mean everything when you're apart, but they may not be enough.

You need to work extrahard to keep the bond alive when you're apart. Absence is said to make the heart grow fonder, but this type of relationship works out best when the common goal is to be together in the end. Relational success ultimately requires proximity—being closer together. Meanwhile, a mutual commitment to see each other routinely is paramount. It's a necessity to have consistent contact. You have to weigh the benefits of being with your love against the effort it takes. Look at the distance as a short-term situation. The key is to have your eye on the eventual plan to be together—the light at the end of the tunnel.

In between regular visits, have frequent phone conversations, send cards, handwritten letters, flowers, videos, talk live by Webcam, instant messaging, and e-mail.

When you can't be together, focus on you, your life, your interests, and your friends.

All the Best, Angelo.

Dear Angelo,
I am twenty-five and I met a guy six weeks ago who is twenty-two. We are going to move in together. What do you think?
Signed, What the Hell

Dear What the Hell,

You might be living in hell if you do this. While I applaud your open heart and your enthusiasm for love, I have to caution you against making a hasty decision that could turn out badly. Some people have to make living arrangements in far less time. For example, you may only meet a potential roommate for several hours before having to make a decision. But six weeks is hardly enough time to build a basis for a couple moving in together. This situation has far greater intimacy and requires more careful consideration. Six weeks may not even be sufficient time to label you a couple yet.

It's normal to yearn for love and "the right one" who will bring it. Most of us long for a Mr. Right. We may want a love so badly, that we can run to someone if they feel right. We want to rush right into it. Excitement is fine. Love is a wonderful feeling. But a broken heart can take a very long time to heal, and living with someone who turns out to be someone else can be quite an unpleasant nightmare.

Yes, it could possibly work out just fine. But my advice is to take it slow. Take the time to get to know each other more before making a rash decision.

All the Best, Angelo.

Dear Angelo,

I met this hot guy outside a gay club. We had a fantastic night. Everything just clicked. It's like we had one rhythm. We danced, kissed, and had incredible sex as one body, laughed, talked, and he says I make him crazy. But he never spends the night, calls me back when he says he will, or makes solid plans, and stuff like that. When we do get together we have a great time, although his eyes roam easily. I don't know what to make of it. I really like him and he says he really likes me. Signed, Is He for Real?

Dear Is He for Real?,
He seems a little shady. Nine out of ten times you have to believe
a guy's actions over his words if there's a discrepancy. He may
rock your world, but if you don't get the feeling that you're his
world, then something's off.

If you can keep it light, have a good time, just taking it for
what it is, then flow with it. But if you're feeling him and think
you're being "played," then you might want to call it an early night
before it gets messy.

It's hard to come by crackling chemistry and it's terrifically
seductive when you find it. It's intoxicating. But be careful not to
let infatuation blind you to what kind of person this guy is, or you
could get hurt. Next time you're together, put his hotness aside
and focus on how he treats you. Make sure he makes you feel
good both in and out of the sheets. If not, tread carefully with
your heart.

All the Best, Angelo.

Dear Angelo,
I just left a three-year relationship with a woman. How do I
plunge into the gay lifestyle? And how can I find out if a hot
dude I like is gay?
Signed, Newbie

Dear Newbie,
Welcome to our community. Plunging into "the gay lifestyle" isn't
quite like putting on your most fabulous Speedo and diving into
a cool pool of water. You can't really jump into a well-defined sea
of gayness because it can be hard to pinpoint what, or where,
exactly, the gay community is. Since gay people are everywhere
and out to varying degrees, the gay community is spread out,
and one's relationship to it varies from person to person. Also,
the gay community itself has many diverse subcultures: twinks,

leather daddies, jocks, bears, drag-queens, muscle-heads—the list goes on. Making a gay life for yourself is about building a life that works for you as a gay person. Enjoy the process of self-discovery, finding your place, and creating a healthy, well-rounded life that's comfortable for you as a gay man.

As for part two of your question, the best way to find out if a guy you like is gay is to ask him. One thing we're up against out there is heterosexism, or the presumption that everyone's straight. A straight guy doesn't ask a single woman if she's heterosexual before he asks her out. He just assumes she is and focuses on mustering up the courage to hit on her. If he's not degrading, the woman usually feels complimented and affirmed by the proposal. If she says "no," he most often takes it as she's simply not interested and moves on. Usually no one is offended in the situation. Her sexuality is rarely an issue.

Well, the same needs to be true for us gays. While we need to use our best judgment in the situation to stay safe from physical harm, we also need to feel uninhibited in expressing our natural attraction to other men. Often we inhibit ourselves from expressing our affection openly because we buy into the idea that being gay is an insult to one's manhood. The belief that it's offensive to ask a guy if he's gay reflects homophobic thinking. It endorses the idea that there's something insulting about being gay—something slanderous, wrong, or bad. If a dude gets offended by a gay man hitting on him (because he thinks it infers he's gay and he's not) that's his problem. Don't take his baggage on—about being "a man's man" (another thing we're up against). There is nothing shameful about being a gay man.

All the Best, Angelo.